THE SQUAD
and the
Intelligence Operations of
Michael Collins

THE SQUAD

and the
Intelligence Operations of
Michael Collins

T. RYLE DWYER

MERCIER PRESS
Douglas Village, Cork
Website: www.mercierpress.ie

Trade enquiries to CMD Distribution
55A Spruce Avenue, Stillorgan Industrial Park
Blackrock, County Dublin
Tel: (01) 294 2560; Fax: (01) 294 2564
E-mail: cmd@columba.ie

© T. Ryle Dwyer, 2005

ISBN 1 85635 469 5
10 9 8 7 6 5 4 3

A CIP record for this title is available
from the British Library

Mercier Press receives financial assistance from
the Arts Council/An Chomhairle Ealaíon

This book is sold subject to the condition that it shall not, by way of trade or otherwise, be lent, resold, hired out or otherwise circulated without the publisher's prior consent in any form of binding or cover other than that in which it is published and without a similar condition including this condition being imposed on the subsequent purchaser.

No part of this publication may be reproduced or transmitted in any form or by any means, electronic or mechanical, including photocopying, recording or any information or retrieval system, without the prior permission of the publisher in writing.

Printed and Bound by J. H. Haynes & Co. Ltd, Sparkford

CONTENTS

	Preface	7
1	'I knew he was the man'	9
2	'Only the beginning'	22
3	'Every damn fool'	35
4	'Almost a miracle I was not landed'	45
5	'I do not defend the murder simply as such I merely applaud it'	58
6	'Shooting of a few would-be assassins'	70
7	'Expect shooting'	83
8	'A little bit of strategy'	96
9	'We are going to have sport now'	106
10	'The first shot was fired from the lord mayor's own gun'	120
11	'No harm would come to Mick'	132
12	'I've my orders to shoot him'	143
13	'Like a town with the plague'	155
14	'The Lord have mercy on your souls!'	170
15	'The most disgraceful show'	186
16	'Too good to be true'	200
17	'Someone has to die for this'	213
18	'She wants to see *General* MacEoin'	226
19	'Miss, you'll be lucky if you get out with your life'	241
	Epilogue	254
	Bibliography	260
	Index of Names	264

This book is dedicated to
Mary Egan Howard

PREFACE

Michael Collins is frequently cited as the originator of modern urban terrorism. The British characterised his Squad as 'the murder gang' and had they knowingly captured members of the Squad, they would almost certainly have executed them. Many were stopped and even captured, but they were usually let go as they were not actually recognised as members of the Squad. They were saved by the great secrecy under which they operated, as were the spies, or moles, within the police force who worked for Collins and his intelligence organisation.

The Squad made a vital contribution to the War of Independence but it did not win it. For one thing, it was effectively disbanded before the Truce and, anyway, the struggle was not a conventional war; it was rarely much more than a police action. The British army was only used sparingly. The Squad's major role was both in helping the Irish side and provoking the forces of the crown. Collins set out with a plan to eliminate the most effective British detectives and thus knock out the eyes and ears of the Dublin Castle regime in order to provoke the British to retaliate blindly. His confident belief was that they would retaliate against innocent Irish people and thereby drive the Irish people as a whole into the arms of the republicans. The genius of Collins was as an organiser and an administrator. The Squad systematically eliminated many of the most effective detectives, with the help of information provided by police spies, or moles, working within the crown's police forces and intelligence services.

In view of the nature of their operation the Squad members and the moles worked undercover and most remained secretive about their activities. Many only spoke out in the early 1950s when the Bureau of Military History began interviewing veterans of the War of Independence with the assurance that the material would not be released in their lifetimes. As a result they could speak more freely and their statements now provide invaluable insights. Of course, the interviews, which were more than thirty years after the events, sometimes show just how much old men forget. But in the case of the Squad, the operations usually had several participants and the files provide not only first-hand accounts of the triggermen but also of those who were backing up the operation. These were more effective witnesses because, unlike innocent bystanders, they would not have been surprised or shocked by the events. They were therefore in a position to observe more keenly.

One does not normally read or hear accounts of the participants in an actual assassination, but the witness statements of the Squad contain many first-hand accounts by the men who pulled the triggers to kill those considered the enemy. They provide invaluable historical insights into what was happening behind the scenes. They help to explain not only what happened but also, in many cases, why it happened, though historians must be careful because Michael Collins was an extremely secretive individual. In most instances he did explain his reasons. When he gave orders for somebody to be killed the Squad carried out such orders without question. The accounts by his various moles also provide insights into the reasons but in some instances Collins probably carried the secrets with him to his grave.

Having studied aspects of the War of Independence in depth for a number of other books, being afforded the opportunity to appreciate the 'new' details and recognise the first-hand confirmation of other information that was already in the public domain has been invaluable. Since such confirmation is of particular historical significance, I have concentrated in this book on the witness statements and have related the accounts as much as possible in the actual words of the men – or in some instances, the women – involved.

I would like to thank the staff of the National Library for their unfailing courtesy and the staff of Kerry County Library for their assistance.

TRD, Tralee, 2005

CHAPTER 1

'I KNEW HE WAS THE MAN'

In January 1919, at the age of twenty-nine, Michael Collins took over as director of intelligence of the Irish Volunteers. It was in this area that he made his greatest mark. After almost ten years in exile in London he returned to Ireland when conscription was introduced by the British in January 1916. He took part in the Easter Rebellion, fighting in the General Post Office, and was interned subsequently in Frongoch.

While interned Collins showed a flair for smuggling messages in and out of the camp. He was recognised in the camp as a 'conscriptible', having only left England after the introduction of conscription earlier in the year. He was released when the camp was shut down just before Christmas 1916. Back in Ireland he played a major role in the reorganisation of the Irish Republican Brotherhood (IRB). He also played a leading part in the election of Joseph McGuinness in the Longford by-election of April 1917. McGuinness and other recognised leaders of the movement were still in jail in England as a result of the Easter Rebellion when Collins came up with the idea of putting him up for election on a platform calling for the release of the prisoner: 'Put him in to get him out,' became the campaign slogan.

Éamon de Valera and the other leaders objected to the idea but Collins ignored their instructions and put McGuinness forward where he narrowly won the seat. As a result, the prisoners were released in June 1917, little over a year after many of them had been sentenced to death or had their sentences commuted to life in prison. Following the release of the prisoners de Valera won election to Westminster in an East Clare by-election, winning the seat vacated through the death of Willie Redmond, brother of the leader of the Irish Parliamentary Party.

The disparate elements of the independence movement came together under the Sinn Féin banner in October 1917 and Collins was elected to the party executive. He was one of the dynamic young men in the movement but he had a tendency to rub many members the wrong way. His nickname, 'the Big Fellow', was a term of derision, born out of his apparent sense of self-importance, although it soon became a term of endearment. Sinn Féin lost the first three Irish by-elections that it contested in early 1918. In April 1918 the British government introduced legislation that would authorise it to introduce conscription in Ireland. The Irish Parliamentary Party walked out of Westminster in protest, which appeared to justify the refusal of Sinn Féin's four MPs to take their seats. They were pledged to establish a national assembly in Ireland. Through de Valera's influence the Irish Catholic hierarchy virtually sanctified the anti-conscription campaign.

Ned Broy, a confidential typist in his mid twenties at the detective division headquarters in Great Brunswick Street, Dublin, was from a farming family in Ballinure near Rathangan, County Kildare and had two great passions, a love of athletics and a hatred of the British empire. He was assigned to type up lists of Sinn Féin members who the crown police intended to round up for their republican activities. He gave a copy of the list to his cousin, Patrick Tracy, a clerk at Kingsbridge railway station. He did not know when the round up was to take place but he promised to warn Tracy in advance. Tracy passed on the complete list to Harry O'Hanrahan, a Sinn Féin sympathiser who ran a shop and whose brother, Michael, was one of the leaders executed following the Easter Rebellion.

On the day of the round up, Broy gave the further warning: 'I met Tracy and told him,' he said. 'Tonight's the night. Tell O'Hanrahan to tell the wanted men not to stay in their usual place of abode and to keep their heads.' Detective Sergeant Joe Kavanagh of the DMP, passed on a similar warning to Thomas Gay, a librarian in the public library in Capel Street.

Broy was summoned to do telephone duty that night at Dublin Castle by Detective Superintendent Owen Brien, the deputy head of the detective division. 'You will be much more comfortable here,' Brien told him. Broy looked forward to what he thought was going to be one raiding party after another coming up empty-handed.

'To my astonishment, continual telephone messages arrived from the various police parties, saying that they had arrested the party they were sent for. A telephone message came from a detective sergeant at Harcourt Street railway station saying, "That man has just left".' That was de Valera who was returning to his home in Greystones.

'That man will get the suck-in of his life!' a smug Detective Superintendent Brien remarked. He immediately rang the RIC headquarters to say that de Valera was on his way home.

'I did not know what to think of the whole raid and what had gone wrong, but I thought that de Valera would surely get out at some intermediate station and not go home all the way to Greystones to be arrested there,' Broy noted. 'To my further astonishment, about an hour afterwards, a telephone message arrived from the RIC at Greystones to say: "That man has been arrested".'

De Valera and the others had apparently allowed themselves to be taken in the belief that their arrest would help their cause. They were purportedly arrested for their part in a 'German Plot'. Ever since being forewarned by American intelligence of plans for the Easter Rebellion, Admiral Sir William Reginald 'Blinker' Hall, the head of British naval intelligence, had been anxious for an excuse to suppress Irish nationalism. He had not tried to stop the rebellion because he believed it would afford an excuse to suppress this nationalism. He gained a great reputation for his handling of intelligence matters in the fight against Germany but exaggerated the significance of German efforts to enlist the support of Sinn Féin in 1918. 'If he believed that the scrappy and inconclusive information which he held was definite proof of an actual plot then he was a fool,' historian Eunan O'Halpin concluded. Hall clearly was no fool; he deliberately deceived his political masters into thinking that the Sinn Féin leaders were involved in some kind of plot with the Germans. While the war continued Hall had enormous influence, but this disappeared with the armistice and naval intelligence faded into the background. No credible evidence of any Sinn Féin involvement in the so-called 'German Plot' was ever produced, with the result that it had little credence in Ireland, where people concluded that Sinn Féin leaders were really arrested because of the success of their campaign against conscription. A few weeks later, Arthur Griffith, one of the founders of Sinn Fein, won a by-election from prison. This was a deadly blow to the Irish Parliamentary Party, which was now essentially moribund. After three successive defeats, Sinn Féin was on the move again.

Collins had managed to avoid arrest and this left him in an even stronger position to exert his influence over the movement in the following months. 'The Sinn Féiners boasted that their most important man had escaped arrest,' Detective Superintendent Brien remarked to Broy a few days later.

Opposition to conscription was so strong that the British did not dare to introduce it in Ireland and Sinn Féin got the credit.

With de Valera and the other recognised leaders in jail, Collins and colleagues like Harry Boland extended their influence. They selected many of the candidates to stand for Sinn Féin in the snap general election called following the end of the Great War. Sinn Féin stood on a platform promising to abstain from Westminster and to establish a national parliament in Ireland that would seek international recognition at the post-war peace conference. The democracies had supposedly fought for the rights of small nations and Sinn Féin was determined to call their bluff. The party won 73 of the 105 seats and that included all but one of the contested seats outside the six counties of the northeast, where the Unionist Party was strongest.

Collins had been functioning as adjutant general and director of organisation of the Irish Volunteers, who were soon to become known as the Irish Republican Army (IRA). In January 1919 he took over as director of intelligence from Eamonn Duggan, who had merely run intelligence as an adjunct of his legal practice and had only one man working for him.

Collins set up a far-reaching network, incorporating intelligence gathering, counter intelligence and matters relating to prison escapes and smuggling (both arms and people). He was the brain behind the whole network and his industry was phenomenal. He retained personal control over work similar to that done by three different intelligence agencies in Britain: MI5, MI6 and MI9.

An intelligence office was set up over the print shop of J. F. Fowler at 3 Crow Street which was just off Dame Street and right under the nose of Dublin Castle. Collins generally stayed away from that office. Joe O'Reilly acted as his main courier to the office and everyone in it. Members of the staff were supposedly 'manufacturing agents', but they spent much of their time in the office decoding intercepted messages.

Liam Tobin, another Cork man, was in charge of the intelligence headquarters in Crow Street. He was an inconspicuous individual, tall and gaunt, with a tragic expression. He walked without moving his arms, which made him seem quite listless, in marked contrast with Collins who bounded from place to place. Tobin's deputy was Tom Cullen, an affable, quick-witted individual from Wicklow who had fought in the Easter Rebellion. He was not only intelligent but also a good athlete and a handsome young man with a fresh complexion and sparkling eyes. Frank Thornton was next in the chain of command at the headquarters, along with Frank Saurin, who stood out as one of the best-dressed men in the movement. He turned out in an impeccable suit and often wore lavender gloves. Some of the British made the mistake of assuming he looked too respectable to be a rebel, with the result that his sense of dress often amounted to a pass allowing him to saunter through enemy cordons.

The developing staff of intelligence officers included people like Joe Guilfoyle, a veteran of Frongoch, and Joe Dolan, who wore a British army badge in his lapel with a red, white and blue ribbon. The badge, which was inscribed 'For King & Country', frequently allowed him to get out of sticky situations as the British assumed that he was a loyalist. Charlie Byrne, another of the new men, was called 'the Count' by colleagues, because of his appearance and his sense of humour. They were joined by Paddy Kennedy from Tipperary, Ned Kelliher and Charlie Dalton, Dan McDonnell from Dublin and Peter McGee.

Each company of the Volunteers had its own intelligence officer (IO) and they reported to a brigade IO, who, in turn, reported to the intelligence headquarters under Tobin. Each IO was encouraged to enlist agents in all walks of life, but especially people in prominent positions who boasted of their British connections. 'It is amazing the number of this type of people who, when it was put to them, eventually agreed to work for us and did tremendous work for us afterwards, whilst at the same time keeping their connection with the British forces,' Thornton noted.

Intelligence was divided into two areas. First there was the gathering of information on the movement of British forces, and second, information on the activity of British agents, whether they were members of the special intelligence service, military intelligence, or members of the various police intelligence units.

'I was given the daily papers to look through,' Charlie Dalton wrote of his first day on the job. 'I was told to cut out any paragraphs referring to the personnel of the Royal Irish Constabulary, or military, such as transfers, their movement socially, attendance at wedding receptions, garden parties, etc. These I pasted on cards, which were sent to the director of intelligence for his perusal and instructions. Photographs and other data, which were or might be of interest were cut out and put away. We often gathered useful information of the movements of important enemy personages in this manner. We also traced them by a study of *Who's Who*, from which we learned the names of their connections and clubs. By intercepting their correspondence we were able to get a clue to their movements outside their strongholds.'

Each of the intelligence officers had an area. 'Mine covered hotels, restaurants, sports meetings and such other places where the auxiliaries and British secret service agents foregathered – Jammets, The Wicklow, The Shelbourne, Fullers, The Moira, The Central, etc.,' Frank Saurin noted. 'We had contacts in these hotels and restaurants, who passed on any information concerning enemy agents that might be of use to us. Through our agents I was enabled to get to know by sign a number of enemy personnel – the object being their extermination if and when the opportunity offered.' He also handled one of the most important Irish agents, Lily Mernin, a young woman typist working in the British army command headquarters under Colonel Hill Dillon, the chief intelligence officer in Ireland. Mernin suggested other typists who were willing to provide information from their perspectives working with different military staffs around Dublin. She was the 'one to whom a large amount of the credit for the success of intelligence must go', according to Thornton.

'One of the earliest jobs given to GHQ intelligence at Dublin was to ascertain the possibilities of getting at least one individual in every government department who was prepared to work quietly and secretly for our Army,' Thornton recalled. 'We were fairly lucky in having one individual who was working with us from the very commencement in records, who secured for us photographs and the names and addresses and history of practically all the typists and all the clerical workers in the most important departments of the enemy. These photographs and descriptions were handed out to the various intelligence officers throughout the areas in which these people lived and in a very short space of time we had a complete and full history of the sympathies and activities of each and every one of these individuals, resulting in quite a number of them, when contacted, agreeing to work for us inside the enemy lines.'

Others worked in the sorting office of the General Post Office or the telephone exchange, and Collins had a number of men who were serving as warders in Mountjoy Jail. They facilitated some of the early escapes, which played a significant part in boosting republican morale. 'There were four warders in Mountjoy who were most helpful and sympathetic to us at the time,' Paddy O'Daly recalled. 'Frawley was one, Daly was another and I am almost certain that Breslin and Berry were the names of the other two.'

Patrick Joseph Berry, a Kilkenny native in his thirties, was a plumber and a warder on the staff in the jail from 1906. It was he who got out word to Liam Tobin's family that Liam was about to be deported to England so that they would be able to come and see him off. Presumably as a result of this incident Tobin informed the Big Fellow about Berry, and Collins approached him. 'I was more or less their intelligence officer in the prison,' Berry explained. 'I was with Collins day and night carrying dispatches from and to prisoners. These were written dispatches. In spite of the fact that the prison authorities must have been aware of my sympathies following the Ashe Inquiry,* no attempt was ever made to search me. Of course I was pretty diplomatic and made no profession of my sympathies.'

In much the same way contacts were made within the police, as Collins set about demoralising the police forces in Ireland. At the time there were two separate police forces – the Royal Irish Constabulary (RIC) and the Dublin Metropolitan Police (DMP). The latter, which functioned only in the Dublin area, was divided

---

* This referred to the inquiry into the death of Thomas Ashe on hungerstrike following a forced feeding in September 1917.

into seven divisions, lettered A through G. Divisions A, B, C and D were uniformed police dealing with different sections of the city, while E and F dealt with the remainder of County Dublin, and G was an overall division of plain clothes detectives.

G Division was modelled on the London Metropolitan Police. It was divided into three sections dealing with routine crime, political crime and carriage supervision. The total strength was between forty and fifty active detectives, under a commissioner, superintendent and a chief inspector. There were five detective inspectors, fifteen detective sergeants, fifteen detective officers and ten detective constables. Most of the men were based at the division's headquarters at No. 1 Great Brunswick Street, but the commissioner, Colonel Walter Edgeworth-Johnson, and Detective Superintendent Owen Brien spent most of their time at Dublin Castle, where the headquarters of the RIC was located.

The members of the intelligence staff were essentially aides of Collins. Their initial task was to gather as much information as possible about the police, especially G Division. Information such as where they lived, and the names of members of their families would prove invaluable to Collins in the coming months. His agents were a whole range of people, with no one too humble to be of use.

'We compiled a list of friendly persons in the public service, railways, mail boats, and hotels,' Dalton explained. 'I was sent constantly to interview stewards, reporters, waiters, and hotel porters to verify the movements of enemy agents.'

Maids in guesthouses and hotels, porters, bartenders, sailors, railwaymen, postmen, sorters, telephone and telegraph operators, warders and ordinary policemen all played an important part. Certain sorters and postmen intercepted mail for British agents undercover, and Collin and his men had mail sent to them under covernames at convenient addresses. The Big Fellow had the splendid ability of making each of the people helping feel important, even though he rarely, if ever, thanked them for what they were doing.

'Why should I thank people for doing their part?' he would ask. 'Isn't Ireland their country as well as mine?'

Central to the success of intelligence gathering was the network of police spies. After Collins took over as director of intelligence in January 1919, one of his first moves was to make contact with Ned Broy, who had provided the information to allow him to avoid arrest in the round-up of May 1918. He had Broy invited to meet with him at 5 Cabra Road, Michael Foley's home.

'I was filled with curiosity,' Broy recalled. 'Would this Michael Collins be the ideal man I had been dreaming of for a couple of years? Looking up the police record book to see what was known about him, I discovered that he was a six-footer, a Cork man, very intelligent, young and powerful. There was no photograph of him at that time in the record book.'

'Steeped in curiosity, I went to 5 Cabra Road and was received in the kitchen by Foley.' This was 'a place where every extreme nationalist visited at some time or another,' Broy continued. 'I was not there long when Greg Murphy and Michael Collins arrived. I had studied for so long the type of man that I would need to act efficiently, that the moment I saw Michael at the door, before he had time to walk across and shake hands, I knew he was the man.'

Collins was dressed in black leggings, green breeches and a trench coat. He struck Broy as being a handsome man, with a quick mind and bundles of energy. He thanked Broy for all the information he had been furnishing and said he felt that the time had come for them to meet, and said there would be no further failure to make proper use of his information. 'We discussed what the Volunteers could do,' Broy added. 'If they did not resort to violence, the movement would collapse, and, if they resorted to violence, there were extreme risks also.' Collins explained that he and his good friend Harry Boland had called on Tim Healy, who had been one of the most prominent politicians going back to the Parnell period of the previous century.

'You are all stark mad,' Healy had told them. He had said that they did not have a chance of succeeding by violence, but he agreed that they were unlikely to get anywhere by constitutional means either.

'I agreed entirely with Michael Collins that force was the only chance, however difficult and dangerous,' Broy recalled. 'I explained to him the police organisation and suggested that as the DMP uniformed service took no part whatsoever in anti-Sinn Féin activities – as unlike the RIC they did not do political duty – they should not be alienated by attacks on them. The majority, at least of the younger men, were anti-British, and had many relatives in the Volunteers.' He added that they had a more liberal outlook than the RIC and were not under as much close supervision as the unmarried men among them lived in barracks scattered throughout the city. 'The result was,' Broy said, 'that they freely exchanged their opinions in the mess halls about home rule, the Ulster resistance, the Curragh mutiny, etc., and there was no authority to prevent them expressing their opinions. I tried to make the difference clear to Mick and he, as usual, was quick enough to grasp the point instantly.'

Morale was low within the force. Even though the majority of the police were Irish Catholics, their prospects of advancement seemed limited as religious and racial discrimination were rife within the police forces. Preferment was given to Protestants and just about anyone other than a Catholic. As a result the rank and file tended to regard the district and county inspectors of the RIC as social climbers and status seekers, rather than committed policemen. It was the same in the DMP, where the men considered their senior officers more ornamental than operational. A double-barrelled name seemed to be an advantage, along with membership of the Masons and Kildare Street Club. To make matters worse the top echelons were reserved for retired army officers.

'We discussed the psychology of the RIC and how it came about that when an ordinary decent young Irishman joined the RIC depot, that within about two months there was an unaccountably complete change in his outlook, and he was never the same afterwards to friends,' Broy continued. Collins said that his friend, Batt O'Connor, from Kerry, had observed the same phenomenon among some young Kerry men who had joined the RIC.

Broy recalled mentioning to Collins the danger posed by the policemen stationed in villages who could easily gather intelligence to arrest local volunteers. 'They were a menace to Volunteers going to such an isolated area. We agreed that ruthless war should be made on the small stations, attack the barracks if the police were in them, and burning them down where they had been evacuated. The RIC would then be compelled to concentrate on the large towns and attempt to patrol the vacated areas from these distant centres. Such concentration would cause the police to lose their grip, psychologically and otherwise, and the inhabitants of the vacated areas, because the police, who returned from a distance to patrol the area, would be in no better position than the British military.'

Broy advocated the Volunteers adopt a twin psychological approach of trying to convince members of the RIC and DMP that, even if they were not prepared to assist the Volunteers in the coming struggle to secure Irish independence, they should not hinder those efforts, at least. At the same time Broy advocated that efforts should be made to persuade the families of the police to convince their police relatives that they would be a disgrace if they hindered the Volunteers. In addition, he said they should try to make contact with policemen in clerical positions, like Broy, who could furnish information to the Volunteers.

After all those efforts he said that 'a ruthless war' should be waged on those police who persisted in resisting the independence struggle. 'As regards the DMP,' Broy argued, 'no attack should be made on the uniformed service, and no attack should be made on the members of the G Division who were not on political duty and active on that duty. In this way, the DMP would come to realise that, as long as they did not display zeal against the Volunteers, they were perfectly safe from attack. In the case of any G man who remained hostile, a warning was to be given to him, such as tying him to a railing, before any attack was made on him.'

CHAPTER 2

'ONLY THE BEGINNING'

On 7 January 1919 twenty-four of the Sinn Féin candidates elected to the British parliament met to consider their next move, Collins among them. They took an oath 'to work for the establishment of an independent Irish Republic' and discussed arrangements for setting up their own national assembly in Ireland, Dáil Éireann, a fortnight later. Collins was opposed to setting up the dáil while so many of those elected to the British parliament were in jail.

On 21 January, the day the dáil was founded, two members of the Royal Irish Constabulary were shot dead at Soloheadbeg, County Tipperary. Although this event is usually seen as the start of the War of Independence, the killings did not in fact have the sanction of the leadership of the independence movement at the time. The leaders in Dublin were furious because Seán Treacy, Dan Breen and their colleagues had acted without authority and had upstaged the establishment of the dáil. The big news story the next day was not the establishment of the dáil but the murders of Constables James McDonnell, a native of Belmullet, County Mayo, and Patrick O'Connell from Clonmoyle near Coachford, County Cork. Dan Breen later wrote that his 'only regret' was that there were only two policemen to kill that day. 'Six would have created a bigger impression than a mere two,' he explained.

McDonnell was a widower with four or five children. 'We must show our abhorrence of this inhuman act,' parish priest Monsignor Ryan told the congregation in St Michael's church in Tipperary. 'We must denounce it and the cowardly miscreants who are guilty of it – aye, and all who try to excuse or justify it.'

'It used to be said "Where Tipperary leads, Ireland follows",' he continued. 'God help poor Ireland if she follows this lead of blood! But let us give her the lead in our indignant denunciation of this crime against our Catholic civilisation, against Ireland, against Tipperary.'

Dick Mulcahy looked on the wild, undisciplined approach to matters of Breen and the Soloheadbeg gang, especially their unauthorised killing of the two policemen, as a kind of nuisance. The volunteers in Dublin did not welcome them and 'the only place in which they could find association and some kind of scope for their activities was on the fringe of Collins' intelligence activity work,' according to Mulcahy.

'It would be incorrect to say in the years before 1916 the RIC were unpopular,' wrote Seán Moylan, one of the heroes of the War of Independence. 'They were of the people, were inter-married among the people; they were generally men of exemplary lives, and of a high level of intelligence.' Many of the younger RIC men resigned in the following years, but the older men felt unable to do so because of their pensions. 'It was a providential thing for the country that these older men remained at their posts,' Moylan added. 'They were a moderating influence that kept within some bounds the irresponsibilities and criminalities of the Black and Tans [the police reinforcements hastily recruited in Britain].'

When those involved in the Soloheadbeg ambush moved to Dublin 'in search of bigger game', in the words of Breen, Collins welcomed them, but other leading members of the movement, such as Dick Mulcahy, the IRA chief-of-staff, virtually shunned them over their upstaging of the establishment of the dáil. Some did wonder whether Collins had been behind the Soloheadbeg ambush, but he had not even been in the country at the time. He was listed as present at the meeting of the first dáil but in fact he was in England personally supervising the final arrangements for springing de Valera, along with Seán McGarry, who was a leading member of the Irish Republican Brotherhood (IRB), and Seán Milroy, from Lincoln Jail.

The prisoners had managed to send out a drawing of a master key on a postcard. This found its way to Paddy O'Donoghue, a Killarney man based in Manchester. 'I crossed to Dublin that evening and contacted Martin Conlan, who, in turn, made an appointment with Michael Collins. I saw Collins that night in Mrs McGarry's house and I showed him the postcard,' O'Donoghue recalled. 'A key was then made from the dimensions given on the postcard by Gerry Boland. Mrs McGarry baked this key in a cake. I took this key with me to England enclosed in the cake and had it sent in to the prison as a gift to the prisoners, but it did not work.'

A suitable blank key together with a file was also sent into the prison to allow the prisoners to fashion a key themselves. When this was ready Collins went to England to supervise the final arrangements personally. 'I accompanied him to the vicinity of the prison,' O'Donoghue recalled. 'We walked round the precincts and had a good look at the escape gate selected, and Collins was quite satisfied with everything he saw. Before Collins [went] back to Dublin, I was working out plans for the escape, such as the hiring of taxis and the position they would take up, and where the prisoners would be taken to following the escape. Collins was satisfied and returned to Dublin to await the selection of the night of 3 February for the escape attempt.'

'A few days before the date fixed for the escape Harry Boland and Michael Collins and Fintan Murphy came over from Dublin,' O'Donoghue continued. 'I was not married then and I had a house to myself. As the Manager of Beecham's Opera Company was a friend of mine we went to an opera on the night before the proposed escape. After the opera we were invited to supper by Sir Thomas Beecham in the Midland hotel. We were all naturally in very good form. I introduced Collins and Boland to Sir Thomas Beecham under their proper names and he expressed his delight at meeting prominent people interested in the Irish Independence movement.

'On Saturday afternoon the four of us – Collins, Boland,

Murphy and myself went to Lincoln. We left Fintan Murphy at Worksop with instructions to have a car at his disposal about the time we would arrive there. Petrol restrictions were very severe at the time and we could not extend beyond Worksop on the first stage. Leaving Murphy behind, the three of us went to Lincoln and I engaged a car there. I had used the driver of this car on several occasions before and had become very friendly with him. I instructed the driver to remain with his car at a certain hotel on the verge of the town. I stayed with the driver and Collins and Boland left me and went to the gates of the gaol which was about a quarter of a mile distant.'

The two men approached the jail from a nearby field and gave a prearranged signal with a flashlight indicating everything was ready. Milroy responded from the jail by setting light to a whole box of matches at his cell window.

Collins tried to open a side gate with a key he had made, but it jammed. With characteristic impetuosity, he tried to force it, only to have the head of the key snap off in the lock. By this time he could hear de Valera and the others approach the other side of the gate.

'Dev,' he exclaimed, 'the key's broken in the lock!'

De Valera managed to knock the broken piece out with his own key and the three prisoners then emerged to the immense relief of those outside. Collins gave de Valera a jubilant thump of the shoulder, and they all made for the taxis. By the time they arrived at the hotel with the three prisoners the whole thing had taken less than half an hour. Collins and Boland left at that point to take a train to London.

'The three prisoners and myself got into the car and went along to Worksop,' O'Donoghue took up the story. 'I dismissed my driver and we walked a couple of hundred yards to the point where Fintan Murphy had his car. We got into the car and drove to Sheffield. When passing near the railway station at Worksop the driver started gibbering about going further because he would be disobeying petrol regulations and suggested we should take the Sheffield train which was in at the station at the time. I tactfully explained to him that the train would not suit us as we had a call to make en route. So the driver accepted the position and continued his journey with us.'

In Sheffield, Liam McMahon was waiting with a friend's car at a nearby hotel. O'Donoghue escorted de Valera to the Manchester home of a Fr O'Mahony from Tralee. He was chaplain at the workhouse in Crumpsall and de Valera stayed with him for several days until word was received from Detective Sergeant Thomas Walsh of the Manchester police that 'it was dangerous to leave de Valera any longer at the priest's residence, as the police suspected he was staying there,' according to McMahon.

Disguised in a colonial uniform, de Valera was taken from Crumpsall to Victoria Park to the home of an Irish woman, Mary Healy. By then, McGarry and Milroy had made it to Liverpool by mixing with the Irish crowds going home after the Waterloo Cup. McGarry dressed as a bookmaker and was provided with a bookie bag for the occasion, while Milroy dressed as a strolling musician and dyed his grey hair brown. He carried a violin in a case to boost his disguise.

De Valera had planned to go to the United States but Collins sent for Liam McMahon and asked him to return to Manchester to get de Valera to come to Dublin first. He said that differences had developed within the party in Dublin. 'The only one who could reconcile the difference would be de Valera. He gave me a letter which I was to deliver to him,' McMahon noted.

McMahon crossed to Manchester that night and met de Valera the following morning. 'I told him the object of my visit, and handed him the letter,' McMahon continued.

'My own idea is that I should be allowed to go to America, where I could come out in the open,' de Valera replied, 'but if they want me at home, my own ideas do not matter ... When am I to go?'

'Today,' McMahon replied.

Neal Kerr and Steve Lanigan made arrangements for de Valera to cross that night from Liverpool to Dublin.

Collins had been hoping that de Valera would lead a military confrontation with the British. 'As for us on the outside,' Collins wrote to Austin Stack on 6 February, 'all ordinary peaceful means are ended and we shall be taking the only alternative actions in a short while now.' But de Valera believed Ireland's best chance of success still lay in enlisting American help in view of President Woodrow Wilson's eloquent pronouncements. Collins tried unsuccessfully to dissuade him. 'You know what it is to argue with Dev,' he complained to a friend. 'He says he thought it out while in prison, and he feels that the one place where he can be useful to Ireland is in America.' Although some people were already saying the American president would not look for justice for Ireland, de Valera called for patience. 'Pronounce no opinion on President Wilson,' he advised. 'It is premature, for he and his friends will bear our country in mind at the crucial hour.'

De Valera was spirited back to Britain to await a ship to the United States.

Meanwhile Collins was active in assisting the escape of others, especially Robert Barton, from Mountjoy. The two had developed a close relationship. In December 1918 they had been part of an Irish delegation, along with Seán T. O'Kelly and George Gavan Duffy, which had tried to meet the American president, Woodrow Wilson, to make the Irish case for independence. 'We went over to London and tried to get in touch with Wilson,' Barton recalled. 'We never got any nearer to him than a second secretary in the American embassy. We had no success at all.'

Collins was so annoyed he suggested kidnapping the American president to make him listen. 'If necessary,' he said, 'we can buccaneer him.' Fortunately nobody took the suggestion too seriously, but the proposal provided an insight into why some colleagues thought Collins was sometimes inclined to allow his enthusiasm to get the better of his judgment.

'I was on very friendly terms with Michael Collins and we used to see one another almost every evening,' Barton recalled. 'Collins had an office under Cullenswood House, which was known to us as the "Republican Hut". Here he was relatively safe and Tom Cullen and Joe O'Reilly could always find him at 9 p.m. and bring persons he wanted to see. Cullenswood House was in the street where I was living and, if I did not turn up, he often sent down for me. I used to hear from him all that was going on. We discussed things in general and he used to urge me to join cabinet meetings to support his point of view.'

Soon after his incarceration in Mountjoy Barton managed to re-establish contact with the Big Fellow. 'Through friendly warders I got in touch with Michael Collins,' he explained. 'Joe Berry, a plumber warder, was one of them. I devised the means of escape. If I had a saw with which to cut one of the bars, I could get out of my cell, they could throw over a rope ladder, and I could climb up the ladder over the wall and get away.'

Collins arranged for Dick Mulcahy, the IRA chief-of-staff, to visit Barton in the jail. He went in posing as a clerk to Barton's solicitor. 'These two came to interview me about my pending court martial and they brought me the tools I was asking for. While the warder was not looking, Dick Mulcahy pushed the tools towards me and I hid them in my riding breeches. I was not in prison garb. With the saw, I cut out the bar.'

On the night of 16 March Barton rigged up a dummy in his bed so that when the warder checked during the night he would think Barton was still in bed. He threw a bar of soap over the wall at a certain spot, which was a prearranged signal for volunteers, led by Rory O'Connor, to throw a rope over the wall with a weight attached. By pulling on the rope Barton was able to pull over a rope ladder attached and use it to scale the twenty foot wall and then jump into a blanket being held by the volunteers. 'Mick Collins was in a street nearby waiting to congratulate me,' Barton added.

'This is only the beginning,' a jubilant Collins declared at Batt O'Connor's home at 1 Brendan Road, Donnybrook, that night. 'We're going to get Beaslaí and Fleming out next.'

'At this time,' Beaslaí noted in his biography of Collins, 'he was sending letters to me continually in which he discussed plans of escape.' He had big escape plans, but then de Valera, who had returned to Britain en route to the United States, decided to return to Ireland again. Pierce McCan, one of the prisoners arrested in the 'German Plot' round-up the previous May, had died of the deadly Spanish Influenza and the British had decided to free all of those being held in connection with the 'German Plot'. De Valera was therefore free to return to Ireland without being apprehended. His impending return was announced with the following statement to the press:

> President de Valera will arrive in Ireland on Wednesday evening next, the 26th inst., and the Executive of Dáil Éireann will offer him a national welcome. It is expected that the homecoming of de Valera will be an occasion of national rejoicing, and full arrangement will be made for marshalling the procession. The Lord Major of Dublin will receive him at the gates of the city, and will escort him to the Mansion House, where he will deliver a message to the Irish people. All organisations and bands wishing to participate in the demonstration should apply to 6 Harcourt Street, on Monday the 24th inst., up to 6 p.m.
> H. Boland
> T. Kelly,
> Honorary Secretaries.

Such arrangements were usually reserved for royalty, so Dublin Castle banned the reception. The Sinn Féin executive held an emergency meeting. Arthur Griffith presided at what was for him and Darrell Figgis the first meeting since their arrest the previous May. Cathal Brugha had complained privately to Figgis some days earlier that Collins and his IRB colleagues had essentially taken over the movement from within while the others were in jail. 'He told me that he had seen what had been passing, but that he had been powerless to change events,' Figgis wrote. 'It was at this meeting I saw for the first time the personal hostility between him and Michael Collins.'

When the executive met to discuss what to do about Dublin Castle's ban on the planned reception, Figgis asked to see the record of the executive meeting authorising the honorary secretaries to announce the plans to welcome de Valera. He was told that the issue had never come up. 'I therefore asked Alderman Tom Kelly on what authority he, as one of the signatories, had attached his name as secretary, and he answered with characteristic bluntness that, in point of fact, he had never seen the announcement, and had not known of it, till he read it in the press.'

There followed a 'tangled discussion' before Collins rose. 'Characteristically, he swept aside all pretences, and said that the announcement had been written by him, and that the decision to make it had been made, not by Sinn Féin, though declared in its name, but by "the proper body, the Irish Volunteers",' Figgis wrote. 'He spoke with much vehemence and emphasis, saying that the sooner fighting was forced and a general state of disorder created through the country (his words in this connection are too well printed on my memory ever to be forgotten), the better it would be for the country. Ireland was likely to get more out of a state of general disorder than from a continuance of the situation as it then stood. The proper people to take decisions of that kind were ready to face the British military, and were resolved to force the issue. And they were not to be deterred by weaklings and cowards. For himself he accepted full responsibility for the announcement, and he told the meeting with forceful candour that he held them in no opinion at all, that, in fact, they were only summoned to confirm what the proper people had decided.

'He had always a truculent manner, but in such situations he was certainly candour itself,' Figgis continued. 'As I looked on him while he spoke, for all the hostility between us, I found something refreshing and admirable in his contempt of us all. His brow was gathered in a thunderous frown, and his chin trust forward, while he emphasised his points on the back of a chair with heavy strokes of his hand.'

Although Figgis may have been impressed at the way that Collins had 'manipulated' the organisation, Arthur Griffith was certainly not. He had no intention of meekly succumbing to such an arrogant display. Tapping the table in front of him with a pencil, Griffith emphasised that the decision was one to be taken by the meeting, and by no other body.

'For two hours the debate raged fiercely,' according to Figgis. Going ahead with the announced plans would undoubtedly lead to trouble, while abandoning them could have disastrous implications for the morale of the whole movement. Parallels were drawn with the disastrous consequences of Daniel O'Connell's decision to accede to the British decision to ban the monster meeting at Clontarf some seventy years earlier.

De Valera was consulted and he duly requested that the welcoming demonstrations be cancelled rather than risk a confrontation in which lives might be lost. 'I write to request that you will not now persist in your idea,' he explained. 'I think you must all agree with me that the present occasion is scarcely one on which we would be justified in risking the lives of the citizens. I am certain it would not.

'We who have waited, know how to wait,' he advised the executive. 'Many a heavy fish is caught even with a fine line if the angler is patient.'

Thus Big Fellow's plans to provoke an early confrontation with the British were frustrated and he was obviously disappointed. 'It is very bad,' he wrote to Stack. 'The chief actor was very firm on the withdrawal, as indeed was Cathal. I used my influence the other way, and was in a practical minority of one. It may be that all arguments were sound, but it seems to me that they have put up a challenge which strikes at the fundamentals of our policy and our attitude.'

Whatever harm Collins had done to his own standing by his arrogant display at the party's executive meeting it was more than offset by the mass escape from Mountjoy Jail on Saturday afternoon, 29 March. The plan was to spring Piaras Beaslaí, J. J. Walsh, Paddy Fleming, and Thomas Malone. Paddy O'Daly was involved in the escape plans from the inside, though he had no intention of trying to escape himself. His wife was dying in a Dublin hospice and he had only been sentenced to six months in jail. If he escaped and went on the run, he would not be able to visit his wife. In the circumstances the prison authorities accorded him parole to visit his wife, and he used this to contact republican leaders on the outside, including the chief-of-staff of the Volunteers, Richard Mulcahy, and Peadar Clancy who was in charge of those designated to help the escape from the outside.

They selected a Saturday afternoon because they had more freedom then than on any other afternoon, as there were fewer warders on duty than on other days. 'I had a feeling that there was something in the air,' Joe Berry noted. 'I had been carrying dispatches between them and Michael Collins and one heard bits of conversation.

'I used to meet Liam Tobin, Tom Cullen, Frank Thornton, Mulcahy and others who spoke openly to me,' he added. 'But there was no actual statement to me by either Collins or the prisoners of the proposed escape.'

'All the criminal sections of the prison were locked up from dinner-time, and we had the grounds to ourselves, with only one or two warders,' O'Daly explained. 'We were supposed to be good boys then and were not causing any trouble.'

He made final arrangements with Clancy on the Friday. 'Clancy would go to Whitworth Road to find out if he could see my signal, which was the wave of a handkerchief, and he would give a signal in return,' O'Daly recalled. 'We fixed the time and everything else. I wanted to make sure that anyone on Whitworth Road could see the window at the end of the corridor on C Wing, from where I was signalling. The rehearsal went off perfectly, he saw my signal all right.'

On the afternoon of the escape there was a snow storm and for a time it looked like the men would not be allowed out to exercise, but then it cleared. There were just three warders with them and two of those were friendly. 'We did not want one prisoner to hold the three warders in case they would be dismissed afterwards.' O'Daly explained. Six men were chosen to initially hold off the warders. 'Any of the six men were told they could [then] escape but the last three or four of these would have to stay behind to hold the warders.'

With Clancy and his party outside, everything was ready. 'When I gave the signal he threw a rope with a stone on the end of it over the wall,' O'Daly continued. The men in the prison grounds saw his signal from the window and staged a snowball fight in the prison yard. Fleming pulled the ladder over the wall. 'Although the three warders were on the ground,' O'Daly said, 'everything went according to plan. In fact, the last man over the wall stood at the end of the ladder and said, "Any more of you coming?" I believe that if everyone of us had tried to escape we could have managed it.'

'Damn it, Joe,' a warder named Kelly said to Joe Leonard, 'that's no way to hold a man on the ground. Tear my coat a bit.' Leonard duly pulled the buttons off Kelly's coat in order to simulate a struggle.

'I think, Paddy, that you had better sit on me,' the warder Murphy said to O'Daly. 'Get another man to hold me as well.'

The other warder, Jones, had tried to resist and he got a punch on the jaw. 'He was the only one who had violence used on him, to keep him quiet,' according to O'Daly. In all twenty men escaped.

'We ran along the canal,' Malone recalled. 'Someone gave me

a bicycle. I went with J. J. Walsh to Jones' Road, where I spent the night in O'Toole's. The whole thing went off better than anyone could have expected. Collins was waiting impatiently at the Wicklow hotel for word of the escape, when his aide Joe O'Reilly arrived breathless having cycled from Mountjoy.

'Is Fleming out?' Collins asked.

'The whole jail is out.'

'What! How many?'

'About twenty when I came away.'

'Various rumours are abroad as to the number who escaped,' the *Evening Herald* reported that evening. 'Some say twenty-seven, and others thirty-five. We are reliably informed that the number did not exceed twenty.'

Collins and Harry Boland went round to O'Toole's in Jones' Road. 'My clothes were in a bad state,' Malone recalled. 'Without a word, Boland, who was a tailor, took out a tape from his pocket and measured me. "I'll have you right in a couple of days".'

As he sat in his office in Cullenswood House that night, Collins put down his pen and burst out laughing. They had brought off a coup and boosted party morale and more than offset whatever damage had been done when they cancelled the welcoming ceremonies for de Valera.

CHAPTER 3

'EVERY DAMN FOOL'

At G Division headquarters Ned Broy typed up daily reports for the government on the activities, associates and movements of suspects. He also typed weekly reports summarising the week's activities and providing a general review of political activity in the district, with monthly reports on similar lines. 'The majority were typed by me, several copies being made of each report,' Broy explained. One copy was sent to the commissioner of the DMP, Colonel Edgeworth-Johnson, and another copy to the director of military intelligence, Major Price. A further copy went to 'the government', and in some cases a copy went to the RIC. Making so many copies, Broy used to slip in an extra carbon and give those reports to Collins.

Joe Kavanagh – a short, dapper, sixty-year-old Dubliner, with a waxed moustache – had taken part in identifying leaders of the Easter Rising at Richmond barracks, and he clearly regretted his role. He was now secretly committed to Sinn Féin. His earliest contacts with Collins were made through Tom Gay, a librarian in the public library in Capel Street. Gay was a diminutive Dubliner who suffered from bronchial trouble which limited his physical ability, but he nevertheless provided invaluable assistance to Collins. Once Collins gave Gay £5 for Kavanagh in return for certain information. Gay recognised that there was something contemptible about the gesture and he returned the money to Collins a few days later.

'You didn't give him the money!' Collins exclaimed.

'No.'

'You didn't think he'd take it?'

'No.'

'A bloody queer G man!'

It was, of course, still early days and Collins was very raw. In his contempt for the police force, it had not immediately dawned on him that there could be patriotic Irishmen in the force as in any other walk of life. But, unlike others in the movement, he soon learned this lesson and turned it to the advantage of the cause.

Collins had a fairly clear vision of what he wished to do and how he wished to do it. He wanted a military confrontation with the British, but not a conventional war. 'If we were to stand up against the powerful military organisation arrayed against us,' Collins later explained, 'something more was necessary than a guerrilla war in which small bands of our warriors, aided by their knowledge of the country, attacked the larger forces of the enemy and reduced their numbers. England could always reinforce her army. She could replace every soldier that she lost.'

'But,' he added, 'there were others indispensable for her purposes which [sic] were not so easily replaced. To paralyse the British machine it was necessary to strike at individuals. Without her spies England was helpless. It was only by means of their accumulated and accumulating knowledge that the British machine could operate.' He basically considered the DMP and RIC as spies.

Detectives from G Division had, after all, segregated the leaders from the rank and file at Richmond barracks after the Easter Rising. And the British had relied on the RIC to select those to be deported from other parts of the country in the aftermath of the rebellion. 'Without their police throughout the country, how could they find the men they "wanted"?' he asked.

The British administration was dependent on such people and would be virtually blind without them. Thus Collins determined that the first step should be undermining the political detectives in G Division of the DMP. He anticipated that once the detectives were neutralised or eliminated, the British would inevitably react blindly and in the process hit innocent Irish people and thereby drive the great mass of the people into the arms of the republicans.

When the dáil met on 1 April 1919 de Valera was elected *priomh aire* (prime minister), and he then proceeded to name a cabinet that included people like Griffith, Plunkett, MacNeill, Collins, Brugha and Constance Markievicz. The cabinet were representatives of the various factions within Sinn Fein.

The audacity of Collins seemed to know no bounds in his quest to understand the working of G Division. He asked Broy to smuggle him into the division's document room one night so that he could see the records for himself. There would usually be one man on night duty in the detective office but it often happened that the detective on duty would have to be in court next day, so Broy was often called on to do temporary duty. On meeting Collins at Foley's on 6 April 1919 he was able to tell Collins that he would be on duty the following night from 10 p.m. until 6 a.m. They arranged for Collins to call him at midnight to ensure that he could smuggle him in. They agreed that Collins would use the name Field, and Broy would use Long. The office where the records were kept was a semi-circular office, with a large steel safe and many windows. As the blinds only covered the bottom of the windows, they would not be able to turn on the electric light without attracting the attention of the uniformed inspector on duty. It was therefore going to be necessary for Collins to use a candle.

At midnight Collins telephoned. 'Field here. Is that Long?' he asked.

'Yes,' Broy replied. 'Bring a candle.'

Collins arrived at about 12.15 with Seán Nunan, who was one of a number of IRB colleagues with whom he met frequently at Vaughan's hotel. Collins had asked Nunan to come for a walk with him and it was only then that he told him that he was actually going to the detective division headquarters

Broy had said they should be armed just in case something went wrong. 'I duly let them in, showed them the back way and the yard door to Townsend Street, in case anything happened, and gave them the general lie of the land. No sooner had I done so that a stone came through the window.'

'I told them to go into a dark passage and to wait near the back door, in the shadow,' Broy continued. On looking out on Great Brunswick Street I saw a British soldier in custody of a policeman. I opened the door and inquired of the constable what was wrong.'

'This fellow is drunk and he is after throwing a stone in through the window next door,' the constable replied.

Broy took charge of the soldier and brought him to the police station next door and went back to Collins and Nunan. He brought them upstairs and pilfered a box of candles and matches, because Collins had thought he was joking about the candle. Broy locked the dormitory room on the top floor and used a master key to open the detective's room. He then opened the steel safe with the records. He had just left Collins and Nunan in the room with the candles and gone downstairs again, when there was a loud knock on the door. 'I opened it and found the same constable back again, inquiring as to the value of the window broken glass. I gave him a rough estimate and he left. I went upstairs, told the boys what the noise was about, and came down to look after telephones, etc.'

Collins wanted to learn first hand the extent of the British knowledge of the Volunteers, to gauge the mentality behind the records, and to use this knowledge to construct an organisation to undermine it. He and Nunan stayed in the office until about 5 a.m. They then walked to their respective residences – Collins in Mountjoy Street and Nunan in Botanic Road.

Among the files that Collins checked was one that the DMP was keeping on him. He later bragged, with characteristic vanity, that his file mentioned he came from 'a brainy' family. The report, dated 31 December 1916, was written by the district inspector of the RIC in Bandon. He noted that Collins 'belongs to a family [of] "brainy" people who are disloyal and of advanced Sinn Fein sympathies.' His file included police reports on his involvement in the Longford by-election of April 1917 and some of his more controversial speeches, especially those he gave in Ballinamuck and Skibbereen for which the authorities had wished to prosecute him. The various files gave him an invaluable perspective on what G Division knew, and who were its most active detectives. He also got an insight into the people who were providing information. Before leaving, Collins pocketed a bound volume of all telephone messages received by G Division during the week of the 1916 Rising. Some of the messages were from loyalists providing information about where Irish Volunteers had occupied positions in small numbers, or where rebel snipers were posted on roofs or in windows. Others messages were from people who later posed as republican sympathisers. Collins had many cynical laughs listening to protestations of patriotism by some of those who had sent messages to G Division.

Although Collins had no sleep the night he spent in the detective division headquarters, he was in fine form next day when Sinn Féin had a special árd fheis at the Mansion House. De Valera was doing his balancing act in accommodating both sides. He sought to keep militants like Collins in check both by getting the árd fheis to give the standing committee of Sinn Féin a strong voice in policy matters and by debarring members of the cabinet – other than himself and Griffith – from membership of this committee. He undoubtedly had Collins in mind when he explained the standing committee's consultative role. He said, for example, that if a minister decided that the Irish people should no longer pay income tax to the crown, the proposal would need the approval of the standing committee, or it would be dropped.

Collins had been arguing in favour of such a scheme within the cabinet, but he had come up against the resolute obstinacy of Brugha. De Valera, as was his wont, had assumed a detached position in the dispute, but his remarks at the árd fheis certainly leaned towards Brugha's more cautious position on the issue.

Collins was busy lobbying for the election of his friend and IRB colleague, Harry Boland, as one of the joint national secretaries of Sinn Féin. When it was all over and Boland had won, Collins seemed quite pleased with himself.

Collins was a young man in a hurry, operating at break neck pace in at least three different spheres. Within Sinn Féin he was trying to strategically position IRB colleagues, in his ministerial capacity he was charged with organising the national loan, and, as director of both organisation and intelligence in the Volunteers, he was preparing to initiate a war of independence.

On the night after the árd fheis, detectives of the DMP were given a very public warning. Volunteers raided the home of Detective Sergeant Nicholas Halley, and held up Detective Constable Denis O'Brien in the street, binding and gagging him. O'Brien, a native of Kanturk, had been particularly active in the DMP, especially against his fellow Corkmen in the city. Neither man was hurt, but it was a warning to them and their colleagues that the Volunteers could and would strike at them in the streets or in their homes.

When O'Brien was brought to Dublin Castle to explain what had happened, Detective Superintendent Owen Brien asked why he had allowed himself to be tied up.

'I would like to know what anyone else would do in the same circumstances?' O'Brien responded. He later told Broy and some colleagues, 'They were damned decent men not to shoot me, and I am not doing any more against them.'

Addressing the dáil next day, 10 April 1919, de Valera advocated moral rather than armed resistance. Collins wished to kill those police who did not heed the warnings to lay off, but de Valera instead called for the ostracism of all policemen, whom he accused of 'brutal treason', because they were acting as 'the main instruments' in keeping the Irish people in subjugation. 'They are spies in our midst,' he added, echoing the sentiments of Collins. 'They are the eyes and ears of the enemy.'

Of course, some of these detectives were becoming invaluable to Collins. Broy was particularly friendly with Detective Sergeant Joe Kavanagh, who was working out of Dublin Castle. He was godfather to Kavanagh's eldest son. Kavanagh ridiculed Detective Superintendent Owen Brien as 'Butt' Brien. 'Get your faces ready for the Superintendent's joke, boys,' he would say as Brien was about to enter a room. 'I did not know that Joe hated England, in addition to hating the officers, but I knew that we were such friends that I could trust him,' Broy said. Collins had asked him about Kavanagh only once or twice. One evening while walking in Stephen's Green Kavanagh and Broy suddenly realised that they were both giving information to Collins. 'I told him about Mick's visit to No. 1 Great Brunswick Street,' Broy explained. 'He nearly fell, laughing, knowing the mentality in the G Division office and knowing Mick. He got me to tell it to him a second time, and he laughed so much that people looked at him as if he were drunk or mad. He asked me what did Mick look like in the office, and I said he looked like a big plain-clothes man going out on duty, with a stick.'

Collins apologised to Broy for not telling him about Kavanagh. 'I told him that that was what I had been preaching to him since I met him, not to tell anything, that the Irish people had paid too big a price for carelessness like that, in the past.' Michael similarly apologised to Joe the next time he met him, but was glad the two of them now knew and understood each other. Thereafter Kavanagh joined Broy's meeting with Collins at the home of Tom Gay. They were later joined by another detective, Jim McNamara, who was a confidential clerk for the assistant commissioner of the DMP in Dublin Castle. The son of a police officer, McNamara was a light-hearted individual who would playfully trip colleagues up while walking. With his charm and guile he won his way into the trust of both his superiors and Collins. The three detectives were subsequently joined by another, David Neligan. The detectives would go to Clontarf separately by tram, while Collins usually cycled there. If any of them wished to contact Collins at other times, they could do so by leaving a message with Gay at the Capel Street library.

In early May a three-man delegation of Irish-American politicians, which had tried unsuccessfully to get President Woodrow Wilson to secure a hearing for a delegation from the dáil at the Paris Peace Conference, visited Ireland. The dáil held a special public session for them at the Mansion House on 9 May 1919, and there were some dramatic developments in which Collins essentially upstaged everyone. 'A few of us had a very interesting experience', he wrote to Stack a couple of days later.

Collins had been arrested in March 1918 for incitement to riot and incitement to raid for arms in Longford. He put up bail in April 1918 during the conscription crisis, but did not appear in Londonderry on 19 March 1919 to face trial. A bench warrant was issued for his arrest the next day. He was also wanted for illegal drilling in Skibbereen. The bench warrant for that offence was issued on 14 April and provided a description of him: 'Clean shaven – youthful appearance – dresses well – dark brown eyes – regular nose, fresh complexion, oval face, active make, 5' 11" height – about 30 years – dark hair. Generally wears a trilby hat and fawn overcoat.' His address was given as 44 Mountjoy Street, which was correct at the time, but he promptly moved, and the police reported that they were unable to locate him there.

But some detectives recognised Collins and a couple of other wanted men as they entered the Mansion House for the special session and they called G Division headquarters to raid the place. 'I heard about this almost on the spot,' Broy said. He could not telephone a warning from the police station, so he went outside to a public telephone and called de Valera. As the telephone service of the day was notoriously insecure, Broy gave the warning in French, but the Long Fellow could not understand his French. Piaras Beaslaí therefore took the message from Broy that the building would be raided that afternoon.

'We'll have our lunch first,' Collins replied rather nonchalantly when Beaslaí passed on the warning. The Big Fellow was obviously enjoying the prospect of becoming the centre of attention. He sent Joe O'Reilly to fetch his uniform. O'Reilly, a fellow Cork man, was a lively individual, totally dedicated to Collins. 'About five o'clock the enemy came along with three motor lorries, [a] small armoured car, machine guns, probably 200 or 250 troops,' Collins wrote. 'They surrounded the building with great attention to every military detail. They entered the Mansion House and searched it with great care and thoroughness but they got nobody inside. The wanted ones codded them again.'

Collins, Robert Barton and Ted Kelly had slipped out a back window and hid in an adjoining building. When the military left they returned, only this time Collins was dressed in his Volunteers uniform. It was a show of bravado that went down well with most of the gathering, though some felt that the Big Fellow was showing off again. 'By this time everybody should know that it is by naked force that England holds this country,' Collins wrote with obvious satisfaction. 'Our American friends got an exhibition of the truth while they were here.'

Tim Healy, the old parliamentarian, happened to be in the vicinity and saw the raid in progress. 'Nothing that the wit of man could devise equalled the Mansion House raid of the military in folly,' he wrote. 'Every damn fool seems to be in the employment of the British government in Ireland.'

Meanwhile Collins was growing ever more impatient for a fight. He encouraged local units of the Volunteers to raid police barracks for arms. This, in addition to affording an opportunity of acquiring much needed weapons, had the advantage of acting as a kind of training operation for the Volunteers. It soon led to the withdrawal of the RIC from isolated areas and the abandonment of hundreds of police barracks throughout the country.

He complained in a letter to Austin Stack about Sinn Féin politicians making things 'intolerable' for militants like him. 'The policy now seems to be to squeeze out anyone who is tainted with strong fighting ideas, or should I say the utility of fighting,' he grumbled. He was particularly critical of the party's executive committee, which he described as 'a Standing Committee of malcontents' who were 'inclined to be ever less militant and more political and theoretical'. In short, they were talkers and thinkers, rather than men of action, and he was a man of action. 'We have too many of the bargaining type already,' Collins grumbled. 'I am not sure that our movement or part of it at any rate is alive to the developing situation.'

Describing himself as 'only an onlooker' at the executive committee meetings, he complained that the moderates were in control. When Harry Boland went to the United States to make preparations for de Valera's forthcoming tour, the party replaced him as national secretary with Hannah Sheehy-Skeffington, the wife of a pacifist murdered during the Easter Rising. Collins was appalled. Not only had Boland been replaced by a woman, but the party also went on to announce that his replacement was necessary because he was out of the country. With this announcement, Collins fumed: 'our people give away in a moment what the Detective Division had been unable to find out in five weeks.'

He clearly felt a lot of hostility towards himself and his militant views. There were 'rumours, whisperings, suggestions of differences between certain people', he wrote, describing this as 'rather pitiful and disheartening'. It belied the national unity of which de Valera boasted and it tended towards confusion about the best way of achieving the national aims. 'At the moment,' Collins exclaimed, 'I'm awfully fed up.'

'Things are not going very smoothly,' he was still writing three weeks later. 'All sort of miserable little under currents are working and the effect is anything but good.'

He would soon have a freer hand to do his own thing though, as de Valera was to set out for the United States in early June.

CHAPTER 4

'ALMOST A MIRACLE I WAS NOT LANDED'

In the spring of 1919, de Valera had restrained the Big Fellow's desire for a military campaign by ensuring that the political wing of the movement had a big say in policy. Shortly after de Valera went to the United States however, Brugha and Mulcahy authorised Collins to kill one of the DMP detectives who had refused to be cowed by the Volunteers.

Many policemen were resigning because of their social ostracisation. Those who were nearing retirement, having spent the bulk of their working lives in the police force, were too old to find other employment. They stayed on but most kept their heads down and ignored all political activities.

In July Collins was authorised by Richard Mulcahy as chief-of-staff and Cathal Brugha as minister for defence to kill Detective Sergeant Patrick Smyth, because he was a particular thorn in the side of the republicans. He had been warned on a number of occasions 'to lay off republicans or he would be shot', one of those who took part in the assassination later explained.

'I'm not letting any young scuts tell me how to do my duty,' Detective Sergeant Patrick Smyth had declared. He had arrested Piaras Beaslaí for making a seditious speech and had found some incriminating documents on him. Collins and Harry Boland warned Smyth not to produce the documents in court, but the detective ignored them. As a result Beaslaí was sentenced to two years in jail, instead of the two months he might have otherwise expected.

Jim Slattery recalled a meeting at 35 North Great George's Street around the middle of July 1919. A number of men were selected by Dick McKee and Mick McDonnell and brought to an inner room. McKee asked if any of them objected to shooting enemy agents.

'The greater number of Volunteers objected for one reason or another,' Slattery said. 'When I was asked the question I said I was prepared to obey orders ... I recall that two men, who had previously told Mick McDonnell that they had no objection to being selected for special duty, turned down the proposition at that meeting ... McDonnell seemed very annoyed at them and asked them why they had signified their willingness in the first instance.'

Among the men who agreed that night were Tom Keogh, Tom Kilcoyne, Jim Slattery and Joe Leonard. These four, together with Tom Ennis and, later, Paddy O'Daly, were to become the nucleus of the famous Squad, but there was no mention of this that night.

'We were merely told that we were to be given special duties,' Slattery added. He received his orders from McDonnell to shoot Detective Sergeant Smyth, who was living in Millmount Avenue. A native of Dromard, County Longford, Smyth was in his early fifties and had helped identify some of the leaders following the Easter Rebellion.

'McDonnell instructed me to go to Drumcondra Bridge and take with me Tom Keogh, Tom Ennis and Mick Kennedy, who knew Smyth by sight,' according to Slattery. 'McDonnell told us that Smyth usually came home by tram, alighted at Botanic Avenue and walked across the bridge. We were to wait at the bridge and shoot Smyth when the opportunity offered. We waited at Drumcondra bridge for about five nights.'

The first time he came along they did not strike because Kennedy was not sure it was Smyth. They expected him to turn into Millmount Avenue where he lived, but he passed the entrance and walked to Milburn Avenue, which was adjacent to his home. It was too late before his would-be assassins realised what had happened. Fearing that they had aroused Smyth's suspicion, they did not come back for about a week, until the night of 30 July.

They waited that night with .38 revolvers, which they soon

found were not powerful enough. They had expected that Smyth would fall as soon as he was shot. 'But after we hit him he ran,' Slattery noted. 'The four of us fired at him. Keogh and myself ran after him right to his own door and I think he fell at the door, but he got into the house.'

Smyth gave a statement next day. 'When I got off the tram at the end of my own avenue, I saw four or five men against the dead wall, and a bicycle resting against the curb stone. Just as I turned the corner into Millmount Avenue, I was shot in the back. I turned and said to them, "You cowards" and three of them fired again with revolvers at me.' Even though one bullet had hit his right leg, he had still managed to run towards his home.

'They pursued me to within fifteen yards of my own door, and kept firing at me all the time. In all about ten or twelve shots were fired at me. I called for assistance but no one came to me except my own son.'

Smyth's teenage son, Thomas, had witnessed the whole thing; he was just over five yards from his father when he was shot.

Smyth was hit four times, the most serious wound was from a bullet that entered his back, passed through a lung and lodged in his chest, just above the heart. At the time Smyth's wife and three of their seven children were in the country on holiday. In the commotion his six-year-old second son raced from the house vowing 'to catch those who shot Dada'. He returned later saying that the men had run off.

'Was it not a cowardly thing to shoot him in the back without giving him a chance of defending himself?' Smyth's sixteen-year-old daughter said next day. 'He always carried a revolver,' she added, 'but he hadn't it with him last night, so he could not put up a fight against his would-be murderers.'

'We had made a right mess of the job,' McDonnell complained next day.

'But I can assure you,' Slattery said, 'I was more worried until Smyth died than Mick was. We never used .38 guns again; we used

.45 guns after that lesson.'

Although Smyth was mortally wounded, he lived for five weeks before finally succumbing as a result of complications caused by an abscess of the lung resulting from a bullet wound. He died on the afternoon of 8 September 1919.

The reaction in Dublin Castle was to use the killing as an excuse to ban Sinn Féin. It was an ill-conceived act that played directly into the hands of Collins, who would henceforth have little difficulty in outmanoeuvring Sinn Féin moderates and implementing a more militant policy. The checks that de Valera had placed on the militants were wiped out by the banning of the political wing of the movement. To some Irish people this amounted to a British declaration of war, and it was intended to appear as such.

Back in the spring of 1919 Ian Macpherson, the chief secretary for Ireland, had wished to ban Sinn Féin, the Irish Volunteers, the Gaelic League and Cumann na mBan, and had written to Bonar Law on 16 May 1919 acknowledging that it would mean '*open war* with all its horrible consequences'. Law and Edward Carson, the two staunchest unionists, thought this would be a mistake. 'To proclaim Sinn Féin means putting an end to the whole political life of Southern Ireland and that could not be effectively done,' Law had warned. In the circumstances Macpherson had to back off, but after an attack on British soldiers in Fermoy on 7 September, followed by Detective Sergeant Smyth's death next day, Dublin Castle announced the drastic measures that the chief secretary had predicted would amount to 'open war' just four months earlier – Sinn Féin, the Gaelic League and Cumann na mBan were all banned, along with Dáil Éireann. 'We had allowed these members to sit together *in consultation* if they wished,' Macpherson wrote to Bonar Law on 13 September, but when they 'conspired by executive acts to overthrow the duly constituted authority then we could act.'

Sir Warren Fisher, the head of the British civil service, would later conclude that the Dublin Castle regime was 'almost woodenly stupid and quite devoid of imagination'. He could hardly believe the folly of banning Sinn Féin and Cumann na mBan. 'Imagine the result on public opinion in Great Britain of a similar act by the executive towards a political party (or the women's suffrage movement)!' he exclaimed.

The DMP raided Sinn Féin headquarters at 6 Harcourt Street on 12 September 1919. Collins was in the building when the police arrived at 10.30 a.m., backed up by two army lorries with British soldiers. 'We had no warning of this raid at all,' Eibhlín Lawless, one of the young secretaries recalled. 'Collins was upstairs in our room.' J. J. 'Ginger' O'Connell had come in to talk to Collins and had left the door to the room open as he left.

'I was getting up to shut it when I saw a policeman standing on guard outside,' Lawless said. 'I shut the door and told Mick it looked like a raid.'

'I think only Mick was armed,' she continued. 'If any of the others were, the girls took the arms from them. I stuck Mick's revolver down my stocking and anything else incriminating we girls took charge of. The police seemed to start the raid systematically from the bottom up thus giving us time to take these precautions. When they arrived, we had disposed of everything and they found nothing of any importance. They searched the men but not us.'

'There was no means of escape,' she noted, 'as the military had occupied the narrow entrance in the back as well as the front.' The police had locked the front door and they were not letting anyone in or out. Detective Inspector George Love was in charge of the raid.

'We are caught like rats in a trap and there is no escape,' Collins said. He sat at his desk, quite calm and collected until Detective Inspector Neil McFeely came in. 'It was Inspector McFeely who came to our room, looking a little bit frightened,' Lawless reported. 'He went round searching the different desks, and seemed desperately anxious to finish his task and get out. Mick sat very casually on his desk with one leg swinging and told him in no measured terms what sort of work he was engaged on. He was scathing in his remarks about it.'

McFeely had only recently been promoted inspector in charge of political duty. 'He was about the least efficient officer that could be allocated to such work, as he was a man completely without guile or ruse,' according to Ned Broy. 'He had been all his life a clerk, could do some "finger and thumb" typing, and frequently was given such duty as making maps of the scene of accidents, burglaries and suchlike. He was directed to take a party of detectives and raid No. 6 Harcourt St.' He was told to arrest people like Paudeen O'Keeffe or Paddy Sheehan, but nobody suggested to arrest Michael Collins because they would not have believed he would be at such a well-known Sinn Fein address as party headquarters. The detectives accompanying McFeely recognised the people on the ground floor, but McFeely wandered upstairs alone. He did not know Collins and he apparently assumed that Collins could not be of much importance if he was upstairs working with a bunch of women.

Broy had advised Collins that McFeely was a staunch home ruler and the way to confront him would be to say that 'by his activities against Sinn Féin he was sowing up disgrace for himself, his family and descendants for years to come.' Thus, according to Lawless, when the detective inspector asked Collins about some documents in his hands, he was met with a torrent of abuse.

'What have they got to do with you?' Collins snapped. 'A nice job you've got, spying on your countrymen. What sort of a legacy will you leave to your family, looking for blood money? Could you not find some honest work to do?'

'The inspector was writhing under the attack,' Lawless added. 'At that stage they left the room.' They then searched the caretaker's quarters overhead.

In the course of the search, the DMP found Ernest Blythe hiding in a small store-room, so he was arrested along with Sinn Féin secretary Paudeen O'Keeffe. 'It was Mick's coolness that saved him from being recognised,' Lawless thought. 'From time to time the girls would take a peep out at the corridor to see if the coast was clear and, as soon as we got word that the police had left the caretaker's room, Mick managed to slip up the stairs, which were now empty,' she added. Some of the other police came into the room later but they just looked and did not question anybody.

'It was only by almost a miracle I was not landed,' Collins wrote next day. 'It so happened the particular detective who came into the room where I was did not know me, which gave me an opportunity of eluding him.'

McFeely would never have confided in someone as junior as Broy, but he did tell Inspector Kerr about the raid. 'McFeely says there is going to be serious trouble,' Kerr told Broy afterwards. 'He has met a very determined young man, a clerk in 6 Harcourt Street, and if they are all as extreme as he is, there is plenty of trouble coming.'

Detective Constable Daniel Hoey, a native of King's County (now Offaly), would find himself on the receiving end of that trouble that night. Although only in his early thirties, he had been a particular irritation for the Volunteers going back to before 1916. He would have recognised Collins but had missed his chance and would not get another.

Mick McDonnell called on Jim Slattery at 9 Woodville Road that evening and asked him to go on a job. 'They very nearly got the man we want to guard,' McDonnell said.

'That was the first inkling I got that Collins was the heart of things,' Slattery noted. 'It became very urgent to get Detective Officer Hoey, because he was the leading spirit in the raiders.' He was the detective on the ground with most knowledge and O'Daly and Kilcoyne had been trying to get him for a couple of weeks.

'Ennis, Mick McDonnell and I came down to Townsend Street,' Slattery recalled. 'Mick said he thought that Detective Hoey would be going off duty at about ten o'clock, and he did not go off. Hoey crossed over from College Street towards the police headquarters in Brunswick Street. I asked Mick if he was sure that this man was Hoey?

'"I am not quite sure, but we will go after him," he replied.

'We intended that if he went straight to the door of the building we would shoot him, but instead of going there he went down Townsend Street nearly as far as Tara Street. We passed him by when he was looking at a window and Mick said, "It is Hoey all right." He went into a shop and passed back up to the corner of Hawkins Street. When we saw him approaching again, we crossed over to the side of the street, which was at the back of the barracks, and we shot him at the door of the garage.'

After the shooting, Mick McDonnell said, 'we had better go to Mick Collins and report to him.' They were confident that they had killed Hoey, who was rushed to Mercer's Hospital, where he was dead on arrival.

Paddy O'Daly had not been at the original meeting in July at which the nucleus of the Squad was formed as he was not released from Mountjoy until 2 August but he did tell of another meeting. 'Dick McKee told Joe Leonard and myself to report to 46 Parnell Square – the meeting place of the Keating Branch of the Gaelic League – on 19 September 1919,' O'Daly recalled. Mick McDonnell, Joe Leonard, Ben Barrett, Seán Doyle, Tom Keogh, and Jim Slattery were at this meeting, which Michael Collins and chief-of-staff Richard Mulcahy addressed.

'They told us it was proposed to form a Squad,' O'Daly said. 'The Squad would take orders directly from Michael Collins, and, in the absence of Collins, the orders would be given to us through either Dick McKee or Dick Mulcahy. We were told that we were not to discuss our movements or actions with Volunteer officers or with anybody else. Collins told us that we were being formed to deal with spies and informers and that he had authority from the government to have this matter carried out.'

Collins gave 'a short talk, the gist of which was that any of us who had read Irish history would know that no organisation in the past had an intelligence system through which spies and informers could be dealt with, but that now the position was going to be rectified by the formation of an intelligence branch, an Active Service Unit or whatever else it is called.' Collins went on to emphasise 'that under no circumstances whatever were we to take it on ourselves to shoot anybody, even if we knew he was a spy, unless we had to do it in self-defence while on active service. He also told us to remember that all members of G Division and the police were not our enemies, and that indiscriminate shooting might result in the death of friends. We discovered afterwards how many of them were our friends.'

'Collins only picked four of us for the Squad that night – Joe Leonard, Seán Doyle, Ben Barrett and myself in charge,' according to O'Daly. 'He told the others that he had special work [for them] to do, but he told the four of us that we were to leave our employment and that we would be compensated for loss of work. We were to have a fixed point where we could be mobilised, and I gave him No. 10 Bessboro Avenue, North Strand, where I had relations and where I practically lived at the time.'

The special work for McDonnell was to go to London to investigate the possibility of killing prominent people there. 'I was approached by Dick McKee and asked to make myself available to go to London for special duty with the object of looking the situation over in London and coming back and reporting as to the possibility of wiping out the British cabinet and several other prominent people including editors of newspapers, etc., who were antagonistic to this country' he recalled. 'I went with Liam Tobin in charge and George Fitzgerald who remained with me for two weeks.'

'Our chief job in London was to familiarise ourselves with the then Ministers of the British cabinet, their haunts, habits, etc.,' George Fitzgerald explained. 'We were to attend any meetings at which they were tabled to speak or any function at which they were to attend. In addition, we were to get any information we could about the geography of Whitehall, especially No. 10 Downing Street. After about a fortnight of this work Mick McDonnell left us and returned to Dublin.'

'I first reported to General Mulcahy at Harcourt Street and made an appointment to go to 41 Parnell Square that night and meet Michael Collins, Cathal Brugha, General Mulcahy and a few others,' McDonnell noted. 'I could not report favourably owing to lack of assistance on the part of the London Volunteers and to the impossibility of making a simultaneous swoop on the entire cabinet and the other people who were earmarked for execution. Michael Collins who had lived in London and knew the situation existing there, agreed with this report, but Cathal Brugha insisted that it could and should be done.'

Wiping out the British cabinet had long been one of Brugha's pet ideas. He knew it would be a kind of suicide mission, but he had already led a similar team to London to kill cabinet members in the House of Commons in 1918 if they had introduced conscription in Ireland. In the course of his planning he had gone into the parliament building to check out first hand the possibility of killing the cabinet there, but the whole thing was called off when the conscription plan was dropped. Brugha was a man of great determination but rather limited vision. He was as 'brave and as brainless as a bull' noted Mulcahy.

'I then told him it would take at least thirty of the best men we could find and they did not hope to return alive, but he still agreed it would be worth while to lose thirty good men,' McDonnell noted. 'This ended the matter as far as I was concerned and I did not go back to London.'

Collins was still supposedly wanted in connection with the illegal drilling in Skibbereen, but the attorney general had ruled that 'no further proceedings need to be taken' in regard to the Longford charges. Collins felt secure enough to move back into Myra McCarthy's Munster hotel at 44 Mountjoy Street. He bragged that the police were afraid to arrest him. In October 1919 he went to Britain primarily in connections with plans to spring Austin Stack and Piaras Beaslaí from Strangeways jail in Manchester. He had taken a particular interest in arranging Stack's escape over a number of months, first from Dundalk Jail, and then from Belfast Jail, but each time Stack was transferred before the escape plans could be implemented. Collins actually visited Stack in Strangeways to finalise the escape arrangements for 25 October 1919.

There were no houses on the street that ran by the back of the jail so the outside escape party decided to block this road during the escape attempt. People would be allowed to enter it from either end, but then they would be compelled to remain until the operation was over. Matthew Lawless and another volunteer were dressed as window cleaners moving about the area ready to do their part with an extended ladder when required.

'When everything was in readiness Rory O'Connor blew a whistle which was the pre-arranged signal and this signal was answered inside by one of the prisoners,' remembered Paddy O'Donoghue. 'Almost immediately a rope with a weight on it was thrown over the wall. The weight fell on the inside but it only brought the rope a few feet over the wall and dangled about twenty feet above the heads of the prisoners inside. The rope was pulled back and thrown over again but with no better result. A third time it was thrown over and this time we succeeded in getting it a couple of feet further but not sufficiently far down for the prisoners to grasp it.'

With the help of Lawless and the other volunteers, Peadar Clancy put the extended ladder against the wall and succeeded in pulling the rope ladder over to within the grasp of the waiting prisoners. 'Austin Stack was the first man to come over the wall in safety.' O'Donoghue continued. 'Beaslaí was next and he got stuck against the wall half way up because his other escaping comrades were trying to use the rope at the same time as he was endeavouring to make the assent. It was then realised that only one man could climb the rope at a time, and the men got safely over.'

Four other prisoners also made it over – Seán Doran from Loughinisland, County Down; D. P. Walsh from Fethard; and two Cork men, Con Connolly from Clonakilty and Paddy McCarthy from Freemount. Stack, Beaslaí, Walsh and Connolly were put into a taxi that was at the ready, while there were bicycles for the other two. O'Donoghue cycled off with Doran and McCarthy but they got separated in the heavy traffic and O'Donoghue lost them. The two were in a strange city so they sought out a Catholic church. Then, pretending to go to confession, they told a priest of their predicament. He contacted a Clare woman living in Manchester and she brought them to the house of George Lodge, an Irish friend who was living in the suburb of Prestwich, about six miles from the city centre. Lodge, a chemist with the Imperial Chemical Company, was already putting up Stack and Beaslaí. It was just a sheer coincidence that the woman took the two men there.

Following the escape Collins went to London to meet with Tobin and Fitzgerald. 'We met him and he walked around London with us, and in the course of our walk we had a good look at Scotland Yard and the principal government offices in Whitehall,' Fitzgerald recalled. He was already impatient to get home. 'Our work was becoming very monotonous,' Fitzgerald explained. 'We were getting tired hanging round having very little to do. We were asked from time to time to get information concerning some matter that GHQ at home was interested in. For example, if a political meeting, banquet, etc., was to be held and was to be addressed by some member of the cabinet, one of us was to go there and report on the Minister who addressed the meeting and say what precautions were taken to guard him, his method of getting to the meeting and getting away from it. This procedure was followed at any political meetings held in the vicinity of London. On one occasion I travelled to Colchester and was present at an "Oyster

Banquet" at which the prime minister was the principal speaker. This information would be conveyed back to Dublin through Sam Maguire.'

Collins returned to Manchester and met the escaped prisoners hiding in Lodge's house and made arrangements for them to be smuggled back to Dublin during the first week in November.

CHAPTER 5

'I DO NOT DEFEND THE MURDER SIMPLY AS SUCH I MERELY APPLAUD IT'

While some people believed that Collins moved about the city in disguise, highly armed and well protected, he in fact usually went alone, unarmed, on a bicycle, without any disguise. Some of the detectives knew him, but he had so terrorised the DMP that they were afraid to apprehend him lest the faceless people supposedly protecting him would come to his rescue, or take revenge on them. They knew only of his ruthless reputation, and he exploited it to the full.

If he took a tram and he saw a detective who would recognise him, Collins would confidently sit by the detective and ask in a friendly way about the detective's family. If one of the children had made their first communion or been confirmed he would mention this, and anything he might know about the wife. He would, for instance, asked how the wife was, using her name. It was all a very subtle way of saying that he knew so much about the man's family that if the detective did not want anything to happen to them, he would not interfere with Collins. It would have been out of character for Collins to attack any member of a person's family in this way, but the detectives did not know that. As Collins would get off the tram, he would tell the detective that it would be safe for him to get off at a subsequent stop.

One day in the street Batt O'Connor became uneasy at the way two DMP looked at Collins. They seemed to recognise him, but he was unperturbed.

'Even if they recognised me,' Collins said, 'they would be afraid to report they saw me.' And even if they did report, it would take the DMP an hour to muster the necessary force to seize him. 'And, of course,' he added, 'all the time I would wait here until they were ready to come along!'

He never stayed in any one place very long. He always had something to do, somebody to see, or somewhere to go.

Although he was always on the go, he never thought of himself as being 'on the run'. Wanted men frequently developed a habit of venturing forth only with care. Before leaving a building they would sneak a furtive glance to make sure there were no police around, whereas Collins had contempt for such practices. He just bounded out a door in a carefree, self-confident manner without betraying the slightest indication he was trying to evade anybody.

'I do not allow myself to feel I am on the run,' he explained. 'That is my safeguard. It prevents me from acting in a manner likely to arouse suspicion.'

Following the raid on the Sinn Féin headquarters at 6 Harcourt Street in September, the headquarters were moved down the street to number 76 Harcourt Street. The police had captured so much material at Number 6 that Batt O'Connor suggested building some hiding place into the new headquarters. 'It would be worth trying anyway.'

He had already built this hiding place, into a wall, when the police raided the office on 8 November 1919. The staff had time to slip the books and papers under a sliding door before the police burst into the room. They searched the building but did not find the secret cupboard. Beaslaí had just arrived back in Dublin that day following his escape from Strangeways. He was at O'Connor's house when Joe O'Reilly arrived with the news that 76 Harcourt Street was being raided and that Collins was in the building.

One of the uniformed policemen involved in searching the building was Constable David Neligan, who was shortly to become another of Collins' police spies. He had no intention of trying to find anything. 'I went upstairs and counted the roses on the wallpaper until the raid was over,' he explained.

Collins headed for the skylight and escaped across the roof, climbing through the skylight of the nearby Standard hotel and boarding a tram outside while the raid was still in progress. The staff working in the building were arrested and each member was sentenced to two months in jail. They included Dick McKee, Diarmuid O'Hegarty, Fintan Murphy, Frank Lawless, Seán Hayes, Seán O'Mahony, Patrick Sheehan, Michael Lynch and Dan O'Donovan. 'They made a clean sweep of the entire male staff, with the exception of the writer [himself] who evaded them,' Collins wrote. 'You will be pleased to know that they got no documents of importance, so that the only disorganisation is through the seizure of the staff.'

Detective Sergeant Thomas Wharton, whose regular beat included Harcourt Street was shot and seriously wounded a couple of days after the raid. He, along with the ill-fated Detective Sergeant Patrick Smyth, had previously arrested Beaslaí. Wharton, who was from Ballyhar near Killarney, was walking on the western side of Stephen's Green towards Grafton Street. He had come down Harcourt Street when a lone shot rang out.

This seemed very different from the shooting of Smyth or Hoey. Wharton was not shot by a gang acting in concert, but by a lone gunman, with an unarmed accomplice. There had been plenty of backup firepower when Smyth and Hoey were shot, but in this instance the would-be assailant's gun jammed after he got only one shot off.

Learning on the night of 10 November that Detective Sergeant Wharton was supposed to be in Harcourt Street, O'Daly and Leonard had gone to look for him, but he was not there. They then went to the vicinity of G Division headquarters. 'After spending some hours around College Street waiting for Wharton's return to barracks, we decided to give it up as a bad job,' O'Daly said. 'Joe Leonard got into the No. 15 tram to go home, and he had only just gone when I saw Wharton going up Grafton Street with two other detectives. I followed them as far as Harcourt

Street. I immediately went to Joe Leonard's house, No. 3 Mountpleasant Avenue, Ranelagh.

'When I got there I discovered that Joe had no gun in the house, so we decided to go down, get Joe's gun and then go after Wharton. On our way down we met Wharton face to face at the corner of Cuffe Street, with three other detectives. I told Joe it would be a pity to let the opportunity pass; that one of the detectives walking side by side with Wharton was the man we were not to shoot.

'I fired at Wharton and he fell,' O'Daly continued. 'The other detective turned round but seemed to make very little effort to draw a gun. I discovered then that the parabellum I had was choked and I could not fire the second shot. I kept my eyes on the other three detectives as we made for Cuffe Street, and I noticed that the friendly detective walked between me and the other two detectives. I saw the gun in his hand but I did not hear him fire it. I think he tried to get between the other detectives and myself in order to prevent them firing.'

O'Daly added that they were surprised to hear the following day that the bullet had hit Wharton in the back of the right shoulder, passed through his right lung, exiting in the front and had then struck Gertrude O'Hanlon, a young female student from Sligo who was walking in front of him. She was particularly lucky because although the bullet tore through her velvet cap and drew an amount of blood from her scalp, it was fortunately only a scalp wound.

Later James Hurley, an innocent news vendor and veteran of the First World War, was charged with the attempted murder before a military court. He had spent fifteen years in the British army before he was discharged in 1917 having been wounded, shell shocked and gassed. The main witness was William F. Bachelor, a former British army officer living on South Circular Road. He testified that a week earlier he had seen Hurley standing at the corner with three other men whom Bachelor had confronted after some remark was made. Bachelor testified that he noticed Hurley in the area on other nights, and on the night that Wharton was shot, he said he saw Hurley run from Cuffe Street into Harcourt Street and fire a shot as two tall men were crossing the street. One was struck and staggered.

Nine days later Bachelor pointed out Hurley to Detective Sergeant Johnny Barton, 'I can swear he is the man,' Bachelor said. Barton arrested Hurley, who put up no resistance. When Barton and a colleague searched him, they found nothing more lethal than a couple of ballads. Among the newspapers that he used to sell were *The Irish Volunteer* and *The United Irishman*.

Bachelor testified that he chased the gunman down Cuffe Street and Wexford Street in the direction of Camden Street but that his progress was obstructed and he lost him. Olive Warrington testified that she was standing on the corner talking to a friend when she heard the shot and saw two men running down Cuffe Street being pursued by Bachelor, but she could not describe the men running away.

A policeman on point duty testified that Hurley normally sold newspapers at the corner between 3 p.m. and 7 p.m. At the time of the shooting on the evening in question Hurley's defence contended that he was in Little's Bar at the corner of Harcourt Street having a drink. Patrick Clitheroe, another newspaper seller, testified that he was with Hurley in the bar when a newsboy, John Ratigan, rushed in and told them about the shooting. Ratigan confirmed that he told them in the public house.

But this was a military court and they were just newspaper vendors contradicting the word of a former officer who was presumed to be a gentleman. Hurley was convicted and sentenced to fifteen years in jail. Had Wharton died, he would probably have been executed. According to Paddy O'Daly, Hurley was released after the truce but was killed during the civil war while helping a wounded soldier into Jervis Street hospital.

The more the notoriety of Collins grew, the more willing some people were to work for him, and the fact that he was president of the supreme council of the IRB probably helped in recruiting spies. A person in his position in a secret society was someone they could trust.

He continued to make new contacts. Kavanagh and Broy introduced him to a new detective, James McNamara, who was administrative assistant to the assistant police commissioner in Dublin Castle.

Tadgh Kennedy, the intelligence officer in Kerry, was on friendly terms in Tralee with another future contact, the Special Crimes Sergeant Thomas O'Rourke, who confided in Kennedy that he was anxious to channel information to the republican leadership. 'I hadn't such experience of intelligence at the time and I was scared to have much to do with the RIC,' Kennedy explained. He therefore consulted Michael Collins, who told him to ask O'Rourke to furnish a copy of the key to the RIC code.

'I asked him for the key,' Kennedy added, 'and he delivered it to myself. I sent it to Mick Collins and henceforth I was able to supply it to Headquarters every month and after each change where the RIC suspected we had got it. Mick told me afterwards that it was the first time he was able to procure the key regularly and it laid the foundation of the elaborate scheme of intelligence in the post offices.'

In September Collins learned that a Sergeant Jerry Maher of the RIC in Naas might be sympathetic. When an emissary asked Maher about working for Collins, his eyes immediately lit up. 'You're the man I've been waiting for,' Maher replied.

He was working as a clerk for the county inspector, Kerry Leyne Supple of the RIC, and he was able to pilfer the code that was confined to county inspectors. He also recruited the district inspector's clerk, Constable Patrick Casey, who became another source of the code being supplied by O'Rourke. At times Collins would have dispatches decoded and circulated to brigade intelligence officers before some of the county inspectors could decode their own messages.

Collins also had at least two other sources for the police codes. Maurice McCarthy, an RIC sergeant stationed in Belfast was one, and the other was a cousin of his own, Nancy O'Brien, who had spent some years working in the post office in London. She was brought to Dublin as a cipher clerk to decode messages. She was selected, she was told, because the Dublin Castle authorities wanted someone they could trust because Collins was getting some messages even before the British officers for whom they were intended. She, of course, promptly went to Collins.

Following his return from Britain McDonnell headed a different section of the Squad but neither section knew of the other's existence initially. McDonnell's group included his half-brother, Tom Keogh, who was an easy-going individual with great courage who had been a shop assistant in Wicklow; and two former inmates of Frongoch, Bill Stapleton from Dublin and Jim Slattery from Clare.

While the plan to kill the British cabinet and leading public figures in England had been called off, it had been substituted with a plan to kill the lord lieutenant, Sir John French. Mick McDonnell said that he had been approached to act as a sniper to get the lord lieutenant on a reviewing stand during a public parade in late November 1919 but that this had been called off by Cathal Brugha because 'the people would not stand for it'. Some of the details of this story were so confused however that one needs to be very careful. There was no parade in later November, but there was one within the grounds of Trinity College on 11 November. Irish secretary, Sir Hamar Greenwood, who was supposed to be with French within Trinity College on the occasion, was not actually appointed to the post until some months later. However, there was no doubt whatever that Collins was anxious to kill French.

As a teenager in London a decade earlier Collins had taken a particular interest in the Phoenix Park murders of 1882 and the

1904 murder in Finland of Nicholai Bobrikov, the Russian governor general. The consequences of the Bobrikov murder were like a 'fairy tale', according Collins. The Russian tsar, fearing revolution, agreed to free elections and the establishment of a national parliament in Finland, based on proportional representation and universal adult suffrage. Even though that freedom did not last long, the fact that it happened at all was enough to encourage the young Collins.

'As a rule I hate morals and hate moralists still more,' the teenage Collins wrote. He approved of the actions of the rebels who assassinated the lieutenant governor in the Phoenix Park in 1882 and he condemned 'the foolish Irish apologists' who were critical of the killers. 'I do not defend the murder simply as such,' he wrote. 'I merely applaud it on the ground of expedience.'

The Finns helped themselves by aligning with Russian revolutionaries. 'May not we also find it beneficial to allow our best to be helped by the English revolutionists?' Collins asked in 1907.

In reality he was prepared to make use of anyone he thought would be helpful to the cause. Dan Breen and some of his colleagues from Tipperary came to Dublin 'looking for bigger game' according to Breen, although Dick Mulcahy, the IRA chief-of-staff, believed it was because Tipperary had become too hot for them. Whatever the reason, Collins welcomed them and enlisted them in his efforts to kill the lord lieutenant. He even took the unusual step of taking an active part in one planned ambush involving the Squad, the Dublin brigade and Breen's men.

They waited to ambush Lord French in the city on his return from Dun Laoghaire in November. 'Mick Collins was with us on the first occasion that we lay in ambush,' Breen recalled. They planned to ambush him at the junction of Suffolk Street and Trinity Street but the viceroy never showed. On another occasion they knew that he would be attending a function so they waited in ambush, but he again travelled by a different route.

While waiting for a chance to shoot the lord lieutenant, the

Squad killed Detective Sergeant Johnny Barton at the height of the rush hour on the evening of 30 November 1919. He was a genial Kerry man from Firies and was well known to the Volunteers. He would 'engage in pleasantries with our Staff Officers or even common Volunteers', according to Joe Leonard. He also frequently called for a cup of tea at the family home of Ben and Bernard Byrne, two men who later joined the Squad.

Very tall and thin, he wore weird clothes with farmer's boots and looked like something out of an Abbey play. 'Anyone could take him for a simpleton,' Constable David Neligan noted, 'but it would be a major error.' He was easily the best detective in these islands, had plenty of touts working for him and was known to be well off financially.

Neligan believed that Barton extorted money from English people who came to Ireland to avoid conscription during the Great War. Known derisively as Flyboys, some of these people had plenty of money, or at least more money than desire to fight. Barton tracked them down through his touts and then, for a financial consideration, left them alone. Having arrested James Hurley for supposedly shooting Detective Sergeant Wharton, he gave the impression that he was not afraid of Collins or the republicans. This posed a threat, because it could undermine the terrorist tactics that the Big Fellow had been using to demoralise the police.

Jim Slattery had no idea why Collins wanted Barton out of the way. 'I have nothing much to say about him except that I received orders (again through Mick McDonnell) that Barton was to be eliminated,' Slattery said. As usual, none of the Squad asked why.

Vinny Byrne happened to go to McDonnell's house on 29 November and found McDonnell, Keogh and Slattery sitting by the fire. 'Would you shoot a man, Byrne?' McDonnell asked.

'It would depend on who he was,' Byrne replied.

'What about Johnnie Barton?'

'Oh, I wouldn't mind – as he has raided my house,' Byrne said.

'That settles it,' McDonnell said. 'You may have a chance.'

Slattery and Byrne worked together as carpenters at The Irish Woodworkers, owned by Anthony Mackey. Next morning, Slattery told Byrne, 'You had better bring in your gun after dinner.'

After work, they went to College Green, where they met McDonnell and Keogh.

'You had better go up Grafton Street and see if you can pick up Barton,' McDonnell told Slattery and Byrne.

'There he is on the far side of the street,' Byrne said as they were going up Grafton Street.

'We followed him along up Grafton Street,' Byrne related. 'He was walking on the left-hand side, and we were on the right. Somehow I think he had second sight, for from the time we had seen him, he would just walk a few paces and, if possible, look into a mirror in the shop windows and then give a quick glance across to the right hand side. Perhaps he was not looking across at us, but somehow that was the impression both Jimmy and myself got. We tracked him to the top of Grafton Street, where he stopped for a few moments looking into a bookshop, then crossed the road and started walking down Grafton Street carrying out the same actions as he had done on the way up.'

When Barton reached the end of Grafton Street he suddenly vanished.

'We have lost him,' Byrne said to Slattery.

'We carried on to the corner of College Green,' Byrne continued. 'When we looked back, Barton appeared coming out of a hallway. He crossed the street at the narrow part over to Trinity College side.

'At this stage we picked up Mick McDonnell and Tom Keogh,' he went on. 'Then I saw Paddy [O']Daly, Joe Leonard and Ben Barrett. They were on the same errand as we were. Now it was a race to see whose party would get Barton first. Barton sauntered along the railings and around into College Street, keeping to the right hand side. Needless to say, the streets were crowded at the time as it was knocking-off time. As one party would pass out the other to have a go, people would come in between us and our quarry. Barton got as far as the Crampton monument and was in the act of stepping off the path to cross over to the police station in Brunswick Street when fire was opened on him.'

O'Daly, Leonard and Barrett were actually moving in on Barton when the shooting started. Getting Barton was not a race as far they were concerned; they considered themselves the Squad and they had no idea that McDonnell and the others were on the same mission.

'We experienced a grave shock when there was a heavy fusillade of firing,' Joe Leonard said.

He was shot in the back from such close range that there were powder burns on his overcoat. As he crumpled down on his right knee, he said, 'Oh, God what did I do to deserve this?' He pulled out his gun and fired up College Street.

'McDonnell and myself cleared up College Street on the right hand side and, as we came to the corner of College Street and Westmoreland street a peeler tried to stop Mick. I drew my gun and let a shout at him.' With that the two of them made their getaway.

The wounded detective was helped to the door of a nearby club. The fatal bullet had gone right through his body, through his right lung.

'They have done for me,' he said. 'God forgive me. What did I do? I am dying. Get me a priest.'

Barton received the last rites upon his arrival at hospital and died minutes later. His fellow Kerryman, Austin Stack, the deputy chief-of-staff of the IRA, did not know why Barton had been shot as he had been in G Division only a couple of months.

'Can you tell me why Johnnie Barton was shot?' was the first question that Stack asked that night on meeting fellow Traleeman Mike Knightly, a reporter with the *Irish Independent* who worked closely with the intelligence people. 'The whole city is upset.'

'I could not say but I presumed that he had agreed to do political work,' Knightly explained. 'I learned later that that evening he had agreed to do political work and was shot a quarter of an hour later.'

Of course, it was absurd to think that they could have arranged the killing in such a short time but there was apparently a great haste to get Barton as two elements of the Squad had been sent at the same time to kill him.

'Later when we all had decamped and on meeting Mick McDonnell, he told us that he had an independent squad out to do this same job. The difference between the two sections of the Squad was that those under O'Daly were being paid a salary of £4/10 a day, while those under McDonnell were only part-time as they still had their day jobs.'

The fact that there were two elements of the Squad which did not even know of each other's existence was a measure of how Collins operated. He had an obligation to protect the identity of his spies and agents, with the result that he was very secretive. 'Never let one side of your mind know what the other is doing,' was a favourite saying of Collins. Later some people were dogmatic in stating that only a certain number of police worked for Collins, but nobody will ever know the true extent of the co-operation, because that knowledge went with Collins to his grave. Certain handlers knew of the people that they were dealing with, but Collins would only have told them of others on a need-to-know basis. If he had done otherwise, the identities of his agents would inevitably have leaked out to the enemy.

CHAPTER 6

'SHOOTING OF A FEW WOULD-BE ASSASSINS'

Following Barton's killing, a select committee was set up to advise the lord lieutenant, Field Marshall Sir John French, on intelligence matters. It consisted of T. J. Smith, the acting inspector general of the RIC; the assistant under-secretary, Sir John J. Taylor at Dublin Castle; and a resident magistrate named Allen Bell. They warned on 7 December 1919 that 'an organised conspiracy of murder, outrage and intimidation has existed for sometime past' with the aim of undermining the police forces. Even though the first police had been killed in Tipperary, they contended that 'Dublin City is the storm centre and mainspring of it all'. To remedy the situation it was proposed that the Sinn Féin movement be infiltrated with spies and some selected leaders assassinated.

'We are inclined to think that the shooting of a few would-be assassins would have an excellent effect,' the committee advised. 'Up to the present they have escaped with impunity. We think that this should be tried as soon as possible.' Some covert agents were put to work under Bell who reported to Sir Basil Thomson, the director of civil intelligence at Scotland Yard. 'In the course of moving about my men have picked up a good deal of useful information which leads to raids,' Bell wrote to French.

It was ironic that while French was being advised to have selected republicans assassinated, some of them were laying in wait to kill him at the first opportunity. Three nights later the Squad lay in ambush for French but, again, he took a different route.

Collins' determination to get French suddenly became a matter of urgency. McDonnell learned through the son of the railroad official who organised a special train for the lord lieutenant that he would be returning to Dublin on the afternoon of 18 December 1920 and that he would be getting off at Ashtown station, a stop near Phoenix Park. The ambush was set but again French did not show. Next morning when McDonnell enquired about what went wrong he was told the lord lieutenant had postponed his return until that day.

'I hurriedly organised the squad and got to Kelly's public house at Ashtown Cross shortly before 1 p.m.,' McDonnell said. 'I was in charge of that ambush. As everyone was working I found it very hard to make up a sufficient number. Seán Treacy, Dan Breen, Seamus Robinson and J. J. Hogan were up here from County Tipperary "on the run" and Treacy had informed me before this that if they could be of any help to me at any time to call on them. This I did at this time with these four, Paddy [O']Daly, Martin Savage, my half-brother Tom Keogh, Jim Slattery, Vincent Byrne, Joe Leonard, Ben Barrett and myself.

'We had no mode of transportation other than bicycles,' McDonnell said. 'We got into Kelly's public house and some of the boys ordered minerals. I went out the back to look at Ashtown Station to see what I could see.

'While out in the yard I saw a large farm-cart standing on its heels. I told Breen to get it in readiness to push it through the gate, body first, on to the road with the object of running round the corner to block French's convoy of four cars which at this time had gone down to the station. I told him above all to turn it while in the yard so as we could push it towards the first car approaching round the corner from the Navan road.'

McDonnell's plan was upset by the unexpected arrival of Constable O'Loughlin to direct traffic at the corner in order to clear the way for the official party. 'What obstructed us most of all was the arrival of a policeman who came along to do point duty in the middle of the road,' McDonnell said. 'We thought of taking him in but thought again it would hamper our position or maybe give the alarm, then decided to leave him alone.

'French's party took less time than we had expected to get into the cars and come from the station,' he added. 'I gave the signal for the cart to be brought out and I put Paddy [O']Daly and four others inside the hedge with handgrenades.

'After telling them to concentrate on the second car and some other details, I turned to the cart again and found they were bringing it through the gate with the shafts first instead of the way I had told them. I started swearing and shouted: "Why didn't you push it out the way I told you?"

'That delayed them trying to turn it outside the gate,' McDonnell explained. 'We lost much time in doing so. The result was the first car of French's party, which was preceded by a detective on a motor-bicycle, flew by before we got the cart to the corner.' French was actually in the first car.

One of the men threw a grenade and Detective Sergeant Nicholas Halley, who was sitting in the front beside the driver, was wounded in the hand. Constable Thomas Flanagan, the motorcyclist, heard the explosion and was about to turn around when the lieutenant governor's car raced past him, heading for the viceregal lodge. He followed.

The second car with just a driver and luggage was hit by a grenade and largely destroyed, but the driver had a miraculous escape, while the third car, with French's military escort, came through with blazing gunfire. Sergeant George Rumble claimed to have shot one of the attackers in the head as he was throwing a grenade. Martin Savage was hit in the head. He wasn't a member of the Squad or the Soloheadbeg gang; he just happened to be with Mick McDonnell that day and, as a veteran of the Easter Rebellion, he was invited along, with fatal consequence. Dan Breen was wounded in the leg.

'All we could do for Martin Savage was to whisper a prayer, search him for guns and papers and lay him outside Kelly's publichouse,' McDonnell said. Savage's body however was found with two revolvers, fully loaded. They had not been fired, and there was also a grenade ring on one of his fingers. The authorities also found a document linking Savage to the grocery shop where he worked as a clerk. The proprietor, a Scottish Presbyterian with no republican sympathies, was arrested but was not held for long.

'The failure to get Lord French was mainly due to the road not being blocked,' O'Daly later concluded, 'but had the road been blocked I think none of us would have come back alive from Ashtown, because we were out-numbered by at least three to one, rifles against revolvers. All our bombs would have been gone and we would not have had a chance with revolvers. Had we stopped Lord French's car we would have stopped the military lorry, and although the element of surprise would have been in our favour we would have been out-numbered.'

French was highly critical of the Dublin Metropolitan Police (DMP) and only slightly less so of the Royal Irish Constabulary (RIC). 'Our secret service is simply non-existent,' he complained. 'What masquerades for such a service is nothing but a delusion and a snare. The DMP are absolutely demoralised and the RIC will be in the same case very soon if we do not quickly set our house in order.' In figures for the year up to 11 December, which were published the day before the ambush, 169 policemen had been killed throughout Ireland in 1919, and a further 245 had been wounded, while 52 soldiers had been killed and 108 wounded.

Ian Macpherson was appointed the chief secretary for Ireland in 1918 but he rarely visited the country, with the result that the civil servants were essentially in charge at Dublin Castle. As under-secretary of state, James MacMahon was officially the top civil servant. He was a Dublin Castle Catholic who owed his appointment largely to the influence of Roman Catholic hierarchy. He 'is not devoid of brains, but lacks initiative, force and driving power,' concluded a senior British civil servant who was assigned to head a committee evaluating the performance of civil servants at Dublin Castle. MacMahon was by-passed by the assistant under-secretary, Sir John J. Taylor, who was a classic martinet – 'a loathsome character, bigoted and anti-Irish', according to Joseph Brennan. Brennan began his career as a civil servant under the British regime, went on to advise Michael Collins on financial affairs, and ultimately became secretary of the department of finance in the Irish Free State. Taylor, who advocated vigorous actions against Sinn Féin and the dáil, sought to centralise everything in his own office. Hopelessly inefficient and out of date, he was a diehard unionist who sought to block all change. His two main allies were his principal clerk, W. J. Connolly, and Maurice Headlam, the treasury remembrancer and deputy pay-master general for Ireland. These three were totally opposed to the idea of trying to kill home rule with kindness, the policy of previous Conservative governments.

Prime Minister Lloyd George had initially been preoccupied with the Paris peace negotiations and he was slow to give the Irish executive any guidance, with the result that Dublin Castle took on a distinctly Orange hew in late 1919 and early 1920. There was an ongoing debate among the crown authorities on how to cope with the massive police resignations and plummeting morale. General Frederick Shaw, the British army commander in Ireland, advocated as early as 19 September 1919 that the RIC should recruit non-Irishmen, or the government should raise a force of discharged soldiers and put them under the command of the police forces. Neither Sir Joseph Byrne, the inspector general of the RIC, nor Colonel Walter Edgeworth-Johnson, the inspector general of the DMP, liked either idea, but their reservations were put aside. The following month the RIC began advertising for men ready to 'face a rough and dangerous task' to join at one of the recruiting stations established in London, Birmingham, Glasgow, or Liverpool.

Lord French had Byrne effectively removed as inspector general of the RIC in early December by forcing him to go on leave for a month. T. J. Smith, the commissioner of the Belfast police, replaced Byrne in an acting capacity initially but this was quickly made permanent.

'Byrne,' the prime minister wrote to Bonar Law, 'clearly has lost his nerve. It may, of course, very well be that the task in Ireland is a hopeless one and that Byrne has simply the intelligence to recognise it. However, until we are through with home rule, a man of less intelligence and more stolidity would be a more useful instrument to administer in the interregnum.

'Smith is very highly spoken of by all who know him best,' Lloyd George wrote. 'Carson has a high opinion of him.'

Smith, an Ulster loyalist, was so highly partisan in political terms that many of the English took a jaundiced view of the appointment. Edgeworth-Johnson was left in charge of the DMP, but a new man was brought in to take charge of G Division. Detective Inspector W. C. Forbes Redmond was also brought from Belfast, where he had spent fifteen years as a detective. He was appointed second assistant commissioner of the DMP and given the task of reorganising G Division. He brought a number of his own detectives to work under cover. Redmond showed himself to be incredible naïve and his appointment further undermined the morale of the DMP.

He made the capture of Collins a priority. He called all DMP detectives from sergeants up and told them 'that they were not doing their duty, that he would give them one month to get Michael Collins and those responsible for shooting the various detectives, or else he would order them to resign.' They need not have worried because Redmond did not last the month himself.

Frank Thornton was sent to Belfast to get a photograph of Redmond. While there he met Sergeant Maurice McCarthy of the RIC who was a Kerryman stationed at Chichester Street, Belfast. Thornton pretended to be a country cousin when he called on McCarthy, who was already working for Collins. That night there was an amateur boxing championship on at the Ulster Hall, and most of the off duty police were there. McCarthy directed his visitor to the district inspector's office, where he was able to lift a photograph of Redmond and return to Dublin with it the following day.

Not knowing Dublin, Redmond had to have someone as a guide to the city, and he made the lethal mistake of using his administrative assistant, Jim McNamara, who was, of course, working for Collins. However the authorities had been recruiting spies of their own.

Henry Timothy Quinlisk from Wexford was one of the prisoners-of-war recruited by Casement for his Irish brigade in Germany and was given the rank of sergeant major. With such credentials he was easily accepted in Sinn Féin quarters, especially after Robert Brennan introduced him to Seán Ó Muirthile, the secretary of the supreme council of the IRB. Quinlisk, or Quinn as he called himself, cut a dashing figure and was quite a man for the ladies. 'He was always immaculately dressed and one would have said that with his good looks, his self-assurance and general bonhomie, he would have got anywhere,' said Robert Brennan. 'He liked to give the impression that he was in on all of Mick Collins' secrets.'

As a result of his enlistment in the Irish brigade, he had been denied back pay for the period of his imprisonment in Germany. Collins helped him out financially, and Quinlisk stayed for a time at the Munster hotel but he wanted more. On 11 November 1919 he wrote to the under-secretary at Dublin Castle, mentioning his background and offering to furnish information.

'I was the man who assisted Casement in Germany and since coming home I have been connected with Sinn Féin,' he wrote. 'I have decided to tell all I know of that organisation and my information would be of use to the authorities. The scoundrel Michael Collins has treated me scurily [sic] and I now am going to wash my hands of the whole business.'

He was brought to G Division headquarters to make a statement, which Broy typed up and, of course, furnished to Collins. But Quinlisk had taken the precaution of telling Collins that he had gone to the DMP merely to get a passport so he could emigrate to the United States. He said the police put pressure on him to inform on Collins, offering money and promising to make arrangements for him to get his wartime back pay. He told Collins that he was just pretending to go along with police.

Collins arrived outside 44 Mountjoy Street while the resulting DMP raid was in progress and he watched from a distance. Detective Inspector John Bruton was in charge of the raid. The Squad were ordered to kill him but this proved easier ordered than executed because he never ventured outside Dublin Castle without an armed escort and he took the precaution of not developing any routine.

Following the raid on 44 Mountjoy Street, Collins moved, though he did return there weekly for his laundry. The owner, Myra McCarthy, was an aunt of the Sinn Féin activist, Fionán Lynch. For the next nineteen months Collins moved about, never staying in any one place for very long. 'Living in such turmoil,' he wrote to his sister Hannie, 'it's not all that easy to be clear on all matters at all times.' Yet he maintained a very regular daily routine.

After his office at 76 Harcourt Street was raided in November, he opened a new finance office at 22 Henry Street. Like his other offices, it was on a busy thoroughfare with a lot of passing traffic so that the comings and goings of strangers would not attract attention, as they would if the offices had been placed in some quiet, out-of-the-way location. The Henry Street office survived for about eighteen months. He had another finance office at 29 Mary Street and he set up a new intelligence office at 5 Mespil Road. He also had an office in Cullenswood House, which had been the site of Patrick Pearse's school, St Enda's. It had been renovated into a series of flats.

With Forbes Redmond as the new head of G Division, a concerted effort was made by some of the police to find Collins. Quinlisk was told that things had got so hot in Dublin that Collins had moved to Cork. On 1 January 1920 William Mulhern, the crimes special sergeant in Bandon, produced a letter that Collins had written to someone in his area in relation to national loan. His return address was the Mansion House, and Mulhern suggested that Collins was 'seemingly at present staying in Dublin'. The county inspector of the RIC reported from Cork next day that 'Michael Collins, M.P. is carrying on operations from the Mansion House. I am putting all my DI's on the alert re the matter + taking steps to deal with the men likely to be appointed to further the loan in different districts. It is clear that Collins is in communication with the Sinn Féin organisation in all counties in Ireland in regard to the Loan.'

However Detective Superintendent Brien telephoned Cork on 5 January to say that Collins was in the Clonakilty area. That was true but he was back in Dublin by the time word got to Cork.

'Collins cannot be found in this District,' District Inspector Henry Connor reported three days later. He said that careful enquiries had been made and a number of houses searched without result. 'A close watch will be kept and if Collins appears I will have him arrested,' the detective inspector concluded. 'No trace of Collins has been found in their districts,' Sergeant William Mulhern reported of Bandon and Skibbereen on 15 January. 'There is reason to believe this man is in Dublin still according to local information in Skibbereen,' the county inspector added at the end of the report, which was shown to Redmond.

One report from the country suggested that Collins was staying at the Clarence hotel, but Detective Officer Denis O'Brien could find no trace of him there, or at Mountjoy Street. Redmond learned that an undercover agent had made contact with Collins.

Sergeant Thomas J. McElligott had sought to organise a representative body within the RIC in 1918 but was soon dismissed from the force because of his Sinn Féin sympathies. He secretly went to work for Collins as a kind of police union organiser. Ostensibly he was trying to improve the pay and conditions of the RIC, but, in fact, he was engaged in black propaganda, trying to undermine the morale of the force by sowing seeds of discord.

When the police went on strike in London, Collins sent McElligott there to make some useful contacts. At strike headquarters he met John Charles Byrne, a secret intelligence service (MI6) agent who was using the alias of John Jameson while posing as a Marxist sympathiser. Shortly afterwards he turned up in Dublin with a letter of introduction from Art O'Brien, the Sinn Féin representative in Britain. Posing as a revolutionary anxious to undermine the British system, Byrne offered to supply weapons, and arrangements were made for him to meet Collins, Mulcahy and Rory O'Connor at the Home Farm Produce shop in Camden Street. They met again the following day at the Ranelagh home of Mrs Wyse Power, a member of the Sinn Féin executive.

'What he was delaying about that prevented him getting us caught with him, at least on the second of these occasions, I don't know,' Mulcahy remarked. Byrne did make arrangements to have Collins arrested at a third meeting at the home of Batt O'Connor on 16 January 1920.

Redmond had one of his own undercover men watching the house, but that man did not know Collins and by a stroke of good luck Liam Tobin, who also happened to be at the house, left with Byrne. The lookout – assuming that Tobin was Collins – intercepted Redmond on Morehampton Road as he approached with a lorry load of troops to raid O'Connor's house and the raid was promptly called off. Redmond had brought his guide, McNamara, with him that night when he decided to keep O'Connor's house under personal observation.

Redmond had already made a fatal mistake when a detective came to him with a grievance over some of his changes in G Division: he dismissed the complaint with some disparaging comments about G Division as a whole. 'You are a bright lot!' Redmond reportedly said. 'Not one of you has been able to get on to Collins' track for a month, and there is a man only two days in Dublin and has already seen him.'

The disgruntled detective mentioned this to Broy, who

promptly informed Collins. Together with the information from McNamara, the spotlight of suspicion was immediately cast on Byrne. He had not only arrived from London recently but had also had a meeting with Collins at Batt O'Connor's house on the day of the aborted raid.

The thirty-four year old Byrne was clearly an adventurer. Small, with a very muscular build, he had a series of tattoos on his arms and hands. There were Japanese women, snakes, flowers and a bird. He had a snake ring tattooed on the third finger of his right hand and two rings tattooed on his left hand.

Collins wrote to Art O'Brien in London on 20 January saying that he had grounds for suspecting Jameson, as he called him, because he was in touch with the head of the intelligence in Scotland Yard. 'I have absolutely certain information that the man who came from London met and spoke to me, and reported that I was growing a moustache to Basil Thomson,' he wrote.

That same night Collins was tipped off that Redmond planned a raid that night on Cullenswood House, where Collins had a basement office and Mulcahy had a top-floor flat with his wife. Cullen and Thornton roused Mulcahy from his bed, and he spent the remainder of the night with a friend a short distance away. Redmond was becoming a real danger, and Collins gave the Squad orders to eliminate him.

'If we don't get that man, he'll get us and soon,' Collins warned the Squad.

Nattily dressed in civilian clothes, topped off by a bowler hat, Redmond looked more like a stockbroker than a policeman. He stayed at the Standard hotel in Harcourt Street while a residence was being renovated for him in Dublin Castle.

Collins had Tom Cullen booked into the hotel to keep an eye on Redmond and gather information about his habits, such as when he left the hotel and returned, and what he did in the evening and at night. He walked to and from work at Dublin Castle without an escort each day.

Usually one of the intelligence people would accompany the Squad to identify the target. 'We'd go out in pairs, walk up to the target and do it, and then split,' Vinny Byrne recalled. 'You wouldn't be nervous while you'd be waiting to plug him, but you'd imagine that everyone was looking into your face. On a typical job we'd use about eight, including the back up. Nobody got in our way. One of us would knock him over with the first shot, and the other would knock him off with a shot to the head.'

Members of the Squad got their chance on 21 January 1920. 'I saw Redmond coming down from the castle but he turned back and went in again,' Jim Slattery recalled. 'Tom Keogh, Vinny Byrne and myself were waiting and Redmond came out again. Tom Keogh turned to Vinny Byrne and myself and told us to cover them off. Redmond went straight up Dame Street, Grafton Street and Harcourt Street, and we followed him.'

'Michael Collins picked Joe Leonard, Seán Doyle and myself to be between the Standard hotel and the foot of Harcourt Street,' Paddy O'Daly recalled. 'Joe Leonard and myself were walking up and down one side of the street, and Seán Doyle was on the other side.' It was nearly six o'clock when O'Daly spotted other members of the Squad walking briskly: 'I saw Tom Keogh and another man crossing the road to the railings' side of the Green.

'Look out, Joe, here is Keogh and the gang,' O'Daly said to Leonard.

'I had hardly spoken these words when I turned and saw Redmond crossing Harcourt Street about six yards away,' O'Daly continued. 'When Redmond was about two yards from me I fired and he fell mortally wounded, shot through the head.' Keogh was about twenty yards away when he started running and arrived moments after O'Daly had hit Redmond behind the left ear and Keogh had shot him in the back. Byrne and Slattery watched, acting as a covering party.

The shot behind the ear was a fatal wound, because it had severed Redmond's spinal cord at the second vertebrae. The other bullet went through his liver, a lung and his stomach. 'There were a number of British servicemen around, but no attempt was made to follow us and we got away,' Jim Slattery noted.

Following Redmond's death, his own undercover detectives pulled out and returned to Belfast, and thereafter G Division 'ceased to affect the situation', according to British military intelligence. Redmond's post was not filled, but Fergus Quinn, who had been assistant commissioner since 1915, was retired and replaced as assistant commissioner by Denis Barrett.

Dublin Castle offered £10,000 rewards for information leading to the arrest and conviction of the person responsible for Redmond's death. This was probably where the story about a big reward for Collins' arrest originated.

He was behind the killing of Redmond. Rewards of £5,000 had already been offered in connection with the deaths of the three other DMP detectives, Smyth, Hoey and Barton, and these rewards were now doubled. Collins had ordered all four killings, so there was a handsome cumulative reward for the evidence to convict him, though the reward was never specifically offered for his arrest and conviction.

Many of the detectives and policemen knew him by sight, but their failure to arrest him could not be explained by fear alone. Like the police who were working for him, others were undoubtedly passive sympathisers. For example, Collins had come across Inspector Lowry of the uniformed branch of DMP as early as 1917 when he delivered the oration at Thomas Ashe's funeral and ever since Lowry had always seemed to salute and show Collins great respect, but there was never much more between them than the inspector's polite 'Mr Collins'. One night as Collins was cycling before curfew, a couple of uniform policemen were standing by the road, and one of them shouted, 'More power, me Corkman!'

CHAPTER 7

'EXPECT SHOOTING'

Although the Squad had been set up to kill specific individuals, it also engaged in some other operations. They were especially busy on these other operations during February 1920.

Mick McDonnell told Jim Slattery and Vinny Byrne that they would be wanted on the night of 5 February to help the Dublin brigade under Vice-Brigadier Peadar Clancy with a 'bit of a job,' which turned out to be a raid on the navy and army canteen board garage at Bow Lane. They took tools, motor parts, a motorcycle, and two light Ford motor vans, which they first filled with petrol. The Squad later used one of the Ford vans on a number of different operations.

The following week the Squad was involved with the Dublin IRA in an attempt to rescue Robert Barton on 12 February 1920. 'Seán Russell, my Company Captain, informed me that he had orders to send a few men to intercept a military lorry some place in the vicinity of Berkeley Road, as it was believed that this lorry would be conveying Robert Barton from Ship Street barracks to Mountjoy Prison, following his trial,' Jim Slattery recalled. 'Peadar Clancy was in charge of this operation. The entire Squad, plus a few men from E Company, second battalion, assembled at Berkeley Road fairly early in the day.'

Mick McDonnell arrived on his motorbike to say that the canvas-covered military truck with Barton had left Ship Street barracks. There were some repairs being done to a nearby house and there was a forty-foot ladder on a handcart outside the house. Some volunteers were working on the house and they wanted to help. 'But we did not let them join us because they were too well known and we had sufficient men at the time,' O'Daly noted. 'We told them that we would take the ladder and the handcart.'

It was shortly after one o'clock in the afternoon and there were many pedestrians in the vicinity, while trams were passing to and from Phoenix Park and Glasnevin. As the military truck approached on Berkeley Road, opposite Nelson Street, a short distance from Mountjoy Jail, the handcart with the ladder was pushed across the road. As the lorry came to a stop, Clancy jumped into the cabin and, pointing his revolver, held up the driver and the two officers travelling with him who had taken part in the case against Barton. They were unarmed. But Barton was not in the lorry, he was being taken to Marlborough barracks, not Mountjoy Jail. In the back there was only a private and a military prisoner.

The raiders were wearing trench coats and had soft hats pulled down over their eyes but they were not masked or disguised in any way, according to witnesses. Each had a handgun. The occupants of the truck were ordered out and told to line up at the rear.

'He's not here,' some of the men shouted having checked the back of the lorry.

A number of the men had remained at the front of the truck while the others covered the soldiers with revolvers or automatic pistols. Suddenly a revolver shot rang out from the front. The military shouted that it was one of the rebels who fired the shot. It was an accident in which the man had shot himself in the left leg. He was taken away in the sidecar of a motorcycle in the direction of Phibsborough.

'Although the whole affair lasted only four or five minutes, it attracted a great deal of attention, as tramcars going to and from the city were held up. People were watching curiously from their houses and the upper decks of the trams. Other than the firing of the one shot, there was no other incident. The driver was ordered to return to the city. 'I do not know why,' O'Daly said, 'except that we did not want him to know why we held him up.' Nobody was fooled.

'It is believed that the purpose of the attacking party was to rescue Mr Barton on his return from the court martial to Mountjoy Prison,' the *Irish Times* reported next day. 'This is borne out by the remark, "He's not here", which was made by some members of the attack party after they had made a search of the motor wagon.' Barton's trial continued and he was convicted and sentenced to three years in jail the following week and promptly moved to England.

The Squad was out with the Dublin brigade again the following evening when they learned that a trainload of ammunition would be leaving the North Wall on a certain date and that it was to be fired on.

'The entire Squad, assisted by members of the Dublin brigade and men from the country including General Michael Brennan, assembled in the vicinity of Newcomen Bridge,' according to Jim Slattery. 'We were waiting for the train, but at the last moment the operation was cancelled.' The train with the ammunition consignment was actually approaching. 'At that particular moment I had the pin drawn from my grenade, and, being rather annoyed over the operation being called off, I fired the grenade at the passing train,' Slattery continued. 'I believe that the signalman on the line was wounded.'

Michael Geraghty of 1 Gilford Place, North Strand, Dublin, was actually leaning out of the signal box at the time and it was initially believed that he was shot by one of the twenty or so soldiers on the train. 'It is assumed,' the *Irish Times* reported, 'that the putting out of a flag from the window of the signal box to indicate that the line was clear was misunderstood by the military guard, and that shots were fired.'

A couple of days later there was a report that two armed men had actually stopped the train, that one had got on and ordered the driver to back up and then after some minutes had told him to go forward again. By then the men on the banking had clearly got away, but there were tyre tracks to indicate that the raiders were using two motor vehicles.

Henry Quinlisk, who had lost touch with Collins after the information he had given to Dublin Castle led to a raid on the Munster hotel, had been making repeated efforts to contact him again. He was told that it had got so hot for the Big Fellow in Dublin that he had gone back to Cork. The Squad suspected Quinlisk was a spy and tried to use him as bait to get at Detective Superintendent Owen Brien. The Squad had been trying to kill him for some time but he rarely moved outside the walls of Dublin Castle.

Seán Ó Muirthile was assigned to keep Quinlisk busy while one of the Squad telephoned Dublin Castle to say that Quinlisk had vital information and would meet Brien outside the offices of the *Evening Mail*, just outside the castle, at a certain time. Brien turned up but something spooked him before any of the Squad could get a shot at him. He darted back into the cover of Dublin Castle.

Collins learned afterwards that the detective superintendent suspected he was being set up. He blamed Quinlisk, who explained that he had been detained all night by Ó Muirthile.

'You're in the soup,' Collins told Ó Muirthile with a laugh.

Quinlisk should have had the good sense to quit at that point, but he persisted in his efforts to see Collins. So a trap was set. He was told that Collins was out of town and would meet him that night at Mrs Wren's hotel in Cork city.

Liam Archer intercepted a lengthy telegram from the inspector general of the RIC to the county inspector in Cork. The message was coded, but Collins had the code. 'On leaving the office, I went to the Keating Branch (of the Gaelic League) and there started to decipher it,' Archer recalled. 'While at this Seán Ó Muirthile joined me. The message informed the county inspector that Collins would be in a Wren's hotel, Cork.'

'Tonight at midnight surround Wren's hotel, Winthrop Street, Cork,' the message read when decoded. 'Collins and others will be there. Expect shooting as he is a dangerous man and heavily armed.'

The telegram added that Collins should be taken 'dead or alive'. When Archer showed the telegram to Collins later that night, the Big Fellow remarked 'That ****** has signed his death warrant.' He was, however, amused about what was likely to happen at Wren's hotel. 'They'll play *síghle caoch* with the place,' he said with a laugh.

On the night of 18 February 1920 members of the Cork No. 1 brigade of the IRA met Quinlisk, promising to take him to Collins. Instead they took him outside the city and shot him eleven times. There was one bullet wound through the socket of the right eye, two bullet wounds between the right eye and right ear, and three further bullet wounds on the right side of the forehead, as well as five other bullet wounds to the body. *The Cork Examiner* concluded, 'the medical evidence was that they could not have been self-inflicted.'

Next night in Dublin members of the Squad again joined with the Dublin brigade for a raid, this time on the sheds of the Irish Steam Packet Company at Sir John Rogerson's Quay. There were twenty-five to thirty men involved in this raid for ammunition. They started the raid between 10.30 and 11 p.m.

'One of the party got over the railings and smashed a pane of glass in the lower window, allowing him to slip off the catch and get through,' said Vinny Byrne. He opened a wicket gate from inside. Some men stayed on patrol but the majority entered the sheds. They did not realise that the ammunition had been moved by the military the previous day. The raiders did not know where to look, so they just took pot-luck in opening various cases.

'I remember opening a case and finding that its contents consisted of sticks of black liquorice,' Byrne added. 'I filled my pockets and had a good chew for a day or two.'

The order was given to abandon the raid, as there was obviously little use in their search. 'After all our trouble, we found nothing,' Byrne noted. Most of those involved in the raid lived on the north side of the city, but Byrne was staying south of the Liffey.

As he was on Tara Street he heard some shooting from the College Green area. He went by College Street but did not see anything unusual.

The following night DMP Constable John M. Walsh from Galbally, near Enniscorthy, County Wexford, was killed in Dublin. Pat McGrath and his brother Gabriel had been due to take part in an operation that was called off. As they were returning to their home in Belgrave Square, Rathmines, they crossed Westmoreland Street at the foot of Grafton Street, where they were challenged by two armed policemen. The McGraths fired on the police who returned fire. Pat was hit in the right shoulder. Gabriel raced up College Street, firing as he ran, fatally wounding Walsh. His colleague, Sergeant Dunleavy, was also wounded.

Pat McGrath was critically ill and was taken to Mercer's hospital before being moved to King George V hospital (later St Brichin's), where he eventually recovered. He later told Liam Archer that a man dressed as a priest visited him and tried hard to get him to make his confession. Some instinct made him refuse, even though he was seriously ill. He was later convinced the 'priest' was the British agent, John Charles Byrne, alias Jameson, but it was some thirty years later that Archer recalled this story and he possible confused Byrne with Allen Bell.

Byrne had gone to England but returned with a case of pistols to demonstrate his supposed sincerity. Tobin brought him and the portmanteau of Webley revolvers to 56 Bachelor's Walk where New Ireland Assurance had premises over Kapp & Peterson's at the corner of Bachelor's Walk and Sackville. Byrne handed over the case to Thornton in the hallway of Kapp & Peterson's. His story was that he had got the revolvers through communist sources.

'I immediately walked straight through the hall and down the steps in Kapp & Peterson's basement, and Tobin took Jameson away,' Thornton explained. 'When the coast was clear I handed the portmanteau of revolvers over to Tom Cullen who was waiting at 32 Bachelor's Walk, which was the Quartermaster General's stores.' Thornton had already asked Jim McNamara to keep his ears open at Dublin Castle about any possible raid because of Collins' suspicions that Byrne was in touch with Scotland Yard. 'About mid-day I got a message from McNamara telling me that the New Ireland Assurance Society's premises at Bachelor's Walk would be raided at about 3 o'clock.

'I joined Tobin and Cullen at McBirney's on the far side of the river at 3 o'clock to await developments,' Thornton continued. At 3 o'clock crown forces raided the Bachelor's Walk building. They first went into the cellar and ransacked it. They then searched the whole building, but found nothing other than an Irish Volunteer's cap. They returned at 1 o'clock the following morning and smashed in the front door. They had picks and shovels and proceeded to dig up the basement looking for a secret passage. Byrne's fate was sealed.

Liam Tobin told Joe Dolan that he would be meeting Byrne in d'Olier Street at a certain time on 2 March 1920. Dolan was to take a careful look at Byrne so that he could identify him for members of the Squad who would kill him that evening.

'Paddy [O']Daly, Tom Kilcoyne and Ben Barrett were to carry out the execution,' Dolan recalled. 'Tom Kilcoyne, Ben Barrett and myself met outside Gardiner Street Church and proceeded on bicycles to the place of execution as pre-arranged.'

That evening [O']Daly met Byrne at the Granville hotel on Sackville Street. He was supposed to be bringing him to see Collins out in the grounds of the lunatic asylum in Glasnevin. 'When he came along the road I identified him to Barrett and Kilcoyne. We held him up and searched him and took all his documents. Paddy [O']Daly stayed back and didn't take part in the search.'

Byrne tried to bluff them about his friendship with Collins and Tobin, but the Squad members knew better. They asked him if he wished to pray.

'No,' he replied.

'We are only doing our duty,' one of the Squad said to him.

'And I have done mine,' he replied, drawing himself to attention as they shot him twice, in the head and through the heart.

'The documents found on him were incriminating,' said Dolan. When Liam Tobin and Tom Cullen saw Byrne being taken away by Paddy [O']Daly they searched his room in the Granville hotel and took all his effects away, which were said to be very incriminating also.

'All the facts so far disclosed and the probabilities point to the conclusion that the deceased was a secret service official, acting under the direct authority of the Secret Service Department in London,' the press reported after the body was found. Walter Long, the first lord of the admiralty, told the British cabinet in May that Byrne was actually 'the best Secret Service man we had'.

On the morning after the killing of Byrne many of the part-time Squad took part in the seizure of the mail from Dublin Castle as it was being transferred to the main sorting office. The sorting office was now in the Rotunda Rink since the destruction of the GPO during the Easter Rebellion. Those engaged in the seizure on 3 March 1920 included Jim Slattery, Paddy Kennedy, Joe Dolan, Charlie Dalton, Tom Keogh and Vinny Byrne. Pat McCrae was driving the van they had stolen in the raid on Bow Lane stores three weeks earlier. The mail was being transferred in a two-wheel, horse-drawn van, in the charge of a driver and a postman. The van left the main sorting office at the Rotunda Rink for Dublin Castle shortly after 8 a.m. It left via a back entrance into Rutland (now Parnell) Square and then moved into Parnell Street. As it approached the corner of Dominick Street, Slattery stepped off the footpath and grabbed the horse by the head and the reins. Byrne ordered the driver and postman to get down, and Slattery drove the van into Dominick Street where McCrae was waiting with the motor van. The mail was transferred, and McCrae then drove the van to the dump in Mountjoy Court, off Charles Street.

When Byrne and Keogh arrived at the dump they found the

intelligence staff sifting through the mail. They joined Liam Tobin, Tom Cullen, Frank Thornton, Frank Saurin and Joe Dolan in opening the letters. Every so often they would hear the sound of a crisp note as someone found money in a letter. There were many applications for passports with postal orders attached for seven shillings and sixpence. When the intelligence staff finished their work, they left Slattery, Keogh and Byrne to destroy the evidence. Byrne got a brainwave and collected all the postal orders that had been left blank.

'Leave it to you, Vincie!' Slattery exclaimed. 'You would think of something like that.'

'Let's have a shot at it,' Keogh interjected.

'So we waded through the letters flung all over the floor and picked out all the postal orders that were blank. We divided the number among us and then burned all the letters and any papers lying around and left.' They agreed to meet that night and pool the money they had collected and share it evenly. Byrne called at post offices in Parnell Street, Westmoreland Street and Duke Street, before going home for his dinner. Afterwards he cashed further postal orders at Aungier Street, Camden Street, Harcourt Place and Merrion Row, often cashing two postal orders at a time. He got all the money in half-crowns. He ended up with about £4 in half-crowns. They pooled the money and divided it that night.

While the Squad members were cashing the postal orders, the intelligence people were analysing some of the correspondence they had seized. One letter would soon take on a particularly sinister significance as part of the counter-murder scheme first advocated back in December. Captain F. Harper Stove had written to Captain Hardy at Dublin Castle on 2 March. 'Have duly reported and found things in a fearful mess, but think will be able to make a good show,' he wrote. 'Have been given a free hand to carry on, and everyone has been very charming. *Re* our little stunt, I see no prospects, until I have got things on a firmer basis, but still hope and believe there are possibilities.'

It was around this time that the two elements of the Squad were joined into one whole time unit. There is no specific date for when the amalgamation took place, but Vinny Byrne put it at early March 1920 because he and Jim Slattery quit their jobs together on 9 March in order to go full time with the Squad. The IRA had been almost exclusively part time, so they had to have time off work for any operations during working hours. As a result most of their activities had been at night or on weekends. As the British began to reorganise their intelligence service in Ireland, they were free to operate in relative safety during the day when their opponents were busy at work. Hence it was decided to put the whole Squad on a full time basis. It began with twelve men, and they were irreverently dubbed the twelve apostles. They were: Mick McDonnell, Tom Keogh, Jimmy Slattery, Paddy O'Daly, Joe Leonard, Ben Barrett, Vinny Byrne, Seán Doyle, Paddy Griffin, Eddie Byrne, Mick Reilly and Jimmy Conroy.

They reported directly to Collins as director of intelligence, or to his deputy, Liam Tobin. They met daily at 100 Seville Place, where they waited for the call to duty in what was a private house. They passed their time reading, playing cards or just chatting at what was a particularly secluded site. From there they conducted operations on orders from GHQ intelligence. Many operations consisted of searching the city for individuals or small enemy units. Pat McCrea acted as a driver for them.

Later they moved to a school house in Oriel Street, which was deep in the docklands, but it took so long to get from there to a central place that the Squad moved its headquarters to a builders' yard off Abbey Street. Paddy [O']Daly and Vinny Byrne were both carpenters, so they set up a cabinet-making business as a front. They acquired carpentry tools and equipped a small office with a rough desk, some calendars and building literature. 'I painted on the gates in large white letters on a brown ground: Geo. Moreland, Cabinet-Maker,' Bill Stapleton recalled. 'There we came together daily dressed in our white aprons – under which we were fully armed – and engaged in amateur carpentry under Vinny's expert instruction. Vinny met prospective customers and discussed their requirements in detail, took notes, promised to submit an estimate but pointed out, rather sadly that, due to pressure of work he could not promise when the job could be started. On hearing this the customer invariably said, "thank you!" and left.'

On 10 March 1920 in Cork, District Inspector McDonagh was shot. Having supervised the transportation of ballots to the count centre following municipal elections, he was walking to the Blackrock police barracks with a head constable when they were ambushed by some men standing at the corner of Sawmill Street. McDonagh was hit on the left side and his injuries were described in hospital as very serious. Members of the Cork No. 1 brigade of the IRA carried out the ambush. They were under the command of Tomás MacCurtain, who also happened to be the lord mayor of Cork. On 16 March he received a threatening letter on dáil notepaper: 'Thomas MacCurtain, prepare for death', it read. 'You are doomed.'

Constable Joseph Murtagh, a twenty-three-year-old veteran of the RIC from County Meath, was shot and killed on Pope's Quay near the Dominican church in Cork at about 10.40 p.m on 19 March. He was not on duty at the time and was in civilian clothes, returning from the Palace theatre. Residents of the area said that they heard two shots followed by a pause and then a burst of shots in quick success. Constable Murtagh was dead on arrival at the North Infirmary. Like District Inspector McDonagh before him, Constable Murtagh was shot by men who were nominally under MacCurtain's command, though in this case they acted without his authority. A few hours later MacCurtain would pay with his life.

Shortly after one o'clock in the morning some men raided his home above the flour and meal business that he ran at 40 Thomas Davis Street. Armed men with blackened faces demanded entry when MacCurtain's wife answered the knocking and kicking at the front door. Some eight men entered the premises. 'Come out, Curtain', one of them shouted.

'All right!' MacCurtain said as he came to his bedroom door. Two revolver shots rang out, as Tomás MacCurtain stepped out of his bedroom in his pants and nightshirt; he fell back into the room, mortally wounded. His five children, whose ages ranged from ten years to ten months, were in the house, and they began screaming.

MacCurtain's brother-in-law, James Walsh, who lived there also, was on the stairs with a candle when the shooting started, and he promptly extinguished the candle and went to a room where the children were screaming. He called out the window for assistance but the men below shot at the window. He then went into another room where his younger sister and two nieces were sleeping and told them to lie on the floor as he shouted, 'Help, Tomás is shot!'

MacCurtain was moaning, so Walsh went to him and struck a match. 'The children, Jim,' MacCurtain said.

'You are only wounded, boy,' Walsh said.

'I am done for,' MacCurtain insisted

After the killing the threatening letter was used to suggest that there was an internal feud among the republicans, but it was given no credence in Cork, where people believed that the police were behind the killing. 'Certainly British propaganda is at work, but like everything else British the Free People have begun to know it and it is, therefore, not so powerful or dangerous a weapon as it was formerly,' Collins wrote to Donal Hales in Italy on 26 March. 'Their agents here, whether military, police or civil, are doing all they can to goad the people into premature actions.' He added that everybody was gloomy over the murder of MacCurtain and 'all the circumstances of the ghastly affair', but that it was not the full story. 'Revelations are yet to come,' he continued, 'revelations which will show that it was planned and executed by agents of the British government.

'The English in their usual way are trying to make the world believe that poor Tomás was shot by his own friends. That is the English way always,' Collins wrote to a friend from Clonakilty on 31 March. 'They will continue until they have no longer the power. The feeling here about the occurrence, and, as far as I can judge, elsewhere throughout the length and breadth of Ireland, was the same as it was in Cork, and many a person who was far away from the scene of the tragedy felt the awful deed in his own very presence.'

The coroner's jury came to the sensational conclusion that 'Alderman Tomás MacCurtain, lord mayor of Cork, died from shock and haemorrhage, caused by bullet wounds and that he was wilfully wounded under circumstances of the most callous brutality; and that the murder was organised and carried out by the Royal Irish Constabulary (at this point the verdict was interrupted by loud applause), officially directed by the British government, and we return a verdict of wilful murder against David Lloyd George, Prime Minister of England; Lord French, Lord Lieutenant of Ireland; Ian Macpherson, late Chief Secretary of Ireland; Acting Inspector General Smith of the Royal Irish Constabulary, Divisional Inspector Clayton of Royal Irish Constabulary; District Inspector Swanzy ("hear, hear", people cried and applauded) and some unknown members of the Royal Irish Constabulary.'

Of course, the coroner's jury had exceeded its authority in functioning like a jury in a criminal case by actually finding people guilty of the murder. But the verdict clearly reflected what people were thinking.

CHAPTER 8

'A LITTLE BIT OF STRATEGY'

Private Fergus Bryan Molloy – who was introduced to Collins at the home of Batt O'Connor by Dr Robert Farnan, a dáil deputy – depicted himself as the son of a Mayoman forced to emigrated. He operated as a double agent for the British. He was working for Colonel Hill-Dillon, the chief intelligence officer of the British army at Park Gate Street, but he was pretending to be sympathetic to the republicans by offering to provide guns. All the while, however, he was really loyal to the British.

Lily Mernin, was supplying information to Collins on the British army similar to what Broy was supplying on the DMP. A cousin of Piaras Beaslaí, she was a typist for Major Stratford Burton, the garrison adjutant at Ship Street barracks for the Dublin district. Burton assigned her to type reports in connection with both the Volunteers generally and court martial proceedings. The duty included typing reports on the strength of various military posts throughout Dublin. Beaslaí introduced Collins to her as a 'Mr Brennan'. 'I promised to give him all the assistance that I possibly could,' she recalled.

'Each week I prepared a carbon or a typed copy which ever I was able to get. Sometimes I would bring these to the office placed at my disposal at a Captain Moynihan's house, Clonliffe Road. He had a typewriter there and I typed several copies of the strength returns and other correspondence, which I may have brought with me that I thought would be of use. I left them on the machine and they were collected by some person whom I did not know. I had a latchkey for the house and nobody knew when I came or went. It was arranged for me that if anything special requiring urgent delivers to the intelligence staff that I would deliver it at Vaughan's between certain hours and Máire Ni Raghalleigh's bookshop, Dorset Street.' She also left messages at Collins' shop, Parnell Street.

Lily warned that Molloy was really working for the British. At one point he had asked one of his Irish contacts to write the names and addresses of prominent members of Sinn Féin, such as Count Plunkett and Countess Markievicz, on Dáil Éireann notepaper that had been seized in the raids on Sinn Féin headquarters. In the light of what happened to MacCurtain, his request took on a sinister appearance.

'We have to shoot that fellow,' Tobin told Collins.

'Well shoot him so,' Collins replied.

Frank Saurin, who was Lily Mernin's handler, was meeting with Molloy on 23 March 1920, and Vinny Byrne was told to get a good look at him so that he could identify him for other Squad members afterwards. Saurin and Molloy went into the Cairo Café on Grafton Street and when Bryne sauntered in, Saurin invited him to sit with them.

'Our friend is very anxious to meet Liam Tobin and I am sure you could arrange it,' Saurin said.

At first Byrne hesitated. Molloy mentioned that he could be a great help to the movement, and Vinny then agreed. 'I made arrangements to meet him the following evening at 5.30 p.m. at the corner of South King Street and Grafton Street,' Byrne recalled. 'We would each wear a flower on our coats, so that we would know one another.'

Next day McDonnell and Slattery were to do the killing while Keogh and Byrne covered them. Molloy hung around waiting for Byrne. 'He waited about three-quarters of an hour and then moved off down Grafton Street,' Byrne recalled.

'We followed Molloy down Grafton Street into Wicklow Street and shot him at the corner of South William Street and Wicklow Street,' Slattery continued.

According to a witness, the gunman brushed aside Annie

Hughes, a domestic servant. She was between him and the victim. 'My God,' she said, 'don't shoot the man.'

As Molloy turned to look he was shot in the right knee and he fell to the ground.

'Stand back,' one of them said sternly to the shocked young woman. Byrne and Slattery then shot Molloy twice more, in the abdomen and in the right temple.

'Help, Help,' Annie Hughes shouted. 'The man is killed.' With that she fainted.

'The crowd started shouting and made attempts to stop us getting away, but Tom Keogh and Byrne, who was covering us, drew their guns. In this way we succeeded in getting away safely.'

'Stop them,' a number of civilians shouted, according to Byrne. 'This was the first time anything like that had happened.' When they discussed what happened among themselves next morning, they concluded that, after what had happened in Cork, people mistook them for British military, dressed in civilian clothes.

'I had to run down towards St Andrew Street,' Byrne continued. 'The majority of the squad made for College Green, but I had to go a different way, as I had to report to Liam Tobin and Tom Cullen whether the operation was successful or not.' While running by St Andrew's church, where the path narrowed, a civilian tried to block Byrne's way with a bicycle. 'I did not pull my gun and fire at him,' Byrne said. 'Instead, I used a little bit of strategy. I shouted at him, at the same time pointing towards Suffolk Street, "Stop them, stop them" and he looked around. I darted by and made my escape to Liam and Tom.'

A couple of days later the target was Allen Bell, the resident magistrate who had served on the secret committee that advised the lord lieutenant on the desirability of the 'shooting of a few would-be assassins.' Bell was from Banagher, King's County (Offaly) and had served in the RIC for many years. He was responsible for the arrest of the American journalist Henry George during the Land League troubles of the 1880s and he rose to the rank of district inspector before leaving the service to become a resident magistrate. He served in that capacity in Claremorris and later in Lurgan, before being transferred to Dublin in 1919. He opened a much-publicised inquiry into Sinn Féin funds in March 1920. He was empowered to examine bank accounts in order to locate money deposited in the names of a number of party sympathisers, but the threat he posed was much more than party funds. He had actually been handling the spy John C. Byrne (alias Jameson) and there were published reports that he had been investigating the attempt on the life of his friend, Lord French.

With the help of Mike Knightly, a reporter working for the *Irish Independent*, Collins' intelligence people managed to get a photograph of Bell that was used to trace him. 'We discovered that he was living in Monkstown and that he travelled in to Dublin on the Dalkey tram,' Joe Dolan explained. 'He used to get off the tram at Cooks, opposite Trinity College, where he would be met by two detectives who escorted him from there to the castle.'

Mick McDonnell detailed Slattery, Byrne and Guilfoyle to help in the killing of Bell as he came into the city on the morning of 26 March 1920. They waited for the tram at the corner of Ailesbury Road, where Tobin and Joe Dolan of the intelligence section joined them. Tom Keogh and Paddy O'Daly went out to Monkstown on bicycles to ensure that Bell got on the tram.

'After waiting for some time we saw Keogh cycling towards us as fast as he could go, and he reached us just before the tram did. He was breathless and he pointed out the tram to us,' Dolan recalled.

Byrne and Slattery went upstairs to the open top area, while McDonnell, Tobin, Dolan and Guilfoyle took seats downstairs. There were about sixty people on the tram at the time. Bell was sitting downstairs just inside the entrance on the left hand side. He appeared to have a cold as he had been coughing a lot, according to the conductor. McDonnell and Tobin sat opposite Bell.

'Are you Mr Bell?' McDonnell asked. Bell acknowledged that he was.

'We want you,' McDonnell said as he and Tobin grabbed him and tried to bundle him off the tram.

The conductor had just finished collecting fares on top and was about three steps down the stairs. 'I noticed three men having a hold of Mr Bell,' he said. 'Mr Bell had his hands on either side of the door of the car, but the three men broke his grip, and they all came out struggling on the platform together. One of the three men was behind Mr Bell pushing him and the other two were in front.' None of them were saying anything.

'Then I noticed one of the three men putting his hand in his pocket and taking a revolver from it,' the conductor continued. 'When I saw the revolver I went back to the top of the car. I passed a remark to some gentlemen there that "something terrible was going to happen downstairs." Then I felt very weak and sat down and saw no more.'

'Let me down off this tram,' Byrne cried as he cut the trolley rope. 'Joe Guilfoyle pulled the trolley off the wires and stopped the tram at the corner of Simmonscourt Road,' Dolan said. 'I jumped off the tram to cover it in case any detectives would interfere. Tobin and Mick McDonnell shot Bell, and we escaped down Simmonscourt Road into Donnybrook.

'From our point of view there was a great mistake made that morning,' Jim Slattery recalled. 'The place selected for the elimination of Bell was not very populous, with the result that we had a long distance to run before we could mingle with people and lose ourselves. We always felt very secure when a wanted man was shot in a thickly populated district, because when the shooting was over we could easily mix with the crowd and escape the watchful eyes of enemy agents. Such was not the case in the shooting of Bell. There was scarcely anybody on the road that morning, and if enemy forces had come along we would have had no chance of escaping. That was a lesson that we took deeply to heart and remembered for future occasions.'

As they were running down Simmonscourt Road a motorbike

with a sidecar passed them. 'We should have stopped that fellow on the bike,' Tom Cullen cried. Some of them ran for the Donnybrook tram.

'Here come the Harriers,' the conducted remarked. Others ran up to Clonskea. While passing the Donnybrook DMP station they noticed the motorbike with the sidecar outside, which looked 'as if the cyclist was reporting the plugging,' according to Byrne. 'Unfortunately, no one got the number of the bike.'

One rather colourful story told by a priest about Bell was published the following September in an Irish-American newspaper. It stated that Bell had 'arranged for a Scotland Yard detective to go to Mountjoy Prison, pose as a priest and "hear" confessions of political prisoners there.' The IRA supposedly learned of this and shot both Bell and the detective the next day. The fact that no DMP detective was killed in the whole month of March was not allowed to get in the way of a colourful story.

Bell's elimination acted as a very public warning to various individuals not to go looking for the national loan money. Despite early misgivings Collins achieved the goal of raising a quarter of a million pounds. In fact the loan was over-subscribed by some forty per cent and more than £357,000 was collected. Of that the British captured only £18,000. 'From any point of view the seizure was insignificant,' Collins wrote, 'but you may rely upon it we shall see to the return of this money just as someday Ireland will exact her full reparation for all the stealings and seizures by the British in the past.'

Detective Constable Henry Kells of the DMP was also on the Squad's list for elimination. They went out to look for him on the morning of 14 April, the day of a general one-day strike. Kells had been a detective for only a couple of months, after about twenty years service. His home was at 7 Pleasants Street and they believed that he would walk to work down Camden Street that day as there were no trams running.

'On our way we picked up Hugo MacNeill, a nephew of Eoin

MacNeill, the initial president of the Irish Volunteers,' Paddy O'Daly recalled. MacNeill was not a member of the Squad but he asked to come along.

'We told him he could help us,' O'Daly added. 'We divided up and patrolled in twos.'

MacNeill was with Joe Leonard. O'Daly then heard a couple of shots and saw MacNeill sauntering down Pleasants Street as if nothing had happened.

'What was the shooting about?' O'Daly asked.

'Kells is up there if you want him,' MacNeill replied.

'Where?'

'On the footpath.'

Apparently nobody witnessed the killing other than the assailants. Jack Jones, who lived on the street, initially thought the shots were a bread van but, hearing a commotion, he went out to see Kells lying about ten feet from the corner of Upper Camden Street. A passing car had stopped to bring Kells to Meath hospital. He was dead on arrival. A bullet had passed right through his chest. It was suggested at the time that the killer had simply vanished into one of the houses.

Detective Constable Laurence Dalton had only been a member of G Division for some months. A stout man in his thirties, he had a charming disposition, according to David Neligan, with whom he was quite friendly. He had recently arrested J. J. Walsh, but that was the only time he had impeded Sinn Féin. He was suspected of fingering IRB people arriving at the Broadstone (now Connolly) railroad station.

'The intelligence section got to know of his activities, with the result that we were instructed to have him put away,' Jim Slattery explained. 'Liam Tobin was the man who pointed Dalton out to us.'

'Mick McDonnell, Tom Keogh and Jim Slattery were detailed to shoot him,' according to Joe Dolan. 'Vinny Byrne and myself were to be the covering party.'

Dalton was walking towards Broadstone station with Detective Constable Robert Spencer at about 12.30 on the afternoon of 20 April 1920. They were planning to meet the 1.10 train from the west. It was raining heavily when they came under gunfire from behind while passing by St Mary's church.

Spencer raced off towards Dorset Street and Dalton headed towards the railroad station. Two of the men followed him and one brought him to the ground with a shot to the leg, as they believed he was wearing a steel vest. 'Let me alone,' the wounded detective pleaded. An eyewitness stated that one of the gunmen fired three shots at him on the ground from a short distance. Dalton was mortally wounded and died at the Mater hospital about two hours later. 'All that can be said now is that personal antagonism brought about this man's death, which I deeply regret,' Neligan wrote in *The Spy in the Castle*. 'It was one of the tragedies of the time.'

Some of the Squad were uneasy that they were merely providing back up cover and not doing the actual shooting. None of the reports of the killing were even written, and Paddy O'Daly noted that many felt that headquarters would think they were doing nothing of importance. 'I promised that they would carry out the next operation, which happened to be the elimination of Sergeant Revell,' O'Daly added. 'As in the majority of the executions which we carried out, we were not aware of the reason for his elimination, we simply got orders to carry out the execution. The reason did not concern us.'

Revell slept at home in Connaught Street off Phibsborough Road, and Vinny Byrne was sent to observe how he came into the city to Dublin Castle, where he worked. One morning, as he was waiting, unarmed, Revell came along. 'I tried to look as innocent as I could,' Byrne explained. 'He walked down Phibsboro Road towards the city on the righthand side. As he came right opposite to me, he stopped and stared very hard over at me. I halted and pretended to look at my watch.

'Looking up and down the road, he moved off again,' Byrne continued. 'I made no further attempt to follow him, as I could see that he had me under cover. The next thing, he went over to the policeman, who was on point duty at Phibsboro.

'It's about time I made myself scarce,' Byrne said to himself. 'I boarded a tram going towards Glasnevin, got off it at Lindsay Road and proceeded to Mick McDonnell's house to make my report.' McDonnell and Tobin were there together when Bryne told them what had happened.

'We had better have a go in the morning,' one of them remarked.

The Squad was in place the following morning. 'The two men detailed for the actual job were standing about twenty-five yards from Connaught Street on the left side coming from the city. As he came within a few feet of them they stepped out on the roadway and let him have it. He was beaten across the street with gunfire. When the job was finished they made off towards the Cross Guns Bridge.'

A policeman on duty on the Phibsboro Road came running up to the spot with a pistol in his hand and gave chase as far as the bridge. There were a number of men outside a mill, and the policeman asked, 'Why did you not stop them?'

'Not bloody likely,' one of the men replied. 'Do you want us to get the same as the fellow got down there?'

'The last I saw of Revell was when he was lying on his back on the road.' The job was finished as far as O'Daly was concerned and he took off. Tom Keogh caught up with him. 'These fellows will do a bit of crowing now,' he said.

'We were perfectly satisfied that Revell was dead, and we were mesmerised when we read in the paper that night that he had only been wounded,' O'Daly noted. Vinny Byrne was particularly worried about an interview that Revell gave because he mentioned: 'I would know one of them very well, as I had seen him the previous morning.'

'Needless to say, we were disappointed that he was not finished off completely,' Byrne noted. 'It left me in the position that I could never be arrested after this, as Revell was in the castle and would identify me at any time.'

CHAPTER 9

'WE ARE GOING TO HAVE SPORT NOW'

Prior to 1920 the British cabinet was too preoccupied with other problems to devote much attention to Ireland, but the need to do something about the deteriorating situation gradually dawned on Lloyd George and his colleagues. Giving the orange clique at Dublin Castle a virtual free hand had been disastrous. Far from reforming the RIC and the DMP, the police forces had only become more demoralised.

The general officer commanding in Ireland, Lieutenant-General Sir Frederick Shaw, had advocated and secured cabinet approval for using British recruits to bolster the RIC back in October 1919. Field Marshal Sir Henry Wilson, the chief of the imperial general staff, has often mistakenly been credited with the idea, but he did support the new force. 'The state of Ireland is terrible,' Wilson noted in his diary on 13 January 1920 after a cabinet meeting. 'I urge with all my force the necessity for doubling the police and not employing the military.' Wilson's impact was in reinforcing General Shaw's initial intent of keeping the involvement of the British military to a minimum. Winston Churchill, the secretary of state for war, advocated raising the auxiliary division, a special force of 8,000 former soldiers to reinforce the RIC. Like Wilson he was proposing to bolster the RIC rather than involve the British army in Ireland. There was clear opposition from a military committee appointed by the cabinet under the chairmanship of General Sir Nevil Macready, the new general in charge of the British army in Ireland. The son of a famous Shakespearian actor, Macready had served in the First World War, before being appointed commissioner of the London police. He was then moved to Dublin, from whence one of his grandfathers had emigrated.

Churchill refined his pet scheme so so that the new force consisted of two distinct elements – one, former enlisted men, and the other, former officers, who became known as auxiliaries. The enlisted men were so hastily recruited that they did not have proper uniforms, so they wore a blend of military khaki and the dark green uniforms of the RIC. They acquired the sobriquet Black and Tans. They made little or no pretence to be policemen. They were an irregular military force with little or no discipline. Some stole everything they could lay hands on, and as a force they committed terrible outrages, often against non-combatants.

The auxiliary division of the RIC was established with an initial intake of 500 men in July 1920. By November, 5,498 new recruits had bolstered the RIC. Those consisted of 4,501 Black and Tans and 997 auxiliaries. The auxiliaries were former officers from various branches of the service with the RIC rank of 'temporary cadets'. Their number ultimately grew to about 1,500 men, in comparison with some 12,000 Black and Tans. The auxiliaries received £1 a day, 'all found', which was double the pay of the Tans.

The British set about a thorough spring-cleaning of the personnel in Dublin Castle. 'Administration in Ireland is, I believe, as bad as it is possible for it to be,' the lord lieutenant wrote to Bonar Law on 18 April. Hamar Greenwood, a Canadian, replaced Ian Macpherson as chief secretary of Ireland. From the outset, even before he had ever been to Ireland, the new chief secretary was determined to follow a hard-line policy. The cabinet secretary, Sir Maurice Hankey, noted in his diary on 30 April that Greenwood 'talked the most awful tosh about shooting Sinn Féiners on sight, and without evidence, and frightfulness generally.'

There were calls for the removal of James MacMahon as undersecretary, but Sir Warren Fisher came out strongly against it, even though he characterised him as lacking initiative and driving force. Fisher wished to retain MacMahon as a kind of token Catholic. He warned that it would impolitic to remove him as he could be a propaganda asset, while a more dynamic individual, such as Sir John Anderson, could be appointed as a joint under-secretary to carry out the more important duties. Anderson was duly appointed to the joint position with MacMahon, and Alfred Cope replaced John Taylor as assistant under-secretary. Mark Sturgis was also effectively an assistant under-secretary, but he was given the title of private secretary to Anderson instead. Taylor's two unionist henchmen, W. J. Connolly and Maurice Headlam, were also removed. The new regime under Anderson was essentially moderate in comparison with the hard-line unionists surrounding Taylor. The new men all favoured the concept of dominion home rule for Ireland, and they were prepared to co-operate with more nationalist minded civil servants like William E. Wylie and Joseph Brennan. Unfortunately for them, it was too late: a dreadful evil had been allowed to develop and fester in the Irish body politic.

Éamon de Valera had wished to block the killing of policemen, but in his absence, Collins had been authorised to kill Detective Sergeant Patrick Smyth. Macpherson had retaliated by introducing policies which he knew would provoke war. Within a matter of months, under the influence of a rabid Irish unionist element, the British had introduced a policy which effectively amounted to counter murder to combat the policies of the IRA in general and Michael Collins in particular.

General Sir Nevil Macready became commander-in-chief of the British army in Ireland, and Major-General Henry Tudor was placed at the head of all the police forces. But there was always tension between them because Tudor did not insist on proper discipline from his forces. Forbes Redmond was not replaced as second assistant commissioner of the DMP, but the assistant commissioner, Fergus Quinn, was retired and replaced by Denis Barrett. General Sir Ormonde Winter, known as 'O', became chief of overall intelligence. Mark Sturgis described him as 'a most amazing original' because he was 'clever as paint' and was probably entirely without morals. '"O" is a marvel,' he wrote, 'he looks like a little white snake and can do everything!'

While Hamar Greenwood was advocating a militant policy against the IRA, the latter was planning to shoot him before he even set foot in Ireland. George Fitzgerald was sent to Sunderland to gather information which would help the IRA to kill Greenwood. Fitzgerald, who was born and had spent some time in the United States, met some of Greenwood's people and got an invitation to hear him speak. He was afterwards introduced to the new chief secretary and his wife. 'He gave me a pass to admit me to any other meetings that were to be held,' Fitzgerald said. 'I got all information possible about his cars, their numbers, etc., the number of bodyguards he had with him, where he was staying, etc ... I came back to Dublin some ten days later, and handed in this information. This was before Greenwood had actually arrived in Ireland.'

Threatening letters similar to the one sent to Tomás MacCurtain were already being sent to prominent republicans. Through intercepted letters Collins realised the British were planning to exterminate certain republicans whose names were already listed, in the words of one British official, 'for definite clearance'.

The British were clearly out of touch with the temper of the Irish people, as was evident from some of the ideas advocated at high level meetings in London during May 1920. When General Macready explained that he planned to take on the IRA with more mobile forces who would surprise rebel elements, Field Marshal Sir Henry Wilson, the chief of imperial general staff, dismissed Macready's plan as useless. Wilson suggested instead that lists of hostages be issued. What was needed, he argued, was 'to collect the names of Sinn Féiners by districts; proclaim them on church doors all over the country; and whenever a policeman is murdered, pick five by lot and shoot them! My view is that somehow or other terror must be met by greater terror.'

Hamar Greenwood told the cabinet the following week that 'thugs' were going about the country shooting people. 'We are certain they are handsomely paid, that their money comes from the USA,' he said. 'The money is paid out to the murderers in public houses.'

'It is monstrous that we have 200 murders and no one hung,' the minister for war, Winston Churchill, complained. He even advocated that the British should behave in Ireland like the Bolsheviks were behaving in Russia. 'After a person is caught he should pay the penalty within a week. Look at the tribunals, which the Russian government has devised. You should get three or four judges whose scope should be universal and they should move quickly over the country and do summary justice.'

'You agreed six or seven months ago that there should be hanging,' he said to Lloyd George.

'I feel certain you must hang,' the prime minister replied. 'Can you get convictions from Catholics?'

'There is no detective department in Ireland,' General Macready complained. 'We are at present in very much of a fog but are building up an intelligence system.'

'The best secret service man we had,' Walter Long said, referring to John C. Byrne (alias Jameson), 'was shot near Glasnevin some time ago.'

'We must try to get public opinion in Ireland in favour of bringing this state of things to an end,' Lloyd George argued. 'Increase their pecuniary burdens.' He was in favour of intensifying economic pressure by compelling the people to pay for local damage in the form of rates and taxes. 'There is nothing the farmers so dislike as the rates,' he added. If they could be got to support the law, 'then you could deal with the terror'.

'The difficulty is that a large percentage of the adult population carries arms,' Greenwood argued.

'Why not make life intolerable in a particular area?' Churchill asked. He went on to suggest 'recruiting a special force'. He got his way and the elite force of 1,000 former officers known as auxiliaries was recruited.

In view of the way that Greenwood, Churchill and Macready were talking, not to mention the even more volatile Sir Henry Wilson, it was hardly surprising that the troops on the grounds were thinking on the same lines.

Between 3.45 and 4 p.m. on 1 June 1920 members of the Squad were involved with the local IRA in a daring daylight raid for arms on the sentry and guards at the King's Inns, Dublin. There were some twenty-five to thirty soldiers at the post at the time. They had planned the operation for a fine sunny afternoon, reasoning that the soldiers would be out in the grounds at the back in the good weather.

'Peadar Clancy was in charge of this operation, which was to be carried out by members of the Squad, assisted by some men from the first battalion,' recalled Jim Slattery. 'Joe Dolan was told to cover the sentries at the main entrance gate. When Keogh and I reached Dolan he was to hold up the sentry, which he did very slickly. Keogh and I then slipped into the guardroom smartly and held up the guard.' The soldiers were caught by complete surprise and none of them had a weapon at hand. 'The operation was carried out without any casualties and no shots were fired,' Slattery continued. 'The rifles were locked in racks and we had difficulty in getting the keys. The soldiers stated that they had not got the keys, but Keogh noticed one of them acting suspiciously, and ordered him to hand out the keys, which he did.

'Captain Jimmy Kavanagh brought some of his Company in and collected the arms, which were loaded on a Ford car and driven away by David Golden,' Slattery continued. 'Keogh and myself travelled with him in the car.' The haul consisted of thirteen rifles and a similar number of bayonets, as well as a Lewis machine gun.

Two weeks later members of the Squad went to County Wexford to kill District Inspector Percival Lea Wilson in Gorey on the afternoon of 15 August. Wilson had been a constable in Charleville before joining the British army in 1915. He had served for a time in France and was in charge of the Rotunda Gardens while the republicans prisoners were being held there following the Easter Rebellion. He became notorious for mistreating prisoners and had reportedly humiliated Tom Clarke and Seán MacDermott.

'Tom Keogh, Pat McCrae, Tom Cullen and other Wicklow men were picked to carry out his execution,' said Paddy O'Daly. 'Men who knew the country were sent, because they would have to take to the hills.'

Dressed in civilian clothes, Wilson had been to the RIC barracks in Gorey and was walking to his home, which was about a quarter of a mile outside the town. He stopped at the railroad station at about 9.25 a.m. to purchase a copy of the *Irish Times*. He had been walking with Constable Alexander O'Donnell, but they had parted about 200 yards earlier.

Wilson was reading his newspaper as he walked so he may not have seen his assailants until the final moments. From the bloodstains and sounds it would seem that two shots were fired and that he went down but got up again and tried to run for about fifteen yards. There were bullet marks on the wall at the side of the footpath. He then went down again and was shot repeatedly on the ground. He died at the scene. Minutes earlier, while on his way to work, Joseph Gilbert, a grocer's assistant, had noticed a car in the area. The bonnet was up and four men who he had not recognised were standing around the engine; there was another man in the car. After the shooting the car was seen going in the Ballycarnew direction.

Joe Sweeney happened to be in the bar of the Wicklow hotel that evening when Collins stomped in. 'We got the bugger, Joe.'

'What are you taking about?'

'Do you remember that first night outside the Rotunda? Lea Wilson?'

'I'll never forget it.'

'Well,' said Collins, 'we got him today in Gorey.'

If Collins had another reason for killing Lea Wilson, he might not have been able to tell Sweeney without compromising his source, but his remarks, the fact that there had been no rebel activity around Gorey,* and the fact that the Squad was sent to County Wexford to carry out the hit, seem to suggest that it was in revenge for what happened outside the Rotunda on the evening in 1916.

However, Paddy O'Daly had a different opinion. 'Captain Lea Wilson was not shot because he had ill-treated Seán McDermott and other prisoners in 1916, because there were other British officers just as bad as he had been and no attempt was made to shoot them,' O'Daly argued. 'I believe he was shot because of the position he held at the time, and for no other reason. I am satisfied from my long experience with the Squad that no man was shot merely for revenge and that any execution sanctioned by Michael Collins was perfectly justified.'

O'Daly recalled that he was once reprimanded by Collins, who thought that O'Daly was planning to take revenge on an officer who had shoved his daughter in 1916. Following his arrest over his involvement in the Easter Rebellion an army officer had informed his wife that O'Daly was in hospital and he looked around her house. As the officer was leaving, a neighbour, Superintendent John Winters of the DMP, arrived, having apparently just got out of bed. The superintendent said there was a large store of guns in the house and, citing his authority as a police officer, began to search the place.

'This is martial law,' the army officer said. 'We are in command and you must get out.'

---

* 'The town has been one of the quietest, if not the quietest in all Ireland,' the *Irish Times* reported the next day. 'Up to the present nothing has occurred.'

When Winters did not comply, the officer called on two soldiers to put him out. As he was leaving, O'Daly's four-year old daughter called Winters 'a traitor' and he pushed her to the ground. Enraged, the officer ordered his men to throw Winters outside the gate.

Somebody told Collins that O'Daly was going to kill Winters, who still lived near him. 'What is this I hear about you going to shoot Winters?' Collins asked him.

'That is the first I heard of it,' O'Daly replied. 'I think it is a joke.'

'That is too serious to be a joke.'

'As far as I was concerned, it was a joke,' O'Daly explained. 'The thought of killing Winters had never entered my head.'

'Collins gave me a lecture on revenge and told me that the man who had revenge in his heart was not fit to be a Volunteer,' Daly continued.*

As part of the British reorganisation, police around the country were being reassigned. Most of the eighteen men stationed in Listowel were being transferred to other stations and replaced by a much larger number of Black and Tans. Only three would remain, essentially to act as local guides for the new men. This led to uproar and the men resisted the move. The new divisional commissioner for Munster, Gerald Brice Ferguson Smyth, went to Listowel to explain the situation. He was accompanied by Major-General Henry H. Tudor, who was in charge of the Black and Tans and the RIC.

---

* It would seem that he did not heed the advice, because he was later responsible for one of the worst revenge killings in Irish history: the Ballyseedy massacre in March 1923 during the Civil War when his men took nine prisoners from jail, tied them around a mine and blew them up. One survived to tell the story. While the evidence that O'Daly ordered the killings may not be conclusive, he was the commanding officer and he unquestionably covered up for the culprits and made no effort to reprimand them.

'Sinn Féin has had all the sport up to the present, and we are going to have sport now,' Smyth told the assembled police at the RIC station in Listowel on 19 June 1920. The thirty-eight year old was a highly decorated veteran of the Great War during which he had risen to the rank of brigadier-general. He had been wounded six times and had lost his left arm. He was appointed as a division commissioner of the RIC on 3 June and believed in a policy of shooting first and asking questions afterwards.

'We must take the offensive and beat Sinn Féin at its own tactics,' Smyth said. 'If persons approaching carry their hands in their pockets or are suspicious looking, shoot them down. You may make mistakes occasionally, and innocent people may be shot, but that cannot be helped. No policeman will get into trouble for shooting any man.'

'By your accent I take it you are an Englishman, and in your ignorance you forget you are addressing Irishmen,' Constable Jeremiah Mee replied, appalled by the thought of such a policy. He took off his cap and belt and threw them on a table.

'These too, are English,' he said. 'Take them.'

Smyth, a native of Banbridge, County Down, informed him that he was not English. He ordered that Mee be arrested, but the constable's colleagues shared his indignation and ignored the order. Afterwards Mee drew up an account of what had happened and thirteen of those present testified to its accuracy by signing the statement, which they gave to a local curate, Fr Charles O'Sullivan, for transmission to Sinn Féin and the media. Five of the constables then quit the RIC. They were Mee, Michael Fitzgerald, John O'Donovan, Patrick Sheeran and Thomas Hughes. Mee offered his services to Sinn Féin and the IRA.

On 14 July 1920 T. P. O'Connor, the Irish nationalist MP from Liverpool, formally asked about the events in Kerry during question time in the House of Commons

'Divisional Commissioner Colonel Smyth made a speech to the members of the force, eighteen in number, stationed at Listowel,'

Hamar Greenwood replied. 'I have seen the report in the press, which, on the face of it, appears to have been supplied by the five constables already mentioned. I have myself seen Colonel Smyth, who repudiates the accuracy of the statements contained in that report. He informed me that the instructions given by him to the police in Listowel and throughout the division were those mentioned in a debate in this House on 22 June last by the Attorney-General for Ireland, and he did not exceed these instructions. The reason for the resignation of the five constables was their refusal to take up duty in barracks in certain disturbed parts of Kerry. They had taken up this attitude before the visit of the Divisional Commissioner. I am satisfied that the newspaper report is a distortion and a wholly misleading account of what took place.'

Major-General Henry Hugh Tudor had also been at the meeting and his presence seemed to suggest that what Smyth said was official policy. O'Connor tried to have a parliamentary debate on the Listowel incident on the grounds that Smyth's address was calculated to produce serious bloodshed in Ireland, but this was blocked by the government.

Mee and a colleague met Collins and others in Dublin the next day. Those present included Countess Markievicz, Erskine Childers (who was editor of the republican news-sheet *The Bulletin*), together with the editor and managing director of the *Freeman's Journal* which was being sued for libel by Smyth for publishing details of Mee's allegations.

'I had always imagined that the IRA leaders who were on the run were in hiding in cellars or in some out of the way place far removed from the scene of hostilities,' Mee recalled. 'I was somewhat surprised then, as I sat with some of these same leaders, and calmly discussed the current situation, while military lorries were speeding through the street under the very windows of the room where our conference was taking place. As a matter of fact there seemed to be nothing to prevent anybody walking into that room and finding Michael Collins and Countess Markievicz.

'For at least three hours we sat there under a cross examination,' Mee wrote. The representatives of the *Freeman's Journal* were trying to build a defence against the libel action, and the republicans were seeking to exploit the Listowel incident.

Smyth was merely reflecting British policy, but the London government was not about to admit this openly, so Smyth accused Mee and the media of distorting his remarks.

Smyth wrote his own explanation on 13 July of what happened in Listowel. He reported that he said 'that if the Sinn Féiners succeed in burning a [police] station we would seize the most suitable house in the neighbourhood, preferably a house of a Sinn Féiner, and fit it up as a police station, that no notice must be given that we intended to seize this house or it would be burnt; that the inhabitants must be turned out of the house on to the streets, and the police put in as quickly as possible. I did not say "let them die there – the more the merrier". A man does not die because he is turned out of his house.'

'I told the police,' Smyth added, 'that they would no longer be tied down by regulations in the police code as to firing on assailants; that a policeman was justified in challenging a man who was carrying arms, or who he had good reasons to believe was carrying arms; that mistakes might occur, but they should not, as the police knew the men in each locality who were likely to carry arms for murderous purposes; that, if such men did not put up their hands when challenged and ordered to do so, the police were justified in shooting.'

Smyth never got his chance to press the libel suit. He had become notorious for nothing yet other than shooting his mouth off but members of the IRA were now determined to get him. Through a waiter working at the County Club in Cork city they learned that Smyth stayed there. They planned to shoot him there on the night of Friday, 17 July, but he went away for the weekend. He returned unexpectedly the following evening and the IRA mobilised a hit squad of six men. They entered the County Club at about 10 p.m., held up the hall porter, Fitzgerald, who was expecting them. Three men went down to the smoking room where Smyth was sitting with RIC County Inspector Craig.

'Were not your orders to shoot at sight?' one of the men said to him. 'Well, you are in sight now, so prepare.'

Smyth tried to rise and take out his pistol but he was shot twice in the head as he staggered towards the hallway. He was shot three more times in the chest, one through the heart. He collapsed dead in the hallway. County Inspector Craig was wounded in the leg.

The coroner was unable to find enough people to serve on a jury for an inquest. Collins proceeded to milk the controversy surrounding Smyth's remarks in Listowel for all the affair was worth in the propaganda war by recruiting two of Mee's colleagues for speaking tours of the United States. In a way it was ironic because the policy advocated by Smyth was not really much different from that being pursued by the IRA in general, and Collins in particular. 'We may make mistakes in the beginning and shoot the wrong people,' Patrick Pearse had written in the article that Collins had enthusiastically endorsed.

Bonar Law, the Conservative leader, told the House of Commons on 19 July 1920 that the government's Irish policy was, 'by the use of all the means in our power, to restore law and order in Ireland and to carry into law the Government of Ireland Bill.' He has previously opposed home rule but was now advocating it along with repressive measures. Law now enjoyed inordinate influence on the government because even though his party was in coalition with Lloyd George's Liberals (they had fought the election on a coalition platform), the Conservatives had an overall majority of their own in both houses of parliament. Thus there was an amount of bewilderment in relation to British policy in London and this led to 'really incredible' confusion in Dublin Castle.

Sir John Anderson warned Greenwood next day that repressive policies would fail. 'We have not in my judgment the instruments at our command which would be essential to secure success,' Anderson warned. A couple of days later, on 22 July, the Irish Situation committee called on the government 'actively to assume the offensive in its Irish policy' and to introduce martial law immediately. When the cabinet met with members of the Dublin Castle regime for the first time the next day, William E. Wylie warned that the British government would be unable to restore law in Ireland because the RIC, bolstered by the Black and Tans, would soon be little better than a mob capable only of terrorism. It was a prophetic warning.

CHAPTER 10

'THE FIRST SHOT WAS FIRED FROM THE LORD MAYOR'S OWN GUN'

Neither the Squad nor intelligence at headquarters had any operational involvement in the killing of Smyth, but Collins did have direct input in the subsequent killing of District Inspector Swanzy in Lisburn, County Antrim. Roger E. McCorley of Belfast was given the task of preparing the groundwork to kill him and he concluded that the best time to shoot Swanzy was coming from church on Sunday, 15 August 1920. A team of five men from MacCurtain's own brigade was selected to kill Swanzy. They were: Seán Culhane, Dick Murphy, Leo 'Stetto' Ahern, C. McSweeney and Jack Cody.

'I met Mick Collins and, after a frank discussion, he remarked that the job was much too big for me,' Culhane recalled. 'I probably looked immature as at the time I was not yet twenty years of age. He said it was a job for experienced men and mentioned about picking selected men from Dublin. I made a strong protest to him and informed him that my orders were very emphatic and that it was solely a Cork brigade job. After thinking it over he said he would leave the decision to the Minister for Defence.

'Later I accompanied Dick Mulcahy to the Minister (Cathal Brugha), where Mick Collins had already arrived,' Culhane continued. 'The Minister questioned me very closely as to my proposed plan of action, which I fully detailed to him.'

After many questions, Brugha relented. 'Go ahead and do the job,' he said.

Culhane stayed at the home of Joe McKelvey and his widowed mother in Belfast. The assassination team hired a taxi to Stoneyford, which was not on the road to Lisburn. They highjacked it at a certain spot and the driver was held in a house nearby while they headed for Lisburn in the taxi. That part of the plan went well, but before they had got very far, the car broke down and they had to abandon the plan. All of the Cork men left Belfast that evening, but McKelvey decided that it was too dangerous using so many strangers.

The following Wednesday Culhane and Dick Murphy returned. It was decided that Culhane would fire the first shot, using MacCurtain's pistol for which Jim Gray, posing as a loyalist, had obtained a permit from Swanzy himself in Cork.

This time they decided to use the taxi of a volunteer, Seán Leonard of Tubbercurry, County Sligo, who worked for a Belfast garage owned by a loyalist. Leonard was acting as driver and would then report to the police that his taxi had been highjacked. Leonard brought Culhane, Murphy and Tom Fox of the Belfast IRA to Lisburn, where McCorley was keeping an eye on Swanzy.

'Everything worked like clockwork,' Fox recalled. 'Swanzy was at church when we arrived. Our taxi was parked about two hundred yards away and as fortune would have it in front of a doctor's house. The engine was kept running. After waiting some time Swanzy appeared, walking in company with two other men.'

'I pointed him out and as had been agreed the first shot was fired from the lord mayor's own gun which had been brought up from Cork,' McCorley explained. Swanzy was in the middle between his father and an army major. The major and his father were knocked to either side from the rear as Culhane moved in for the kill. 'I fired the first shot getting him in the head and Dick fired almost simultaneously into his body,' Culhane recalled. The first shot, fired from almost point blank range, hit Swanzy behind the right ear and the bullet exited on the other side of his head between his ear and his eye.

'Immediately after, we all opened fire on him,' McCorley said. 'When we were satisfied that the execution had been carried out we started off for the taxi.'

As they ran towards the taxi a mob started to run after them. 'I halted and fired back into the mob which then cleared off,' McCorley said. 'This left me a considerable way behind the others. I was then attacked by an ex-British Officer called Woods who seemed to have plenty of courage. Although I was carrying a revolver in my hand he attacked me with a blackthorn stick and by a fluke I shot the stick out of his hand.

'When I got within twenty yards of the car it started off and I was unable to make the necessary speed to catch it,' McCorley continued. The taxi was only capable of reaching 30 mph so McCorley continued to run after it.

When Fox looked into the back seat he realised that McCorley was missing, so he called on Leonard to stop. By that time McCorley had reached the car and he got in one door as Fox was getting out another to look for him.

'I got out of the taxi, which was moving slowly ahead, and as I did so McCorley climbed in on the other side,' Fox recalled. 'The jerking of the car as he climbed in caused him to discharge the last round in his revolver which went through the seat I had just vacated.'

There was only one car around for the police to follow them in. It was a taxi and they had talked about disabling it before leaving. 'But in the excitement it was forgotten,' Fox continued. 'The police commandeered it and followed us. Our car could not exceed 30 m.p.h., while the taxi with the police was much faster. We had a good start, but must have been overtaken before long, if in going round a sharp corner too quickly, the pursuing car had not pulled off two tyres.'

'We had been expecting that we would be pursued immediately and we had grenades and heavier arms in the car to enable us to carry out a running fight or to meet the police on foot if our car was put out of action,' according to McCauley. After the tyres came off the pursuing taxi with the police however, the escape was surprisingly easy.

Culhane and Murphy took the train to Dublin that evening. 'On the train passing through Lisburn we noticed a number of houses on fire, which we heard later were houses of Catholic sympathisers,' Culhane recalled. The killing actually sparked eight days of rioting in which thirty-one people were killed and some 200 injured in Lisburn and Belfast.

'Inspector Swanzy and his associates put Lord Mayor MacCurtain away,' Collins later said, 'so I got Swanzy and all his associates wiped out, one by one, in all parts of the Ireland to which they had been secretly dispersed.' The following Friday the Squad killed Frank Brooke. He was another of those who advised Lord Lieutenant French, and was a frequent overnight guest at the viceregal lodge.

Tom Keogh, Jim Slattery and Vinny Byrne were sent to kill Brooke, a railroad executive, at the company's offices at Westland Row on 30 July 1920. 'I do not know much about him except that we received instructions to shoot him,' Jim Slattery explained. 'Brooke was sitting at his table when we entered his office. We immediately opened fire on him and he fell.'

Brooke was actually armed with a loaded revolver in his right pocket but he never got the chance to use it before he was hit repeatedly. As the three were going back down the stairs they wondered if Brooke was actually dead. 'I said I was not sure,' Slattery said.

'What about going back and making sure?' one of the others asked.

'Keogh and myself went back,' Slattery continued. By then another railway executive, A. T. Cotton, had entered the room.

'When I went into the room I saw a man standing at the left of the door and I fired a shot in his direction at the same time looking across at Brooke on the floor,' Slattery said. 'I fired a couple of shots at Brooke and satisfied myself that he was dead. Although I did not wound the other man who was in the room, I was informed afterwards that it would have been a good job if he had been shot, as he too was making himself a nuisance.'

The killing of Smyth in Cork had sparked a pogrom against Catholics in the Belfast area, and the killing of Swanzy in Lisburn further inflamed the situation. Roman Catholics were burned out of their homes in mixed areas, and some 8,000 Catholic workers were expelled from the shipyards and other industries. The dáil retaliated by sanctioning a boycott of goods from Northern Ireland.

The same day that Swanzy was killed, there was a shooting in Bandon, Cork, that caused particular revulsion. Sergeant William Mulhern, the RIC crimes special sergeant who had been looking for Collins in the Bandon area back in January was shot as he entered the local Catholic church for eight o'clock mass. Daniel Cohalan, the Catholic bishop of Cork, roundly denounced the killing of Mulhern: 'His murder was singularly heinous, for he was murdered in circumstances which added to murder awful irreverence and disrespect to God.' He pronounced the murderers as excommunicated from the Catholic church.

Michael Collins had set out to undermine the morale of the police in order to knock out the eyes and ears of Dublin Castle. Largely with the help of his own agents within the DMP, Collins had managed to uncover the early operation of identifying and killing prominent activists, such as Tomás MacCurtain and had the Squad kill Redmond, Jameson, Bell and Brooke. He also had a number of the politically active police shot, such as Kells, Revell, Dalton and Swanzy.* The British were essentially back where they had been the previous December, before they began reorganising.

While they were building up their forces and introducing new intelligence people, Collins was building up his own counter intelligence. The boycott against the police was intensified. 'Volunteers shall have no intercourse with the RIC and shall stimulate and support in every way the boycott of this force ordered by the dáil,' IRA headquarters ordered on 4 June 1920. This did not just apply to Volunteers, it applied to everyone. 'Those persons who associate with the RIC shall be subjected to the same boycott, and the fact of their association with and the toleration of this infamous force shall be kept public in every possible way,' the circular order continued. 'Definite lists or such persons in the area of his command shall be prepared and retained by each company, battalion and brigade commander.' In short, anyone associating with the police should be blacklisted. This of course was making life intolerable for the police and their families.

Constable David Neligan, the officer who had counted the roses on the wallpaper in the upstairs room during the raid on the Sinn Féin headquarters in November 1919 wished to get out of the DMP but feared that he might be targeted if he returned to his native west Limerick, because local republicans were liable to suspect him of being a British spy. His brother, Maurice, a member of the IRB and a transport union organiser in Tralee, tried to help Neligan by seeking the assistance of Tim Kennedy, the IRA's intelligence officer for north Kerry.

Kennedy, the accountant for Kerry county council, was a small man with a cherubic face and bright eyes. He had already recruited Thomas O'Rourke, the crime special sergeant in Tralee, to provide the RIC cipher on a regular basis. The Neligan brothers met Kennedy one day and explained that Neligan was looking for Collins to secure a safe conduct so that he could return home.

---

* Collins also traced Head Constable John Patrick Ferris to Belfast. He was another of those suspected of involvement in the MacCurtain killing. Headquarters in Dublin warned that 'this operation would have to be very carefully organised because Ferris seems to have a charmed life,' said McCorley. 'One or two previous attempts had been made on him and he came out of all of them unscathed,' he added.

Ferris was shot at point blank range in Cavendish Street in the Falls Road after leaving St Paul's presbytery. He was hit in the neck and the hip. 'We left him perfectly satisfied that the execution had been carried out. To our astonishment, although he was seriously wounded, he recovered,' McCorley lamented.

Kennedy, who spent much of his time working in Dublin between March and October 1920, was unable to locate Collins, so he turned to Stack with unfortunate consequences.

'I saw Stack and said that this fellow should not resign,' Kennedy related. Stack arranged for an aide, Paddy Sheehan, to meet the Neligan brothers. After Sheehan questioned Neligan, however, Stack dismissed the idea of using Neligan as a spy.

'Get him to resign,' Stack told Kennedy. 'He's no good.'

Neligan duly resigned from the DMP on 11 May 1920 and was provided with a note from the IRA for his own protection. Collins was furious when he learned what happened.

'I got a flaming letter from Mick asking why the hell did I take Stack's/Sheehan's advice,' Kennedy noted. 'The result was that I went to Maurice and I told him that I had been sacked for letting Dave leave.' Kennedy also set up a meeting for Neligan with Stack at the Clarence hotel in Dublin. 'He told me that Collins wanted to meet me and that arrangements would be made,' Neligan wrote.

Neligan suggested that he would have an excuse to get back into the force if the IRA pretended to intimidate him by sending him threatening letters to get out of Limerick. This was done and he even burnt some hay that his father had at the back of the family home as a supposed warning. Neligan re-applied to the DMP and produced the threatening letters that had been sent to him. That was good enough and he was accepted back.

'I thought he was the best intelligence officer I ever met in my life,' Tim Kennedy explained. 'I discussed plans with Michael Collins for the re-establishment of Neligan into favour with the castle authorities.' Collins had stuff planted in Findlaters, a loyalist business house. When the auxiliaries raided the place and found the planted material, they nearly wrecked the building, much to the amusement of Collins and company. 'A number of such stunts put up Dave's stock with the castle people,' Kennedy explained, 'and when the castle were looking for one of their G men to train and lead the military raids, they asked for volunteers and Dave came to me, and he volunteered, and I understand with dire consequences to the military.'

Before being invited to rejoin, Neligan was interviewed by the inspector general, Colonel Walter Edworth-Johnson, who asked him about conditions in the country. 'I told him the truth, which was unpalatable to him,' Neligan explained. 'Of course he knew the state of affairs himself, better than I did.' He offered Neligan any division he desired. 'I replied that G Division would suit me,' Neligan noted. 'He agreed.' Hence Neligan went back as a detective working on political crime – the classic double agent. His initial task was protecting Thomas O'Shaughnessy, the recorder of Dublin. Dan McDonnell was Neligan's handler, carrying messages from him back to intelligence headquarters.

Each of the G Division detectives kept a journal in which he entered the names of suspects that he had seen that day. Neligan and McNamara used to check the journals of the detectives based in Dublin Castle and note information that would be of interest to the IRA. 'We used to convey this information to Collins which served as a warning to those political suspects to watch themselves, that they were being seen by the police or under observation with a view to being picked up later,' Neligan explained.

Collins got further information by recruiting Willie Beaumont, a British army officer who happened to be from Dublin and whose brother, Seán, was a Sinn Féin supporter. Willie Beaumont said openly on a number of occasions that he was going to capture Collins to earn a £20,000 reward. Collins had Seán Beaumont arrange a meeting with his brother.

'Tom Cullen and I were present at the interview,' Frank Thornton noted. After a long discussion, Collins revealed himself.

'I am the fellow that is worth £20,000,' he said.

Collins was not taking a huge chance in revealing himself to Beaumont as he knew that Beaumont was already supplying information to them. Dan O'Donovan, who worked for the finance department under Michael Collins, was receiving the information and passing it on to Collins. The Big Fellow, however, resented O'Donovan's interference in intelligence matters.

Beaumont's involvement stemmed from the night he was on a tram that was stopped and searched by auxiliaries. They found a notebook on him that he had kept while serving with the Dublin Fusiliers in France, and they gave him a bit of a hard time until one of the auxiliaries who had been in some of the same places in France realised that he was telling the truth. Beaumont was indignant about the way that he and the other passengers had been treated.

'He said to me that, if I got him a gun, he would shoot some of the auxiliaries,' Seán Beaumont recalled. 'I suggested to him that he should cultivate their acquaintance and pass on any information that he might get to me.'

And so Willie Beaumont began associating with the auxiliaries, going drinking with them at night and then giving the details to Seán when he got home. Seán would write down this information and pass it on to O'Donovan, who passed it on to Collins. Thus Collins knew that Willie Beaumont was disillusioned with the British before he sought to enlist his help.

Collins also enlisted the help of others. Constable Maurice Ahern from west Limerick was stationed at the Bridewell. He helped a Volunteer one night by getting the station sergeant to threaten the British military personnel responsible if they did not bring back a prisoner named Guilfoyle.

'The officer in charge of the military said that it was none of our business, that he was their prisoner, but we told him that if he was not brought back to the Bridewell we would report the fact [to the police],' Ahern explained. 'The military returned with their prisoner to the Bridewell about 4 a.m. I had a chat then with Guilfoyle who told me that he was brought to the Milltown Golf Links and put on his knees there, but added that he gave them no information. He heard a discussion between the officers regarding the attitude taken up by the policeman before he was taken from the Bridewell and he believed that the action of the Sergeant and Constable were responsible for saving his life.'

'It must have been as a result of this,' Ahern added, 'that Constable Matt Byrne called me one day and told me he, himself, was very prominently identified with the Volunteer Movement at the time and that he was in touch with Michael Collins and others. He asked me if I could get into the Movement and give all the information and help I could. I said I would be delighted to give all the assistance and information that might be of use to them which would come my way.

'I remember one particular occasion a British party coming down and the officer in charge saying to me, "Paddy, we are going to raid a couple of houses in the locality tonight. Do you know where Frankfort Avenue is?" I said I did. His next question was: "Do you know McGee's shop?" I said I did. I may mention that this time I knew from Collins' staff where certain wanted men would be residing. This information was given to me so that if I knew beforehand the places where these men were residing were about to be raided I could convey the information to those concerned prior to the raids. When the British officer asked me if I knew where McGee's shop was, it occurred to me that J. J. Walsh was the man they were going to raid for, as I knew him to stay there occasionally. The British officer said to me: "Paddy, come along and show me where these places are." I said to him, "Do you mind delaying, sir, for about a quarter of an hour until I get a cup of tea," and he said, "Certainly not, come to the Station Sergeant's office when you are ready."'

Ahern used the time to warn the people at McGee's of the impending raid. Then, of course, when the raid took place, nobody of interest to the raiding party was caught.

Ahern went with Constable Byrne to Julia O'Donovan's house one night in Rathgar Avenue, where they met Constable Culhane. They were asked to recruit more. 'I went to Fitzgibbons Street

Station and there got in touch with Constable Terence O'Reilly,' Ahern said. 'I put the matter to him as it had been represented to us at the meeting in O'Donovan's house, and he agreed to come in.'

Collins came to O'Donovan's another night, along with Gearóid O'Sullivan, J. J. O'Connell from IRA headquarters and Ned Broy. They had a lengthy discussion about compiling intelligence reports on enemy activities and getting some more policemen to provide information on undercover agents being brought in from Britain. 'Collins addressed us that night and told us he appreciated very much all we were doing.' He added that he still felt that he could rely on them to get more reliable men who were serving in the DMP to come over to their side.

They proceeded to enlist the help of others – Constables John Neary at Kevin Street, Peter Feely at Kingston, P. O'Sullivan at Fitzgibbon Street, Paddy McEvoy, Mick O'Dea and Sergeant Patrick Mannix at Donnybrook. Those were just some of the police who helped to compile information on undercover agents and helped to frustrate their activities.

'I secured information as to where raids were to take place when stationed in Donnybrook,' Sergeant Mannix recalled. 'I was on several occasions detailed for duty at the Show Grounds, Ballsbridge, and, subsequently, had to accompany British Officers from the Show Grounds who were engaged in searching houses in the Donnybrook area. On a few occasions while accompanying the search parties, I saved the lives of men who were found in the houses that were being searched, as I informed the officers in charge that those men were law abiding citizens, although in each case they were much wanted men. The officer, relying on my information, then withdrew and the men got safely away.'

This happened a number of times. On one occasion a volunteer named Burke escaped as the raid was about to begin, but he was spotted next day by a secret service agent named Pat Killeen who informed Donnybrook Station that Burke would be at the address that night. Mannix informed friends of Burke to stay away that night. 'This man escaped last night but he won't escape tonight,' the officer declared as they left Donnybrook station. Mannix took this to mean that the officer was going to shoot the man on the spot, but, of course, he was not there.

Some of the touts that the British brought in were English people who were really of little use to them. Dave Neligan asked Cullen and Thornton to meet him and some of the touts one night at the Rabbiatti Saloon in Marlborough Street. 'I found ourselves with three of these touts sitting around a table having fish and chips,' Thornton remembered.

'Blimey,' one of them said to Thornton, 'how did you learn the Irish brogue? We're here in Dublin for the last twelve months and we can't pick up any of it, yet you fellows seem to have it perfected.' These imported touts were not of much use to the British, but there was a lot of information the IRA intelligence could pick up from them.

CHAPTER 11

'NO HARM WOULD COME TO MICK'

At a few minutes after 7 a.m. on 15 July 1920 a post office official was on the platform of the back entrance of the Rotunda sorting office when he noticed four civilians walking quickly towards him. They produced revolvers and ordered him to put up his hands. They ordered everyone inside and Oscar Traynor, along with some twenty men, descended through a mail shoot. All were armed with revolvers.

'I at once made my way to the office in which I had been informed the emergency telephone was situated,' Traynor said. 'We took possession of the phone, the room and its occupants.' All of the postmen stopped working and gathered to watch what was going on. The postmen were, on the whole, favourably disposed towards the raiders.

The operation was undertaken primarily by the second battalion of the Dublin brigade under Traynor, but one of those involved was Joe Dolan of the intelligence headquarters staff, as well as Charlie Dalton who joined the headquarters staff immediately after the raid. The whole thing was arranged with inside help from the sorting office, where the three main agents were Pat Moynihan, Liam Archer and Dermot O'Sullivan. Moynihan, who was known as '118', provided a map of the layout of the Rink, identifying the sector where the Dublin Castle mail was sorted. A few of the men went straight to the compartment known as the 'State Office' which was where the official correspondence for the various Dublin departments was sorted in four or five bags. These bags were passed out to a car, and the driver then took off slowly so as not to attract any attention.

Ever since the Squad had held up the mail van on 3 March, Dublin Castle mail was collected at about 8 a.m. by an armoured car, but on the morning of 15 July the IRA made off with the mail before the armoured car arrived. 'The raiders apparently were thoroughly familiar with every department and carried out their plans in an expert and thorough fashion,' the *Irish Times* reported.

'After the raid I went off to my job, and while I was there Mick Collins sent word to me to tell me that I had been identified,' Traynor continued. 'Collins said I had been identified by a postman who was an English Jew.' The man had possibly recognised Traynor through his involvement in football, and had told some other postmen that he recognised the leader of the operation. Word was promptly sent to Collins.

'Mick said that if I thought it necessary to get away from work to do so, but he said that he was taking the necessary steps to see that this fellow did not talk any more about it. A couple of fellows were sent to talk to this Cockney Jew, and they told him that if he did not keep his mouth shut they would have it shut permanently. That put the wind up the fellow, and I think he left the country.'

A couple of days later Lord French received mail at the viceregal lodge with a notice stamped on it: 'Opened and censored by the Irish republic'. The letters that the intelligence people did not have any use for had simply been resealed and dropped in an ordinary post box.

In the era before direct dialing the telephone system was notoriously insecure and the mail provided the safest means of communication, other than direct personal contact. For people being planted as undercover agents or for people passing on information to the authorities direct personal contact was too risky. The seizure of the mail bound for Dublin Castle in February and again in July proved an invaluable source of information. Thereafter the IRA held up trains and raided the mail carriages. This not only provided a source of intelligence on communications between Dublin Castle and the local authorities, but the seizure of letters to the RIC frequently uncovered local people who were passing on information. Thus the raids, which became a near daily occurrence from Donegal to Kerry, became a deterrent to people using the mail to inform the police.

With the mounting number of agents, Collins also had to increase his intelligence staff around this time. One of his new men was Dan McDonnell, a sturdy Dubliner with a thick mop of red hair. 'I was invited to become a member of the intelligence staff,' McDonnell explained. He was interviewed by Tobin and Cullen and given the code number 101. 'When I had any written report to make, which was rarely, I just signed it "101",' he explained. 'My first assignment was to go to Leeson Street at 9 o'clock on a Monday morning and to report on all British personnel, whether in cars or on foot, that passed up Leeson Street Bridge. Along came three or four staff cars with staff officers, etc., and with brass hats, red bands, etc. I did this morning after morning. At the same time another member of our staff had been detailed to watch these following from another place, and what we saw, between us, tallied. Nothing that I know of was done in these particular cases.

'We were next taken into the office and our first job was to go through every letter from wherever it came, that went to the castle. Apart from that we got in every morning a complete pile of letters from all over the country, from England, from everywhere, whether to the castle authorities, to GHQ or to the RIC depot. All these letters varied and we got quite an amount of information from them. Especially from people anxious to give crown forces information. Inter-department, official and unofficial also came through our hands. Then I discovered we had a complete organisation within the post office itself.' Soon he became the main contact keeping in frequent touch with Dave Neligan.

With so many Irishmen resigning from the police forces and with the effectiveness of the IRA's counter-intelligence methods, the British were looking for good intelligence about what was happening in Ireland. In September 1920 Ormonde Winter came up with a plan, enrolling the assistance of Scotland Yard to obtain information by correspondence. 'Anyone desirous of giving information was invited to do so by sending an anonymous letter to an address in London,' Winter explained. 'This resulted in a quantity of letters being received, but they were practically all written by irresponsible jesters or active rebels, and led to no satisfactory results, being for the majority, merely accusations against well known loyalists. The experiment was, however, well worth the attempt, as, indeed, is any experiment when faced with so many outstanding difficulties. Many of the anonymous communications were received through various sources, but the vast majority contained false information, intended only to mislead.'

The IRA had been able to use the whole thing to send the British on wild goose chases. When the IRA intercepted such mail, which was often, the intelligence people had no problem recognising their own spoof letters but the genuine letters gave them a real insight into their need for more effective counterintelligence measures, and they frequently learned who was secretly providing the British with information. Many of these people were subsequently killed and left with the note: 'Spies Beware. IRA'.

Crown loyalists were under intense pressure. 'That terrible weapon, the boycott, immensely cruel, was used against them,' David Neligan noted. 'No one would speak to them or to their wives or children, shopkeepers would not serve them, nor undertakers bury them.' Winston Churchill thought 'the prolonged strain' on the crown officials was leading to 'breaking down the officials in Ireland. It was necessary to raise the temperature of the conflict,' Churchill argued according to Assistant Cabinet Secretary Tom Jones. In short, Churchill was arguing that they should turn up the heat in Ireland to make the republicans more amenable to a settlement that would be acceptable to the crown.

In August 1920 the *Irish Bulletin* gave details of nine civilians killed in the previous thirty days by the crown and of various towns being shot up such as Bantry, Kilcommon, Thurles, Limerick, Swords, Templemore, Fermoy, Enniscorthy, Lismore, Tuam, Newcastle West, Newtownmountkennedy and Carrick-on-Shannon. The Black and Tans were trying to beat the republicans with their own tactics by waging a counter terror. Faced with terrorists on either side, the Irish naturally chose their own as they had little to fear from them personally. The republicans were striking at specific targets, while the Black and Tans and auxiliaries were just lashing out blindly, often at anyone who happened to be around.

'I told Lloyd George that the authorities were gravely miscalculating the situation but he reverted to his amazing theory that someone was murdering two Sinn Féiners to every loyalist the Sinn Féiners murdered,' Field Marshall Wilson noted in his diary. 'I told him that this was not so, but he seemed to be satisfied that a counter murder association was the best answer to Sinn Féin murders.'

'Macready issued a proclamation to his soldiers denouncing reprisals in August. Tudor was also to issue a similar statement. Both he and Macready recognised that permitting reprisals would be fatal to discipline, but privately each of them was saying something different,' according to Mark Sturgis. 'If a policeman put on a mackintosh and a false beard and "reprised" on his own book,' Macready admitted, 'he was damn glad of it.' Tudor expressed a similar sentiment. 'If they sometimes give a man, caught red handed in some minor outrage, a damn good hiding instead of arresting all the minnows, it's all to the good,' he remarked, according to Sturgis, who personally had 'no doubt reprisals do a good of a sort'.

There was a distinct lull in the activities of Collins and the Squad in early September. This was largely in response to the hunger strike of the lord mayor of Cork. He had been arrested on 12 August for possession of a police cipher that Collins had given to him during a visit to Cork a few days earlier. 'He had it on him at City Hall that night,' Collins wrote to Art O'Brien. 'Not wishing to destroy it if possible, he hid it outside at the back behind a partition. One of the soldiers saw him hide it and drew the attention of an officer in charge.' A military court sentenced MacSwiney to two years in jail for possession of the cipher. He promptly went on hunger strike demanding to be treated as a political prisoner. Ten others were also on hunger strike, but MacSwiney received most publicity, because he was an elected member of the Westminster parliament as well as lord mayor of Cork.

From August the media took an intense interest in MacSwiney and he was depicted as near to death. 'The lord mayor of Cork isn't dead yet', Mark Sturgis wrote in his diary on 22 August. The following week he was complaining about rumours. 'Another this morning that MacSwiney is dead – he isn't', Sturgis wrote on 26 August. MacSwiney did not die until the last week of October. During September Collins manage to arrange a bloodless propaganda coup when he provided Arthur Griffith, the acting president of Dáil Éireann with the information to expose a criminal working for the British secret service in sensational circumstances.

J. L. Gooding, who was going under the alias of F. Digby Hardy, had written to Lord French on 12 August 1920 offering his services. He had been sentenced to five years in jail for fraud but was released after six months to work for the secret service. He told French he had information about arms and equipment stored in Ireland, but Scotland Yard was not interested in his information. He contacted the IRA intelligence headquarters 'and told them all the nice things he could do for Ireland if they would only take him into their confidence', according to Frank Thornton who was assigned to tail the man for a day.

'I picked up one of our intelligence officers who pointed him out to me,' he recalled. 'My orders were just to watch him and follow him, to find out with whom he made contact and also the places he visited. I can tell you I was footsore and weary walking around the city after him. I remember we walked to Westland Row station, turned back, waited outside the Queen's Theatre for a considerable time, then up to Grafton Street, dilly-dallying all the way, and back across town. He went into the Hamman hotel in Sackville Street and, as I was about to enter the hotel, he came out again and started walking aimlessly about the town. I was not sorry when I was relieved early that evening.'

Collins managed to get a copy of Gooding's letter offering his services to French, so he knew the man was an impostor. Gooding met Griffith and offered to set up the British spymaster, Sir Basil Thomson, on Dun Laoghaire pier, so that the IRA could kill him. This, of course, was probably just a trap to catch republican gunmen. Griffith invited reporters, including foreign correspondents, to a secret meeting on 16 September 1920. 'This man admits he is in the English secret service, and offered to arrange for the presence of the secret service chief at a lonely point on Dun Laoghaire Pier,' Griffith told the reporters. 'He asked me to let him meet leaders of the movement, especially on the military side, and he is coming here this evening imagining that he is to meet some inner council of the Sinn Féin movement.

'I will let him tell you his own story,' Griffith continued, 'but I will ask the foreign gentlemen present not to speak much lest the man's suspicion be aroused.'

Hardy duly arrived about five minutes later, thinking the journalists present were IRA leaders. He told the gathering that he was a secret service agent and that upon his arrival in Ireland he had been met by Basil Thomson of Scotland Yard at Dun Laoghaire pier and given instructions to find Michael Collins. He said that Thomson 'was the man responsible for all the dirty work in Ireland and held the strings of all secret service operating against the Sinn Féin movement.' He offered to arrange another meeting with Thomson on the pier so the IRA could kill him. He also said that he could arrange to lead the auxiliaries into an ambush and he could locate arsenals of the Ulster Volunteer Force. If the IRA could give him information about Collins' whereabouts, he said he would withhold the information for a couple of days and could then impress his secret service superiors by giving them the information.

'And, of course,' he added, 'no harm would come to Mick.'

'Well, gentlemen, you have heard this man's proposal and can judge for yourselves,' Griffith intervened. He then proceeded to expose Hardy as a convicted criminal. 'You are a scoundrel, Hardy,' he said, 'but the people who employ you are greater scoundrels. A boat will leave Dublin tonight at 9 o'clock. My advice to you is – catch that boat and never return to Ireland.'

Griffith furnished the press with detailed information supplied by Collins about Hardy's criminal record. He had been freed from jail to work for the secret service, and it made for good propaganda to show that the British were using criminal elements to do their dirty work in Ireland. Indeed, the Sinn Féin propaganda people would do such an effective job that many Irish people believed the British had virtually opened their jails for any criminals prepared to serve the crown in Ireland. This was absurd but incidents like the Hardy affair lent it credence.

On the morning of 20 September 1920 a small IRA force tried to emulate the raid on the King's Inns for arms, by seizing the weapons of soldiers escorting men collecting bread supplies from Monk's Bakery in Church Street. Between the raiding party and covering parties, more then twenty men were involved with the aim of seizing about a half-a-dozen rifles. One of the British soldiers managed to fire a shot and the raid developed into a firefight in which three of the British soldiers were killed.

Kevin Barry had a pistol that jammed repeatedly and in the course of trying to free it did not realise that his colleagues were withdrawing, so he hid under an army lorry but was spotted and arrested. Later that day British soldiers twisted his arms in an unsuccessful effort to force him to divulge the names of his colleagues. In terms of the way others had been treated by the Black and Tans, his mistreatment was mild, but it would later be categorised as torture in song and story.

Later that evening at around eight o'clock the RIC head constable, Peter Burke, was travelling from the force headquarters in Phoenix Park to Gormanstown Camp, where some 1,000 auxiliaries were based. Burke and his companions stopped off at Mary Smith's bar in Balbriggan, about three miles from Gormanstown. Another party arrived about an hour later. It became raucous in the bar, and the local police were called. Quiet was restored but after the local police departed it became noisy again, and the IRA police came to clear the bar. There were conflicting stories about what happened outside but the end result was that Head Constable Burke was shot dead and his brother, William Patrick, a sergeant in the RIC who had been stationed in Trim for some time before joining the Irish Guards during the Great War, was seriously wounded in the chest. They were natives of Glenamaddy, County Galway. Later that night at around 11 o'clock five lorry loads of auxiliaries who had only recently been transferred from Phoenix Park to Gormanstown, arrived and began terrorising the Balbriggan community.

The *Irish Times*, a unionist newspaper, described the scene witnessed the following day. 'When our reporter visited the town yesterday it presented a most extraordinary spectacle. The spacious hosiery factory, adjoining the railroad station, of Messrs Deeds, Temple, and Co., in which some 400 workers have been employed, was a mass of smoking ruins; while in the principal streets of the town several of the leading business premises chiefly those of grocers and licensed traders – were also smouldering ruins, and one street, containing some thirty small houses – Clonard Street – had been virtually reduced to ashes. People of both sexes and all ages were leaving the town, as though it was stricken with plague.'

The troops went to the home and business of James Lawless, a barber with nine children. They smashed the windows and doors. The children were taken to a neighbour's house and their father was taken to an outhouse in the back and killed. The Tans went to the house of John Gibbons, a local dairy proprietor. They arrested him and told his sister that he would 'be all right'. But his body was later found near the RIC station.

From the outset they were aware at Dublin Castle of what happened. 'Balbriggan was sacked yesterday by the Black and Tans from Gormanstown – reprisal for two officers shot', the assistant undersecretary of state, Mark Sturgis, noted in his diary. He added that the two men killed by the Tans had been 'two prominent bad men' and that General Tudor agreed with him that if the Tans had just been satisfied with killing them, there would have been little problem.

'The burning spoilt the whole thing,' Sturgis added. 'Since worse things can happen than the firing up of a sink like Balbriggan and surely people who say "stop the murders before all our homes go up in smoke" must increase.'

James MacMahon, one of the joint under-secretaries of state, was 'desperately pessimistic about the way things are going' after Balbriggan, Sturgis noted. He was seen as little more than a token Dublin Castle Catholic, a protégé of Michael Cardinal Logue, without any real power. Sir John Anderson and Sir Alfred (Andy) Cope wielded the real power in the Dublin Castle administration.

Another of the prominent civil servants, William E. Wylie, believed that the reprisals would make civil government impossible, but others believed it would be impossible to hold the Tans who went on the rampage at Balbriggan responsible. 'How the devil can we round up and try fifty policemen when we know that they know that the bulk of their officers up to the top agree in principle with the action even if they prefer shooting to burning (as I do, if we must have either!!),' Sturgis wrote on 24 September. 'It's tragic,' he wrote the following week, 'these men cannot see that indiscriminate burning is idiotic and a little quiet shooting equally effective – and shoot a bad man who, if he hasn't just shot your comrade, has no doubt shot somebody else, is morally much more defensible than this stupid blind work.' What he called 'the stupid blind work' was playing into the hands of Collins, who had envisaged that this would happen if he scuppered Dublin Castle's attempts to gather intelligence.

No inquests were held, just a brief military inquiry, which concluded that the two Sinn Féiners 'were stabbed not by bayonets but by some sharp instrument like a knife by unknown members of the police'. What happened in Balbriggan got the most notoriety, but there were similar incidents over the next two nights in Carrick-on-Shannon and Drumshambo, County Leitrim; Tuam, County Galway; Galway city, and the three small County Clare towns of Ennistymon, Lahinch and Miltown-Malby.

CHAPTER 12

'I'VE MY ORDERS TO SHOOT HIM'

John Lynch, a Sinn Féin county councillor from Kilmallock, County Limerick, who had come to Dublin with national loan money for Collins, was shot dead in his room at the Exchange hotel on the night of 23 September 1920. Secret service agents claimed he had pulled a gun on them, but Collins dismissed this.

'There is not the slightest doubt that there was no intention whatever to arrest Mr Lynch,' he wrote. 'Neither is there the slightest doubt that he was not in possession of a revolver.' Neligan informed Collins that Captain Baggallay, a one-legged courts martial officer had telephoned Dublin Castle about Lynch's presence in the hotel, and the men responsible for the actual shooting were two undercover officers using the names Paddy McMahon and Peel, each a *nom de guerre*.

There was a suggestion that John Lynch was mistaken for Liam Lynch, an IRA commandant, but that was hardly likely seeing that there was an extreme difference in their ages. John Lynch was simply a Sinn Féiner and this had become a capital offence as far as the British secret service was concerned. Collins had no doubts and neither had the British, and this was not just the regular officers and men who were involved but the generals at the top, the prime minister, Lloyd George, and the leader of the Conservative Party, Andrew Bonar Law. Field Marshall Sir Henry Wilson feared that the escalating reprisals would undermine the discipline of the British army. He continued to argue that the British government should assume responsibility for the reprisals; that they should order them and draw up a roster of people who would be held as hostages to be executed as reprisals, rather than allowing troops on the ground to select their own victims.

'I had one and a half hours this evening with Lloyd George and Bonar Law,' Wilson noted in his diary on 29 September. 'I told them what I thought of reprisals by the Black and Tans and how this must lead to chaos and ruin. Lloyd George danced about and was angry, but I never budged. I pointed out that these reprisals were carried out without anybody being responsible; men were murdered, houses burnt, villages wrecked (such as Balbriggan, Ennistymon, Trim, etc.). I said that this was due to want of discipline, and this *must* be stopped. It was the business of the government to govern. If these men ought to be murdered, then the government ought to murder them. Lloyd George danced at all this, said no government could possible take this responsibility.

'I have protested for months against this method of out-terrorising the terrorists by irresponsible persons,' Wilson continued. 'We drift from bad to worse and always under the guidance of Lloyd George. Anyhow, neither Lloyd George nor Bonar can ever say that I have not warned them and very plainly spoken my mind.'

Winston Churchill, who was not renowned for either his political sagacity or sound military judgment as this stage of his career, tended to side with Wilson on the need to take formal responsibility for killings. He had been calling for formal executions for months, and was about to get his way. 'You have been right all along,' Churchill wrote to Wilson, 'the government must shoulder the responsibility for reprisals.'

When Wilson met the prime minister to discuss the Irish situation on 14 October, Lloyd George said that he would 'shoulder the responsibility for reprisals', but wanted to 'wait till the American elections are over'. He did not wish to speak out then, because it would give the Democratic presidential candidate, Governor James M. Cox, an issue with which he could exploit Anglophobic sentiment in the United States. Lloyd George essentially agreed with the reprisals – the issue was simply whether he would accept formal responsibility for what British force were doing in Ireland.

Hankey, the cabinet secretary, noted that the prime minister privately argued that 'murder reprisals' had been resorted to from time immemorial in Ireland. 'He gave numerous instances where they had been effective in checking crimes,' Hankey added. 'The truth is that these reprisals are more or less winked at by the government.'

There was no use in saying 'I should shoot without mercy,' Churchill argued. 'The question immediately arises "whom would you shoot". And shortly after that "where are they?"' He actually came to the conclusion that Wilson's reprehensible scheme to take reprisals by roster was justified. 'At last there is some hope that the cabinet will stop whispering from the back parlour and will come into the open.'

The debate about the British reprisals was not confined to the corridors of power; it was also in the public domain. 'I do not think that any truthful or sane person can avoid the conclusion that the authorities in Ireland are deliberately encouraging, and, what is more actually screening, reprisals and "counter-murder" by armed force of the crown,' General Sir Hubert Gough wrote to the *Manchester Guardian* in early October. 'In Ireland at the moment murder and destruction are condoned and winked at, if not actively encouraged. The murders of policemen and others by the "Irish republicans" have been inexcusable. As you say the leaders of Sinn Féin and the Irish priesthood are very greatly to be condemned for not having taken a far more active part against such methods, but that is no excuse for any government, and especially a government of the great British empire, adopting such methods.'

Arthur Griffith publicly accused the British secret service of planning to kill moderate Sinn Féin politicians in order to give the impression that they were victims of an internal republican feud. In this way the movement's international support could be undermined. 'A certain number of Sinn Féin leaders have been marked down for assassination,' he said. 'I am first on the list. They intended to kill two birds with the one stone by getting me and circulating the story I have been assassinated by extremists because I am a man of moderate action.'

Meanwhile, even though he had provoked the current situation, in September and early October 1920, Collins was acting with extraordinary restraint so as not to take the spotlight off Terence MacSwiney's hunger strike. Although hoping that MacSwiney would be released, he secretly called for him to quit the hunger strike because he did not want him to die. The hunger strike became more protracted than anybody had expected. Many had been expecting him to die in August, but MacSwiney survived until the fourth week of October. While his protest continued it attracted the focus of media attention around the world.

The hunger strikes became so protracted that Sturgis noted they 'have faded into insignificance as a topic beside reprisals'. Before the end of September Collins was being goaded into arranging what would have been by far the Squad's most spectacular operation up to then. On the Sunday after the killing of Lynch, he made arrangements for the Squad to kill from eight to a dozen senior policemen such as Owen Brien, John Bruton, and Denis Barrett, as they went to eight o'clock mass at a church near Dublin Castle.

'I was instructed to accompany Paddy O'Daly and Joe Leonard and report with other members of the Squad for an operation to be carried out outside the Upper Castle Yard in the maze of alleyways that approached the rear entrance of Saints Michael's and John's church,' Charlie Dalton explained. 'We took up the various positions indicated by Mick McDonnell ... We were advised that a party of the political branch of G Division would leave from the Upper Castle Yard on their way to eight o'clock mass.' In addition to the Squad the Tipperary gang was present – Treacy, Breen, Hogan and Robinson – Tom Cullen of the intelligence branch, along with Hugo MacNeill and Jim Brennan. They took up positions in Essex Street, outside the back entrance of the church.

'I would say there was between ten and twelve in the group,'

Vinny Byrne recalled. They were waiting for a signal from Cullen. The attack was called off at the last moment because Jim McNamara was among the policemen. They were not in a position to tell so many men not to shoot McNamara as he was a valuable agent. Hence the whole thing was re-set for the following Sunday.

The following Sunday as O'Daly, Leonard and Dalton were making their way from the north side of the city at about 7 a.m., they found that British soldiers had set up a roadblock on Newcomen Bridge and were searching people. The three of them therefore turned down Ossory Road, where they climbed a wall and went down on the railroad track. They took O'Daly's gun from him and he proceeded to join the others outside the church near Dublin Castle. Leonard and Dalton made their way down the tracks from where they could see that the military had taken up positions on a bridge in Drumcondra.

They obviously had no intention of being robbed of what had promised to be an exciting morning. 'We decided to fire on the military on Binn's Bridge,' Dalton continued. 'We emptied both our pistols – I was using a Mauser (a Peter-the-Painter) and Leonard a Colt .45 and we saw two soldiers fall as a result of our fire. The range was approximately 200 yards.' They had, indeed, wounded two soldiers, who were taken to King George V hospital. One had been hit in the thigh and the other in the arm.

The planned attack on the police outside the church had to be called off again that day, this time because the detectives did not turn up. They went to another church – Saint Teresa's in Clarendon Street. The following Sunday the Squad was in Clarendon Street, but the detectives went elsewhere. 'Misters! They're not here today!' a newsboy shouted at them. If the newspaper boy could twig what they were trying to do, they were clearly becoming too obvious.

Tom Keogh had said that if he did not get Bruton that day, he was going to go into church and shoot him at mass, according to Ben Byrne, who believed that Collins learned of Keogh's plan and 'put his foot down in a most determined fashion, feeling that the after-effects on public opinion might not, perhaps, be to our advantage.' Collins actually called off the plans to shoot the men on their way to mass. With Terence MacSwiney and ten other hunger strikers approaching death, killing the police would undoubtedly detract from the enormous international publicity that MacSwiney's hunger strike was attracting, and it would then be easier for the British to allow them all to die.

Although the Squad had been unable to kill Barrett, Brien and Bruton, Collins did manage to exploit the rivalries within the DMP to such an extent that Brien was discredited and forced to retire from the force. The British strongly suspected that arms were being brought from America into Dublin on the Moore-McCormack Line. Inspector McCabe, who was on port duty at the north wall, was directed to have a microscopic search made of these boats. The Americans were inclined to make legal trouble for the inspector as regards international law. McCabe wrote a long report, explaining the position and difficulties, legal and otherwise, and asking for instructions. Detective Superintendent Brien submitted this report to the inspector general, Colonel Edgeworth-Johnson, for instructions.

'This subject ought never to have been raised,' Edgeworth-Johnson wrote in the margin. 'All American sailors are now suspect. Their belongings should be searched and a report made in each case.' Broy gave Collins a copy of correspondence. 'We will make use out of that,' he said.

The Americans had been traditionally irked by the British claim of a right to search American ships going back over more than a hundred years, and Collins sought to exploit this. 'I remember seeing Colonel Johnston's minute in the latest news column of the Dublin *Evening Mail*,' Broy recalled. 'Superintendent Brien hated Inspector McCabe, who was a Unionist, and said that he must have been indiscreet and must have shown the file to some disloyal Customs Officer. Disciplinary action was taken against

Inspector McCabe, and he was about to be compelled to retire on pension.'

'I settled that fellow's hash at last,' Brien remarked to some colleagues that included Broy.

'Apparently they had been life-long rivals,' Broy explained. 'I told this to McNamara who met McCabe in the castle and told him. McCabe got on to some of his Unionists friends at the castle and had the matter reopened. The final result was that McCabe was reinstated and Detective Superintendent Brien was compelled to go on pension.' Collins viewed Brien as a very dangerous man and, having failed to kill him, was delighted to have him discredited and forced out of the DMP, though the whole thing would soon lead to the ousting of McNamara also.

Superintendent John J. Purcell, who replaced Brien, had come up through the uniform branch and loathed G Division and the political detectives. A thirty-year veteran of the force, he had a solemn countenance, close cut hair, rimless glasses and a gruff voice. Neligan, who was working in the superintendent's office as pay sergeant, used to call in to talk to see Broy, on the pretext of looking for more money. They pretended to be hostile to one another because Purcell was liable to burst in on them at any time.

The Tipperary gang was broken up in October. Part of the British reorganisation had involved the setting up of a combined intelligence unit to track down wanted members of the IRA. The Central Raid Bureau under Ormonde Winter soon began to make its presence felt as it tracked down Dan Breen and Seán Treacy. The British mistakenly thought that Breen was responsible for the shooting of the one-armed colonel, Ferguson Smyth, in the County Club in Cork. Major Gerald Smyth had returned from the Middle East to avenge his brother's death and when Winter's people learned that Breen and Treacy were spending the night of 11 October at the Drumcondra home of Professor John Carolan, Smyth was selected to lead the raiding party.

The group burst into the house, but Smyth and Captain A. P.

White were killed as they approached the room occupied by Breen and Treacy, who then escaped through a window. When the shooting started the troops outside raced into the house, thereby allowing the two men to escape. Breen had been wounded in the exchange of fire and was taken to the Mater hospital, where doctors and nurses colluded to hide his identity and the nature of his wounds. Professor Carolan was also brought to the hospital, where he died of his wounds, but not before making a full deathbed statement that he had been shot in cold blood by one of the raiding party.

The funeral of Smyth and White took place the following day, 14 October. The Squad and members of the Dublin IRA were in place at various vantage points to the funeral, while intelligence officers were scattered only along the quays which the funeral procession was expected to pass. 'Our information was that Hamar Greenwood, General Tudor and other prominent officers would take part in the funeral procession, and it was decided that an attempt would be made to shoot them en route,' related Frank Thornton. 'With this purpose in mind Liam Tobin, Tom Cullen, Dick McKee, Frank Henderson, Leo Henderson, Peadar Clancy and I met at the back of Peadar Clancy's shop. Receiving information that none of those whom we sought were taking part in the funeral, the job was called off.'

Thornton and Tom Cullen were almost the last to leave Clancy's shop, with Dick McKee following behind them. 'As we left, Seán Treacy arrived, and on informing him of what had happened he went on towards the shop while we went towards the Pillar,' Thornton continued. 'We had very nearly arrived at the Pillar when the shooting started lower down the street, but to all intents and purposes it looked to us like one of the ordinary incidents which were happening every day in the streets of Dublin.' Treacy was killed along with two innocent bystanders – Patrick Carroll, a young messenger boy, and Joseph Corringham, of 57 Lower Gardiner Street who ran a tobacco shop.

RIC Sergeant Daniel Roche and Constable Fitzmaurice were sent to Dublin to identify Treacy and another Volunteer (Matt Furlong as it turned out) who had been killed in a premature explosion and who seemed to fit Breen's descriptions. David Neligan was given the gruesome task of accompanying Roche to the Richmond hospital morgue, where he identified Treacy, but did not recognise the other body.

'That's not Dan Breen,' Roche said. 'I would know his bulldog face anywhere.'

That evening Neligan mentioned the incident to Liam Tobin and added that he was due to meet Roche on Ormond Quay the following afternoon. Collins decided that the Squad should eliminate Roche, a twenty-year veteran of the RIC, in his mid-forties, and a father of four.

When Neligan saw Tom Keogh, Jim Slattery, Joe Dolan and Frank Thornton at the corner of Capel Street the next day he realised what was about to happen. There is a discrepancy here though as he said that he did not know that they would be waiting to kill Roche, whereas they said he was to identify Roche for them.

'For Christ's sake, what has he done?' Neligan asked.

'I don't know,' one of the men replied. 'I've my orders to shoot him and that's what I'm going to do.'

Dolan claimed that it had been arranged for Neligan to identify Roche. The Squad already had a description of Roche but his presence with Neligan would have made it easy to identify him.

'We took up our position and then we saw Neligan talking to two men near the Ormond hotel,' Slattery noted. 'One of them was a stout man and looked more like a farmer than an RIC man. Joe Dolan and Frank Thornton were supposed to shoot these men, and we got the job of covering them off. We did not take any particular notice for a little while, until we saw Dolan approaching us with a drawn gun in his hand, and the two men who had been talking to Neligan walking in front of him.'

At that time repairs were being carried out on the bank premises at the corner of Capel Street and scaffolding poles were erected, so that there was room for only one person to pass at a time. Roche was walking with Constable Fitzmaurice. 'The two policemen were coming towards us and we let them pass us,' Dolan explained. 'Then I took out my revolver and put six bullets into Roche when he was just in front of me in the passage-way. Tom Keogh and Jim Slattery put a few more bullets into him.'

'When they passed us, Dolan levelled his gun and we knew that they were the men we were looking for, so we fired at them, killing Roche,' Slattery recalled. The wounded man still managed to run some distance as they were shooting him. In the process two bystanders were wounded – a fifteen-year-old girl, Eileen Allen, of 23 Lower Bridge Street, and an elderly man, Daniel Reid, of 34 Little Strand Street.

'The other man [Fitzmaurice] escaped, although we had the place surrounded. He got away before we realised he was one of the men we were looking for.' According to Dolan the other policeman ran to Dublin Castle and promptly resigned from the RIC.

Constable Fitzmaurice reported that he had seen Neligan talking to one of the killers, and Neligan had some difficulty extricating himself. He was summoned before Colonel Walter Edgeworth-Johnson, the head of the DMP.

'This constable says he saw you talking to the men who shot Sergeant Roche,' the inspector general said.

'He is making a mistake, sir.'

'What did you do?' he asked. 'Did you see the men who attacked Roche?

Neligan said that he had run away as he thought the shots were being fired at him. 'I also told him that I was waiting for a tram to go to the Park,' he added. 'I had no sooner said this than I saw there was a flaw in it as I was on the wrong side of the road for an outgoing tram.'

The inspector general could not understand how the IRA learned that Roche was in Dublin. 'Didn't you tell me that some woman at the railway station enquired where you were going?'

'Yes,' Fitzmaurice replied. 'A woman in the magazine stall at Limerick Junction asked me where we were bound for.'

At that point Neligan was told he could leave. He was understandably annoyed that shooting Roche in his presence had jeopardised his cover as a spy. It really demonstrated a dangerous blind spot in the Big Fellow's intelligence operations. As a man of action he was so anxious to get things done that he sometimes acted before the dust had settled to cover his agents' tracks.

Vinny Byrne did not believe the Squad had shot Sergeant Roche just because he identified Treacy's body. 'There is no doubt there must have been some other reason for the shooting,' he argued, 'as it in itself would not warrant such action; but that was of no concern of the Squad's; they got their orders and asked no questions.' Neligan thought likewise. 'Identifying a dead man was certainly not an offence at all, but of course it was not for me to question the ins and outs of the matter,' he explained.

Paddy O'Daly said that Roche and Fitzmaurice had supposedly been recognised in the lorry that raided a republican outfitters, and it was suspected that they were in Dublin to look for Breen. It seemed more likely to Neligan, however, that Roche was just shot as a reprisal for the killing of Seán Treacy. Whatever the real story, Neligan clearly had pangs of conscience. 'That was the one day I regretted my role,' he said. 'If for one second I thought the poor wretch would have been shot, not a word of his visit would have been mentioned.'

Believing that Larry Dalton and Daniel Roche had both been unfairly eliminated, Neligan set out to spare Detective Sergeant Denis Coffey, who had picked out men in 1916 for execution. Coffey knew many of the older Volunteers and could pick them out in the street. There was an even greater danger that someone might tip him off about IRA activities. Hence he was on the Squad's hit list.

'Although, in my opinion, he richly deserved such a fate, I

determined to save his life for the sake of his poor wretch of a wife and young family,' Neligan explained. 'I, therefore, sought him out and told him I'd heard two fellows in a public house saying they'd shoot him next day.'

Coffey was terrified. 'He had no stomach for the business after that,' Neligan said. 'He never came out of the castle (where he lived with his wife and family) again until the Truce ... Hordes of officials holed up there and spent their evenings walking about, some wearing steel waistcoats.'

The first of the hunger strikers to die was Michael Fitzgerald on 17 October, but his death was hardly noticed against the backdrop of MacSwiney's continuing struggle. The lord mayor died eight days later on 25 October, after seventy-four days on hunger strike. Joseph Murphy died some hours later, and Arthur Griffith ordered that the other hunger strikes be called off.

MacSwiney attracted most attention because he was not only an elected member of the Westminster parliament, even though he had never actually taken his seat, but was also the lord mayor of the island's third largest city. After his death Sinn Féin sought to make as much capital as possible out of the funeral. If they had had their way the body would have been brought to Dublin and then brought down through the country, but the British military delivered it straight to Cork, where there was a massive funeral.

MacSwiney was buried in Cork on Sunday, 31 October 1920. Speaking in New York at the polo grounds that day, de Valera said that MacSwiney 'and his comrades gave up their lives for their country. The English have killed them ... Tomorrow a boy, Kevin Barry, they will hang, and he alike, will only regret that he has but one life to give. Oh God!' De Valera then quoted Yeats:

> They shall be remembered forever,
> They shall be alive forever,
> They shall be speaking forever,
> The people shall hear them forever.

CHAPTER 13

'LIKE A TOWN WITH THE PLAGUE'

The execution of Kevin Barry, an eighteen-year-old university student, was the first official British execution of a rebel in Ireland since 1916. He was sentenced to death on 21 October and hanged eleven days later. Collins did consider some rescue plans but Barry's mother was opposed as she thought his sentence would be commuted because of his age.

There was intense public pressure to reprieve Barry, but there was little support for the idea at Dublin Castle, because 'the three soldiers he and his party killed were all under 19,' noted Mark Sturgis, who felt this made a nonsense of the arguments about Barry's age. 'I think the Shinns would gain more sympathy as "sportsmen" if they were a little more logical about this,' Sturgis wrote. 'They seem to see nothing absurd in making their proudest boast that they are a rebel army attacking a tyrant and yet using every sort of plea for mercy whenever one of their brave soldiers is up against it.'

Churchill was finally getting his way, but he could hardly have conceived of a timing that would cause greater offence to the Irish people than by desecrating 'All Saints' Day', a Catholic holy day, with the hanging of a teenage college student. They thereby played right into the hands of Michael Collins. 'Rather a pity no one noticed it is All Saints' day,' Mark Sturgis wrote in his diary. Barry would immediately go into the pantheon of Irish heroes as a martyr and a virtual saint. He was immortalised in song:

> Another martyr for old Ireland,
> Another murder for the crown,

> Whose brutal laws may kill the Irish,
> But won't keep their spirit down.
> Lads like Barry are no cowards
> From the foe they will not fly,
> Lads like Barry will free Ireland,
> For her sake they'll live and die.

IRA headquarters decided on a general attack on British forces on the eve of Barry's execution as a kind of a reprisal. Orders were sent out to this effect to the officer commanding each brigade. Tadgh Kennedy brought the order to the Kerry No. 1 brigade as he was just returning to Tralee after five months in Dublin.

'I conveyed the order to Paddy Cahill,' Kennedy explained. 'A cancelling order was sent out at the last minute but none reached Kerry.'

Four RIC men had been killed in Kerry by rebels since the Easter Rebellion, but within twenty-four hours of Barry's execution no less than sixteen policemen and a radio naval officer had been shot, seven fatally, another two were kidnapped, beaten savagely, and then released. One of those never recovered from the ordeal and committed suicide shortly afterwards.

Hugh Martin of the *Daily News* argued that what occurred next in Tralee was symptomatic of what was happening throughout Ireland. The IRA struck and the crown police lashed out in retaliation against the people as a whole. This had the impact of solidifying local support for the IRA.

On the night of 31 October Constable William Madden, aged thirty, from Newcastlewest, was shot dead in Abbeydorney and a colleague, Constable Robert Gorbey, aged twenty-three, was mortally wounded. He died later in the week. Constable George Morgan, also aged twenty-three, a native of Mayo, was killed in nearby Ballyduff and Constable Thomas Reidy, aged forty-two, from Clare, was shot through the head and two other colleagues were wounded. Black and Tans arrived in Ballyduff a few hours later and proceeded to torch the creamery and some of the principal business houses.

John Houlihan was taken out of his home near the village and shot by the Black and Tans. The military arrived at the house around 4.30 a.m. As the teenager's horrified parents looked on the Tans dragged him from the house across the road, where one stabbed him with a bayonet in the side, shot him three times, and then another finished him off with a blow of a rifle butt to the head.

Two Black and Tans, Constables Herbert Evans, aged twenty-six, from Belfast, and Albert Caseley, aged twenty-four, from London – were killed at Hillville, near Killorglin, that night. Officially they were on patrol, but they had actually just seen two girls home when they were attacked. Two more Black and Tans were wounded in an ambush in Green Street, Dingle.

Killorglin had been relatively quiet over the years, but the Black and Tans went on the rampage in the town that night. They burned down the Sinn Féin hall and an adjoining garage, as well as the Temperance Association hall and the residence of a well-known Sinn Féiner who was in Cork with his family for the MacSwiney funeral. Throughout the night shots were discharged intermittently until about 5.30 a.m. The homes of other known Sinn Féiners were knocked up, but none of the 'wanted' men were found, though Denis M. O'Sullivan was taken from his house in the square and shot four times. He never recovered fully and died the following year.

Meanwhile Tralee was in turmoil. On Sunday evening, Constable Daniel McCarthy of the RIC and Bert Woodward, a naval radio operator, were shot and wounded, while Constable Patrick Waters, aged twenty-three (a four-year veteran from Loughanbeg, near Spiddal, County Galway), and Constable Ernest Bright, a Londoner in his early thirties – were seized by the IRA, taken outside the town and killed. Their bodies were never found. It was variously rumoured that they were thrown live into a furnace at the Gas Works, or that they were shot and their bodies disposed of in the furnace or buried near the lock gates at the end of the local canal outside the town or in the family crypt of the lock keeper.

Assuming that their two colleagues had been kidnapped and were possibly still being held by the IRA, the Black and Tans unleashed a veritable reign of terror in Tralee over the next nine days. The events made front-page news in both Canada and the United States, prompted a series of parliamentary questions at Westminster, and became the subject of some controversy and editorials in the British daily press. News from Tralee was actually reported on the front page of the *New York Times* on three separate days during the siege and on the front page of the *Montreal Gazette* on four different days.

Monday, 1 November, was All Saints' Day, a holy day of obligation, with the result that all the churches were busy. The Black and Tans drove up and down the streets in lorries, discharging their rifles. 'Volley after volley resounded to the terror of the people,' recalled one witness. Shots were fired as people emerged from twelve o'clock mass at St John's parish church and there was a panic as people stampeded back in.

A group of foreign journalists from the Associated Press of the United States, *Le Journal* (Paris), the London *Times*, *Daily News*, *Manchester Guardian*, and London *Evening News* visited Tralee after MacSwiney's funeral and heard of the burning of the local county hall the previous night. Although the local council owned the hall itself, Paddy Cahill, the IRA brigadier in north Kerry, was renting it as a cinema.

The Tans told a group of journalists which happened to include Hugh Martin of the *Daily News* (London) that they were looking for him because of what he had been reporting. The threat to Martin, which made front page news in the *New York Times*, was denounced as a threat to the freedom of the press in an editorial in *The Times* of London: 'An issue of importance to all independent newspapers and to the public is raised by the account published yesterday in the *Daily News* of the threatening attitude of the constabulary at Tralee towards a special correspondent and confirmed in all essentials by the special correspondent of the *Evening News* who accompanied him and heard the threats.'

A French journalist who was with the group visiting Tralee depicted a frightening situation. 'I do not remember, even during the war, having seen a people so profoundly terrified as those of this little town, Tralee,' M. de Marsillac, the London correspondent of *Le Journal* reported. 'The violence of the reprisals undertaken by representatives of authority, so to speak, everywhere, has made everybody beside himself, even before facts justified such a state of mind.'

Shopkeepers were warned by the police to close down for the funerals of their companions, who deserved as much respect as the lord mayor of Cork. All schools were closed and remained closed for over a week. The security forces stalked the deserted streets firing shots into the air, or shooting blindly into windows as they drove up and down the street. Shortly after noon on Tuesday, Tommy Wall, aged twenty-four, an ex-soldier who had fought in France during the First World War and returned to join the IRA, was standing at the corner of Blackpool Lane and The Mall when some Tans told him to put up his hands. One of the men hit him in the face with a rifle butt and told him to get out of the place. As he left they shot and fatally wounded him, claiming that he was shot trying to escape.

'Except for soldiers, the town was as deserted and doleful as if the Angel of Death had passed through it,' de Marsillac continued. 'Not a living soul in the streets. All the shops shut and the bolts hastily fastened. All work was suspended, even the local newspapers.'

In the early hours of Thursday morning the Black and Tans began firebombing the occupied business premises of Sinn Féin sympathisers. 'Scenes of the wildest panic ensued,' *The Cork Examiner* reported. 'The screams of the women and children were heard from the neighbourhood of the burning buildings, mingled with the ring of rifle fire and the explosion of bombs.' The accounts of what was happening were still fairly sketchy on the Thursday when T. P. O'Connor, the nationalist member of parliament from Liverpool, asked in the House of Commons about the deaths of John Houlihan, John Conway, Tommy Wall and Simon O'Connor.

'I have received a report to the effect that John Houlihan was shot by masked men at Ballyduff at 6 a.m. on Monday the 1st, and that Thomas Wall was fatally wounded in Tralee from gunshot wounds,' Sir Hamar Greenwood, the chief secretary for Ireland, replied. 'Courts of inquiry will be held in these cases. In the case of Conway a court of inquiry found that he died from natural causes. I have not yet received a copy of the proceedings of this court, but I am informed by the police authorities that the deceased was found dead near his home on the 1st instant, and the body bore no traces of gunshot or other wounds.'

The London *Times* had already reported that its correspondent had seen the body laid out with an obvious bullet wound in the temple. 'The vital fact in the tragedy is that while the chief secretary is repeating his stereotyped assurances that things are getting better, it is patent to the readers of newspapers the world over that they are getting daily worse,' the *Daily News* commented. 'At the moment the supreme need is to withdraw the troops. If the police cannot remain unprotected, let them go too. Ireland could not be worse off without them than with them. There is every reason to believe her state would be incomparably better.'

On the same day that John Conway was killed in Tralee, Ellen Quinn, a pregnant housewife, was shot dead in Galway while sitting on her wall by a Black and Tan firing indiscriminately from a passing lorry. There was no doubt about the responsibility even in Dublin Castle. 'I wish these lorry loads of police could be restrained from this idiotic blazing about as they are driving along – it can do no conceivable good and yesterday's case of a woman in Galway shortly expecting a child, shot in the stomach and now dead is beastly.'

By Friday, 5 November, separate stories from Tralee were front-page news in both the *Montreal Gazette* and the *New York Times*. By then the British army commander was being depicted as protecting the people from the police but saying that he really did not have the authority to act, because the police terrorising the town were the legal authority.

Saturday, market day, was normally the busiest day of the week in Tralee, but people were not allowed into town. The correspondent of the *Freeman's Journal* contacted his newspaper by telegraph. 'Police persist in taking measures to cut off the necessities of life from the people,' he reported. 'Black and Tans take up positions outside bakeries and provision stores where they suspect food could be secured, and at the bayonet's point send famishing women and children from the doors. Outside one baker's establishment a Black and Tan, brandishing a revolver, told women and children to clear off, adding "You wanted to starve us, but we will starve you".'

By now, people had not been able to do any shopping for a week and there was real deprivation, especially in the poorer areas. The breadwinners had been unable to work and the poorer people could not afford to buy food, even if it had been available. The story on the front page of that day's *Montreal Gazette* was headlined: 'TRALEE IS PARALYZED: Town Near Starvation, Condition is Desperate.'

'The town of Tralee, Ireland is fast approaching starvation in consequence of recent police order forbidding the carrying on of business – until two missing policemen are returned by the townspeople,' the report began. 'Trade is paralyzed, the banks, and bakeries even being closed, and the condition of the people is becoming desperate. An addition military order forbids the holding of fairs and markets or assemblies of any kind within a three mile limit.'

That same day in London T. P. O'Connor asked another series

of questions in the House of Commons about what was happening in Tralee. He asked about the police closing of all businesses in Tralee, whether the poor were in serious distress, and whether the trade of the town was being destroyed.

'The business premises in Tralee were closed for some days following a number of assassinations of police on Sunday last, but not by order of the police.' Greenwood replied. 'I understand shops are now open and business is resuming its normal course.' He said he had already telegraphed Tralee and was waiting for a reply to his question, 'on whose authority were they closed?'

'Is the world expected to believe that women and children went without food for days in the hope that the chief secretary would be blamed for reducing them to starvation?' the *Freeman's Journal* asked. 'That is the only interpretation of Sir Hamar Greenwood's so-called explanation. It gives the measure of the present Parliament that this issue of grotesque fabrications was apparently accepted by the majority, not indeed as the truth, but as a plausible substitute for the truth. Any lie, however clumsy, will serve if the object is to stifle inquiry into the Irish Terror.'

On Monday the bakeries, butcher shops and local factories were permitted to open in Tralee, but all other business were not. The *New York World* reported that an attempt to open others shops in Tralee on Tuesday, 9 November, 'was met by demonstrations by the police, who appeared on the streets shouting and discharging firearms and terrorising those who had attempted to defy the order and open their business places.'

'No coherent account of conditions in Tralee is possible,' the *New York World* correspondent explained. 'Communication is difficult, investigation dangerous, and the reports from the place are so remarkable as to be almost unbelievable. It has been suggested officially that the police are not responsible for the order, but local accounts leave no doubt that the police are enforcing it, perhaps unofficially but none the less effectively. Wholesale starvation apparently is enforced with bayonets and occasionally with bullets, as events have shown. The people cannot understand how this can be done by forces of the crown without crown authority ... A Black and Tan rule has been set up in Tralee. Many of the 10,000 inhabitants have fled, but those unable to find refuge elsewhere are the victims of this awful procedure.'

It was not until around 8 p.m. on Tuesday night, 9 November, that the Black and Tans announced that businesses could re-open the following day. That same evening Lloyd George declared during a highly publicised address at the annual lord mayor's dinner at the Guildhall that the security forces 'had murder by the throat' in Ireland.

While the British had been building up their intelligence service, the intelligence department under Collins and Tobin had been collecting the addresses of the undercover British agents living in private houses around the city. Instead of taking them out one by one, it was decided to hit as many of them as possible at the one time, as they were coming much too close to the IRA leadership for comfort.

Having been introduced by Willie Beaumont and Dave Neligan to some of the British intelligence people, Cullen, Saurin and Thornton began to frequent Kidds Buffet in Grafton Street, where the British intelligence officers and auxiliary intelligence officers met frequently. 'We were introduced in the ordinary way as touts,' Thornton explained. They eventually became great friends with men like Lieutenant Bennett, Captain Peter Ames and a number of other prominent secret service officers. One day, one of these officers turned suddenly to Tom Cullen and said, 'Surely you fellows know these men – Liam Tobin, Tom Cullen and Frank Thornton, these are Collins' three officers and if you can get these fellows we would locate Collins himself.'

'If the ground opened and swallowed us we could not have been more surprised,' Thornton added. 'It was a genuine query to three Irishmen whom they believed should know all about the particular fellows they mentioned. The fact remains that although they knew of the existence of the three of us and they knew of the existence of Collins, they actually had no photograph of any of us, and had a very poor description of either Collins or the three of us.'

'Of all the sources of information, undoubtedly the most valuable was that derived from the examination of captured documents,' Ormonde Winter wrote. 'After the first important capture which, to a great extent, was fortuitous, other searches were made from the addresses noted and the names obtained, and the snowball process continued, leading to fresh searches.' The Raid Bureau was established. According to Winter, 'from August 1920, to July 1921, 6,311 raids and searches were carried out in the Dublin district'. He noted that the British learned an enormous amount about the workings of the IRA because 'the Irish had an irresistible habit of keeping documents'. The British seized a tremendous number of documents from which they learned who was doing what within the IRA, but not what those people looked like. Thus, they quickly knew who they wanted, but they could not identify them.

In the first two weeks of November some of Collins' most trusted associates had close calls. Frank Thornton was arrested and held for ten days, but he managed to convince his captors that he had nothing to do with the IRA. On the night of 10 November they just missed Dick Mulcahy as he escaped through the skylight of Professor Michael Hayes' house in South Circular Road around five o'clock in the morning, but they seized some crucial documents which included the names and addresses of more than 200 volunteers with notations classifying them as 'very good shots, good shots, etc.'

Three days later they raided Vaughan's hotel and questioned Liam Tobin and Tom Cullen, but they managed to bluff their way out of it. In a matter of three days the IRA's chief-of-staff had had a narrow escape and the three top men of Collins' intelligence network had been arrested and let go. The need to disrupt the

British intelligence network was becoming imperative.

Dick McKee took charge of the overall planning. In early November representatives of the four battalions of the Dublin brigade and the Squad were given descriptions of the undercover agents to be eliminated and details about where they were living. These agents were suspected members of what the IRA intelligence people were calling the Cairo gang, so-called because of their tendency to frequent the Cairo Café on Grafton Street.

Liam Tobin told Charlie Dalton to meet Maudie, a maid at 28 Upper Pembroke Street, where some of the undercover agents were residing. 'She described the routine of the residents of the flats, and it would seem from her account that they followed no regular occupation but did a lot of office work in their flats,' Dalton noted. 'I arranged with her to bring me the contents of the waste paper basket. When they were examined we found torn up documents, which referred to the movement of wanted Volunteers, and also photographs of wanted men.'

Although McKee was in charge of the planning, Collins suggested that the morning of Sunday, 21 November would be the best time to strike. This had been the suggestion of one of his own agents, whom he referred to as 'Lt. G.' Collins was not always as careful as he might have been about protecting the identity of his spies, but in this case nobody seemed to know for sure the identity of 'Lt. G.' Florence O'Donoghue, the intelligence officer of the Cork No. 1 brigade, thought it was Lily Mernin at army headquarters. 'While I worked as an agent in Dublin Castle, Michael or any other member of the staff never referred to me by name,' she explained however. 'Michael always referred to me as the "little gentleman".' O'Donoghue believed she signed her notes 'G' and Collins could have added the 'Lt.' to make it more difficult for anyone to guess her identity if his notes were captured. People would naturally assume his agent was an army officer rather than a woman typist at army headquarters.

'It was part of my normal duty to type the names and addresses of British agents who were accommodated at private addresses and living as ordinary citizens in the city,' Mernin explained. 'These lists were amended whenever an address was changed. I passed them on each week.'

'There was a girl in the office who was the daughter of Superintendent Dunne of Dublin Castle,' she continued. 'When he resigned she moved out of Dublin Castle to an address in Mount Street. Stopping at the same address were a number of men. Every morning she would come into the office she would tell us about them; she was puzzled to know whom they were. Her brother also resided there with her and, apparently he used to mix with them, and he discussed their conversation with her. She would report this conversation to us when she would come in to the office in the morning. There was one fellow there by the name of McMahon who was very addicted to drink. While under the influence of drink he was, I believe, liable to talk a lot, and, mainly, his conversation concerned raids and arrests of wanted IRA men. Whatever tit-bits of information that I could glean from Miss Lil Dunne I immediately passed on to the intelligence section.'

One morning Lil Dunne arrived in an excited state, saying that her brother believed there was a spy in their office, because somebody had given information to the IRA about McMahon and Peel, two British agents, who were lodging in the same house as her and her brother in Mount Street.

'Who could be a spy?' Mernin asked. She put the blame on Lil's brother for talking to much.

In fact it was Seán Hyde, a veterinary student living at 21 Lower Mount Street, who had informed IRA intelligence that two of those wanted in the killing of John Lynch – Paddy McMahon and Peel – were living in the same house, along with a number of medical students. 'I was instructed to investigate and I met Hyde, who gave me all the facts,' Charlie Dalton said. 'Those suspects did not go out in the daytime except to an ex-serviceman's club, known as the South Irish Horse Club, in Merrion Square. They also occasionally visited a billiards saloon at the rear of a tobacconist shop in Mount Street. This was owned by a Mr Kerr who was not sympathetic to the movement.'

The Squad was ordered to kill McMahon and Peel, if the chance presented itself. Dalton tried to find them with the help of Tom Keogh and Joe Leonard and others on different occasions. One night, one of Hyde's friends, Conny O'Leary, told Dalton that McMahon and Peel were in Kerr's playing billiards.

'On this occasion I was accompanied only by Joe Leonard,' Dalton recalled. 'We went into the saloon, in which there was one table, and two gentlemen were playing billiards. The only description I had of McMahon, who was the principal party, was that he wore a signet ring on a finger of his left hand.' Dalton and Leonard were waiting to see the ring before they opened fire when suddenly O'Leary rushed in to say that McMahon had already returned to the house. He had apparently only briefly gone upstairs in the billiards saloon to visit a woman. After that night plans to kill McMahon and Peel were shelved in favour of the new plan to kill a much larger selection of undercover agents at the same time.

The search for British undercover agents went on. 'On various occasions I was requested by members of the intelligence squad to assist them in the identity of enemy agents,' Lily Mernin recalled. 'I remember the fist occasion on which I took part in this work was with the late Tom Cullen in 1919. Piaras Beaslaí asked me to meet a young man who would be waiting at Ó Raghallaigh's bookshop in Dorset Street and to accompany him to Lansdowne Road. I met this man, whom I learned later was Tom Cullen, and went with him to a football match at Lansdowne Road. He asked me to point out to him and give him the names of any British military officers who frequented Dublin Castle and GHQ. I was able to point out a few military officers to him who I knew.

'When I got to know the auxiliaries better, I accompanied Frank Saurin (known then as Mr Stanley) to various cafes, where I identified for him some of the auxiliaries whom I knew.'

'Arrangements should now be made about the matter,' Collins wrote to Dick McKee on 17 November. 'Lt. G. is aware of things. He suggests the 21st. A most suitable date and day I think.'

Charlie Dalton met Maudie, the maid in 28 Upper Pembroke St, on the Saturday evening, 20 November, at their usual rendezvous and she told him that all her 'boarders' were at home, with the exception of Peter Ames and George Bennett. She said that they were changing their residence to 38 Upper Mount Street that night.

That same night, at the headquarters of the printer's union at 35 Lower Gardiner Street, McKee met with Brugha, Mulcahy, Collins, Russell, Peadar Clancy and those people selected to head the assassination team to finalise arrangements for the following morning. Brugha felt there was insufficient evidence against some of those named by Collins. There was no room for doubt however in the cases of Ames and Bennett, the two men who knew that Tobin, Cullen and Thornton were the leading intelligence operatives of Collins, nor was there with Captain Baggallay and the two men who had shot John Lynch at the Exchange hotel – McMahon (whose real name was Lieutenant H. R. Angliss) and Peel. Brugha authorised the killing of all these and some thirty other agents the following morning.

'It's to be done exactly at nine,' Collins insisted. 'Neither before nor after. These whores, the British, have got to learn that Irishmen can turn up on time.'

McKee questioned those in charge of operations as to their reconnoitring of their positions and the arrangements they had for getting their men back to the northside of the city. He impressed on them that they were to be careful of the bridges on their way back because the crown forces were likely to cut them off and search people. The second battalion arranged to commandeer a ferryboat to take the men back across the Liffey afterwards.

The four battalions of the brigade were each responsible for a certain area. Most were operating outside their own patch because nearly all of the operations were within the third battalion's region. Seán Russell, the quartermaster general of the IRA, selected the men for the different operations. He put Paddy Moran, a captain of one of the second battalion's companies, in charge of the team that was targeting three secret service men saying at the Gresham hotel in Sackville Street. He insisted on appointing members of the Squad to take charge of all the other teams.

Paddy O'Daly was anxious to take part but McKee insisted that he stay in the background organising things. He remained with some first-aid people at No. 17 North Richmond Street, which was his base for the day, looking after the five operations being conducted by the second battalion under Squad leadership. 'I did not like it,' O'Daly said, 'but I was told that I was not going because I had other business to do.'

'Paddy, I'm not going either,' McKee said. 'Have you not full confidence in the men appointed?'

Of course, O'Daly said that he had full confidence. And that ended the matter.

The various teams met subsequently at different centres. Members of the second battalion met at Tara Hall in Gloucester Street (now Seán McDermott Street). One of the senior intelligence officers explained the nature of the operations about to be put into action. There were between twenty and thirty men present. Tom Keogh had been selected to take charge at 22 Lower Mount Street and Vinny Byrne was supposed to assist him, but a new team was put together at the last moment to kill Ames and Bennett in the new residence at 38 Upper Mount Street.

'I had about ten men under me, which included a first-aid man,' Byrne explained. 'I did not like the idea of taking charge, as Tom Ennis was in my group, and I thought that he, being a senior officer of the second battalion, should be in charge. I made known my thoughts.'

'You take charge of the men and I will carry out the operation,' Byrne said to Ennis. But Ennis would not hear of it.

'Very good, Tom,' Byrne conceded.

CHAPTER 14

'THE LORD HAVE MERCY ON YOUR SOULS!'

After the meeting at 35 Lower Gardiner Street, Collins, McKee and some of the others went over to Vaughan's hotel for a drink. Christy Harte, the porter, became suspicious of one of the hotel guests, a Mr Edwards, who had booked in three days earlier. Edwards had made a late night telephone call and then left the hotel, a rather ominous sign as it was after curfew. Harte immediately went upstairs to where Collins and the others were gathered.

'I think, sirs, ye ought to be going.'

Collins had come to trust Harte's instincts and had no hesitation now. 'Come on boys, quick,' he said, and all promptly headed for the door.

Collins took refuge a few doors down in the top floor flat of Dr Paddy Browne of Maynooth College at 39 Parnell Square. From there he watched the raid on Vaughan's hotel a few minutes later. By then all the guests in the hotel were legitimately registered, with the exception of Conor Clune. He had come to the hotel with Peadar Clancy, and had apparently been forgotten. He was taken away for questioning. Dick Mulcahy later said that Clune had made an inane comment to Seán Kavanagh about being prepared to die for Ireland or something to that effect when questioned. Kavanagh was convinced that Clune was lifted simply because he was not registered and did not even have a toothbrush to suggest that he had planned to stay overnight. It was a mistake that would ultimately cost him his life.

During the night McKee and Clancy were also arrested but everything was already in train for the morning. The plan was to kill at least twenty selected agents at more than a dozen different locations in the city at the same time. Some used church bells, and other waited for clocks to strike before they began the operations, exactly at nine o'clock. Each team contained a member of the Squad and/or an intelligence officer, assigned to search the bodies and rooms for documents.

Most of the men had never engaged in such an operation before and were extremely nervous. While going up the stairs of the Shelbourne hotel, one of the men was startled by the sight of somebody with a gun and shot at his own reflection in a hall mirror. Hearing the shot, the man they were planning to kill apparently slipped out of his room and the operation was aborted.

Captain Crawford was in bed with his wife in their flat in Fitzwilliam Square when somebody knocked at the door. He assumed it was one of his men with a message.

'Come in,' he called out, but nobody came in. He got up and opened the door to find three men pointing pistols at him.

'Put up your hands,' one of them said.

'Is this a joke?' he asked.

'It's no joke! Are you Major Callaghan?'

'There is a Mr Callaghan living upstairs but he is not in the army and has no connection with the army,' Crawford replied.

In reply to their questions he said he was in charge of the motor repair department.

'Why the hell do you come here? Why don't you mind your own business in England?' they shouted.

They then ordered him back into bed with his wife. One of the men covered the couple with his gun and the other searched the room thoroughly for documents. Finding nothing compromising they seemed satisfied and ordered him out of the bed again. He thought they were going to shoot him and he pleaded with them not to do it in front of his wife.

'Shut up,' the leader said.

'Why should this happen to me – what have I done to deserve this?' Crawford's wife asked.

'You shut up too!'

'You bloody well clear out of this country within twenty-four hours or we will come back tomorrow night and do for you.'

Charlie Dalton recalled the details of another operation: 'On the Saturday night I stopped as usual in the "dugout" were we used to stay while on the run … This was located in the unoccupied portion of Summerhill Dispensary, and we gave accommodation for the night to several other Volunteers who were going into action in the morning.' Before curfew he went to Harcourt Street to meet Paddy Flanagan and the men of the third battalion who were to accompany him to 28 and 29 Upper Pembroke Street and they fixed a rendezvous time for the morning.

'When I arrived at Upper Pembroke Street on the Sunday morning,' Dalton continued, 'I met Flanagan and a few other Volunteers. I explained to Flanagan that we had no keys for the hall doors in order to gain admission, so we went over our arrangements.' As it happened, when they reached the front door it was open, as the hall porter James Green was shaking some mats.

About eight men entered the house. Two men stayed in the hall while the others divided into two groups and went up the separate staircases.

'I accompanied Flanagan and two other Volunteers to a room at the top of the house,' Dalton explained.

Meanwhile Major W. Woodcock was heading down for breakfast and his wife was looking out their third-floor window while dressing when she noticed a man slip over the back wall and drop into the back garden. Leo Dunne had been ordered to secure the back entrance to the property and to hold up anybody in the back or the kitchen area of the house. Woodcock took a revolver out of his pocket and checked before creeping forwards towards the building. She screamed to her husband. He came back, witnessed what was happening and told her to keep an eye on the man while he rushed downstairs to warn his colleague, Lieutenant-Colonel Hugh F. Montgomery. As he went downstairs he saw Green talking to two men holding revolvers. The men ordered Woodcock to come down, put up his hands and tell them his name. When he replied one of the men said: 'Are you sure?'

'Yes. Do not forget there are women in the house.'

'We know it.'

Woodcock was ordered to turn around and face the wall. At that point he heard Lieutenant-Colonel Montgomery open the door of his room and he shouted to him to look out.

'Hands up,' one of the men shouted and Montgomery complied.

At that point Dalton and Flanagan had reached the top floor elsewhere in the house. One of them knocked at the door and when Major C. M. G. Dowling, who was already dressed, answered it, they shot him dead. They also mortally wounded Captain Leonard Price in the next room. He died within a matter of minutes.

Once those shots rang out one of the men fired at Montgomery, who fell forward, and the same man then shot Woodcock.

'My husband and myself were awakened by a loud knocking,' Captain B. C. H. Keenlyside's wife recalled. 'Men dressed in overcoats and raincoats, and wearing cloth and felt hats filed methodically into the bedroom. They shouted roughly at my husband, "Get up, and put up your hands", which he did. They hustled him downstairs, clad only in his pajamas. I protested and begged them not to hurt him, holding the arm of one of the raiders. He assured me that I would not be hurt, and pushed me roughly back into the room. I followed them immediately out, and saw another officer being taken downstairs with his hands up.' This was Lieutenant R. G. Murray.

'They then placed him and my husband side by side in the hall, demanded their names, and fired at them, wounding the officer in the back and my husband in the jaw, both arms and upper part of the forehead,' Keenlyside's wife continued. 'I ran down and helped him quickly upstairs to our bedroom. I had roughly bandaged him when doctors and nurses arrived, and he was conveyed to an adjacent nursing home.'

The experienced gunmen had been on the top floor. Most of their colleagues were young and anxious. This kind of cold-blooded killing was something new for them. They were so nervous that they could not shoot straight. Ned Kelliher had been left guarding the front door and had not seen what went on in the house, but the men coming out said that six men had been shot. 'At the time they were under the impression that they were all dead,' said Kelliher. They were so nervous, however, that they could not shoot straight. Although all of the six agents in the residence were shot, three of them survived.

One operation, on the East Road, did not come off at all as the spies had left that address the previous day and there was nobody in the house when the Volunteers arrived. The first battalion had no success either when they raided a house on North Circular Road. The lieutenant colonel was believed to have moved to another lodging on the eve of the attack. The targets in the Eastwood hotel – Colonel Jennings and Major Callaghan – were also missing. They reportedly spend the night in a brothel. Another target was missing from a guesthouse in Fitzwilliam Square.

Captain Nobel, another of the wanted men, was also absent when a group made up mostly of the fourth battalion raided 7 Ranelagh Road. Todd Andrews recalled that he walked the mile from Brighton Square to the canal at Charlemont Street Bridge, where he met up with Francis X. Coghlan, Hubert Earle and James Kenny at about 8.55 a.m. Joe Dolan and Dan McDonnell led the team. 'We got a very ugly mission to perform,' McDonnell explained. They were to kill a 'British agent called Noble, and his paramour … They were both agents, and our information was that they both were the main cause of a member of our organisation, named Doyle, getting a very cruel death in the Dublin Mountains,' McDonnell added.

Coghlan was carrying a walking stick which he stuck in the

door to ensure it could not be closed when a teenage girl answered it. They brushed past her and walked straight up to the front first floor room where they expected to find Nobel. They had their guns out and cocked, ready to shoot him on sight as they burst into the room.

'We found the room empty except for a half-naked woman who sat up in the bed looking terror stricken. She did not scream or say a word,' Andrews recalled. The man they were looking for had apparently got up and gone on some assignment shortly after 7 a.m. When a man came out from the next room, Andrews almost shot him, thinking he was Noble.

'He's all right,' Coghlan shouted. The man was a lodger in the house and was apparently the source of their intelligence.

Dolan and McDonnell turned the place over looking for Noble's papers. There were only women and children in the rest of the house, but that did not prevent Dolan and his colleague from 'behaving like Black and Tans', according to Andrews. 'In their search for papers they overturned furniture, pushing occupants of the house around, and either through carelessness or malice set fire to a room in which there were children.'

'I felt a sense of shame and embarrassment for the woman's sake,' Todd added. But Dolan and McDonnell had no sympathy for her. Their orders were to shoot her and Noble, if the two of them were together, but not to shoot her alone. Hence Dolan took out his frustration on her. 'I was so angry I gave the poor girl a right scourging with the sword scabbard,' he recalled. 'Then I set the room on fire.'

Coghlan, a married man in his mid-thirties with a couple of children of his own, was furious at such conduct. They were witnessing the tactics of the Squad for the first time. 'Having seen the children to safety he directed Kenny to bring two more members of the company into the house, so that we could form a bucket chain from the tap in the basement (the only one in the house) to the first floor where the fire was becoming serious. Nearly half an hour was wasted putting out the fire before we were able to get of the house.' Neither Coghlan nor Kenny mentioned anything about the day, which later became known as Bloody Sunday, in their statements to the Bureau of Military History.

'In our fourth battalion area there were at least four abortive raids,' according to Andrews.

The operation at the Gresham hotel under Paddy Moran seemed to go smoothly. Twelve to fourteen men entered the hotel at 9 a.m. One of the men was carrying a sledgehammer. Some wore hats pulled down, but they wore no masks. They held up the staff and some guests in the lobby and ordered them to raise their hands and face a wall. 'Our first job was to disconnect the telephone,' Paddy Kennedy noted. They then checked the register. 'Our party split up, as pre-arranged, and proceeded to the rooms allotted to them by Paddy Moran,' continued Kennedy. 'I remained with Paddy Moran while the shootings were taking place.'

Hall porter Hugh Callaghan was ordered take them to rooms 14 and 24. L. E. Wilde, aged thirty-nine, occupied the first. They knocked on the door, and he answered in his pyjamas. He was shot two or three times, and fell, fatally wounded, face down. The raiders then forced the door of Number 22 and shot Captain Patrick McCormack of the Royal Veterinary Corps as he was sitting up in bed reading a newspaper. He was hit five times, once in the head. To cries of 'Shame', Hamar Greenwood later told the House of Commons that McCormack's body had been horribly disfigured. 'The hammer was possibly used as well as the shots to finish off this gallant officer.'

Michael Collins later admitted that McCormack was a case of mistaken identity. His interests were in sport, not politics. He was actually due to leave for Egypt shortly, where he was to take up duty as starter for the racing club. The other target at the Gresham was not in his room. 'The third man escaped,' reported Kennedy. 'He was a Catholic, I believe, and had gone out to early mass.' The whole operation lasted less than ten minutes.

The men who called at 28 Earlsfort Terrace asked for Captain Fitzpatrick. They were told that there was no one of that name there, but there was a Captain John Fitzgerald, the son of a Tipperary doctor who had been a prisoner-of-war in Germany. He had joined the RIC some months earlier and had been stationed in Clare, where he was lucky to survive an IRA kidnapping. He had been in Dublin having his wound treated. He was found in his bed, having been shot four times, twice in the head and once in the heart. The other wound was to his wrists as he was obviously protecting himself.

Captain Baggallay, a court martial official who had lost a leg in the war, was shot dead at his residence at 119 Lower Baggot Street.

Captain Newbury was living with his wife in a flat at 92 Lower Baggot Street. A housekeeper admitted about ten men, led by Bill Stapleton and Joe Leonard of the Squad. They asked if Captain W. F. Newbury was in, but the housekeeper did not know. The landlady, seeing the men, immediately fled upstairs and said that she did not see what ensued. But the raiders obviously knew where to look because they went up to Newbury's first floor room and knocked on the door. His wife answered and, seeing the armed men, promptly slammed the door, but they broke it in. Newbury and his wife fled to an inner room and but he was shot through the door. He tried to get out a window, but they shot him some seven more times and he died on the window ledge. His distraught wife, who was heavily pregnant at the time, put a blanket over the body hanging halfway out the window.

'Where are the papers?' one of the assassins asked her, and they then searched the room. She gave birth to a stillborn baby a week later.

The ten-year-old son of Thomas Herbert Smith, the owner of 117 Morehampton Road, answered the knock on their door and some ten men pushed their way into the house. Captain Donald L. MacLean and his wife were asleep in bed when the men entered their room.

'Get up,' one of them said to MacLean. He got up and left the room with them. Kate MacLean tried to follow her husband, but she was ordered back into the room as they took him upstairs. She heard them ask her husband his name.

'MacLean,' he replied.

'That is good enough,' someone said. They shot him, along with the owner of the house (who was living there with his wife and three children), and Kate MacLean's brother, John Caldow, who was a former soldier with the Royal Scots Fusiliers. Although shot just below the heart, Caldow managed to recover. It was Sergeant Patrick Mannix who first identified MacLean as one of the undercover agents. He later explained that Smith was also considered an agent and that was why he was shot.

Tom Keogh and Jim Slattery of the Squad had six men from E Company of the second battalion undertake the attack on 22 Lower Mount Street. 'We knocked at the door and a maid admitted us,' Jim Slattery recalled. 'We left two men inside the door to see that nobody would enter or leave the house, and the remainder of us proceeded upstairs to two rooms.' They already knew the number of the rooms of the men they wanted – McMahon and Peel, both *noms de guerre*.

The group then split up with Keogh and some of the men going to Peel's room, while the others went up to the top floor to McMahon's room.

Peel had locked his door and, sensing trouble, pushed some furniture to barricade the entrance. Unable to get into the room, the men outside began firing into the door, up to seventeen bullets, but Peel was physically unscathed. When he was finally relieved, he was almost incoherent with excitement. As the shots were being fired at his door, a maid shouted out the front window: 'They are killing an officer upstairs,' she cried.

At that moment a lorry with auxiliaries was passing. They had just left their Beggar's Bush base en route to Kingsbridge (now Heuston) railroad station. Hearing her and the shooting inside the building, they stopped and rushed to the door. They tried to gain entry but the two men guarding downstairs were holding the door.

At one point Billy McLean put his hand around the door with a pistol and fired. The auxiliaries returned the fire and MacLean was hit in the hand.

Two of the auxiliaries – Temporary Cadets Frank Garniss and Cecil A. Morris, both Englishmen – were sent back to Beggar's Bush on foot to get reinforcements, while some of their colleagues went in through No. 21 to get access to the back of No. 22.

The second group 'had only just gone upstairs,' Slattery said, 'when we heard shooting downstairs.'

The door to McMahon's bedroom was unlocked and they found him sharing a bed with another officer who was still asleep. The other officer woke up with a start as somebody shouted, 'Hands up'. He later said that he opened his eyes to see some seven men in a semi-circle around the bed.

One of the raiders searched a cabinet but found nothing.

'Where are your guns, Mac?' the same man asked.

'Look here, we are two R.C.'s; the guns are in the bag,' McMahon replied, pointing to a portmanteau.

The portmanteau was put on a table, broken open, and two guns were taken from it. At this stage they could hear shooting in the street. 'Are you fellows all right?' somebody shouted. 'They are surrounding the house.'

The raiders began to withdraw from the room. McMahon and the other man were still in the bed. 'As I was turning over in the bed I saw McMahon raise his right arm,' the other man said. 'I heard a shot, and he rolled over on the right hand side of the bed. Then came a whole lot of shots.'

The other man rolled under the bed and lay on the floor:

'I saw McMahon's two legs stuck out underneath the bed. I spoke to him and felt his heart, but I knew he was dead and he was lying face downward.'

While he lay under the bed, he heard somebody smashing glass as if trying to break out a back way. 'Come out this way,' he heard one of the men shout. 'I lay quiet for some time, as I thought they might come back and I had no revolver.'

'We succeeded in shooting Lieutenant McMahon,' Slattery said. But they left the man who had been sharing the bed, 'as we had no instructions' to shoot him. 'We discovered afterwards that he was an undesirable character as far as we were concerned, and that we should have shot him,' Slattery added.

'We went downstairs and tried to get out but found the British forces in front of the house,' Slattery continued. 'We went to the back of the house, and a member of E Company, Jim Dempsey, and myself got through by getting over a wall.' Frank Teeling followed them but was shot by auxiliaries in the garden of No. 21.

'I am done lads,' Frank Teeling cried as he slumped back on the ground while the others escaped.

'Are you wounded?' one of the auxiliaries asked.

Teeling did not answer. He opened his pistol and shut it again, having obviously loaded it. The auxiliaries shouted for him to throw the pistol away, which he did, over his right shoulder. It was found to be fully loaded.

The officer upstairs remained under the bed for some minutes. He then dressed and went downstairs to look for Peel. He was told at first that there was someone lying in the yard, but that was Frank Teeling, whom he recognised as one of the men who had been around the bed upstairs.

The two auxiliaries who had gone for help had been intercepted crossing the Canal Bridge by the IRA covering party, who took them to a house on Northumberland Road, where they were questioned and then taken out the back and shot dead.

A nurse and another person who had witnessed those shootings raced to Beggar's Bush, where Brigadier General Frank Crozier was reviewing a parade.

Crozier promptly took a lorry load of men to Mount Street and entered No. 22. He remarked that 'the dingy dirty house resembled a bad billet in France shot up by French mutineers.' One of his men had a pistol to Teeling's head and was counting, giving him until ten to start naming his colleagues. Crozier promptly put a stop to this and ordered that the wounded Teeling be brought to King George V Military hospital.

While all of that was going on Vinny Byrne's team had been going about their business less than a quarter of a mile away in Upper Mount Street. They had mobilised outside St Andrew's church, Westland Row, at 8 a.m. Herbie Conroy brought a sledgehammer, in case they had to break in any doors. He had some ten men reporting, including a first-aid man. They all turned up on time. 'As we proceeded up Westland Row, I called my first-aid man and asked him had he got plenty of bandages, etc.'

'I have nothing,' he replied.

'Did you not hear the instructions I gave you last night?'

He found that there was no first-aid stuff when he got home.

'I may be able to get some in Jackie Dunne's dump in Denzille Lane,' Byrne said. 'I went into the dump, met Jackie there and asked him had he any first-aid outfits. He searched around, but found none.'

'Would this be any use to you?' Dunne asked, producing a .38 revolver.

'Give it to me,' Byrne replied. 'It might come in handy.'

'When I returned to my group, I handed the .38 to the first-aid man, telling him he might find use for it.'

They walked up Holles Street, into Merrion Square, and turned into Upper Mount Street. 'When we came to No. 38, I detailed four of five men to keep guard outside,' Byrne said.

Michael Lawless was stationed on the steps outside the front door, while Byrne and Ennis went to the door and rang the bell.

As soon as the servant girl opened the door Byrne put in his foot to ensure that she could not close it again and said they were looking for Lieutenant George Bennett and Peter Ames. He entered the hallway beckoning the other men to follow.

'Lieutenant Bennett sleeps in there,' the maid said, pointing to the front parlour, 'and the other officer sleeps in the back room down there.' Byrne told Ennis and Tom Duffy to go to a back room and look for Ames.

'I gently tried the handle to open the door, and found that it was locked,' Byrne continued.

'You can get in by the back parlour. The folding doors are open,' the maid said.

'Thank you.'

'I went into the back parlour, with Seán Doyle and Herbie Conroy each side of me,' Byrne continued. 'As I opened the folding door, the officer, who was in bed, was in the act of going for his gun under his pillow. Doyle and myself dashed into the room, at the same time ordering him to put up his hands, which he did.'

Doyle went around the bed and pulled a Colt .45 from under the pillow. Frank Saurin entered and began searching through Bennett's stuff. 'I was interested principally in the papers these intelligence officers might have,' Saurin explained.

Byrne noticed a Sinn Féin tie in one drawer along with what he thought were photographs of the 1916 leaders. 'I ordered the British officer to get out of the bed. He asked me what was going to happen.'

'Ah, nothing,' Byrne replied, ordering him to walk in front of him to the back room.

Meanwhile Ennis and Duffy had found Ames in a room at the back of the house. Duffy covered Ames with a revolver as Ennis asked him to identify himself.

'I am a British officer,' he replied. He said he was not armed, but Ennis put his hand under the pillow and took out a .45 Colt automatic, fully loaded, as well as a pouch with about fifty rounds of ammunition. He put the pistol in his pocket and gave Duffy the pouch.

As Byrne and the others were bringing Bennett to the back room, there was shooting in the street and the doorbell rang.

'Open the door,' Byrne ordered.

A British soldier, a dispatch rider with the rank of private, had left Dublin Castle a short time earlier on a motorcycle with a side car. On turning into Herbert Place, near Mount Street, he had been held up by armed men who ordered him off the motorcycle and took it away. It did not seem to be his morning. As he walked along Upper Mount Street he saw Michael Lawless at No. 38 but as he got within thirty yards of him the man produced a pistol and told him to put up his hand and come towards him. He was then ordered to knock on the door, but nobody answered.

'Open the door, boys,' Lawless shouted.

The door was then opened and the private was half pushed and half pulled into the house, while a major's batman witnessed the scene from across the road in No. 28. He informed his officer, Major Carew, who fired at the volunteer outside No. 38. The batman got his gun but could not see the man outside the building so he went out into the street.

Meanwhile the dispatch rider was told to put up his hands and was kept under guard in the hall. Byrne and his prisoner returned to the back room. Ames was standing up in the bed facing the wall, and Byrne told Bennett to do likewise.

'The Lord have mercy on your souls!' Byrne said to himself. 'I then opened fire with my Peter. They both fell dead.' Doyle had joined in the shooting.

'As I came into the hall, the servant girl was crying,' Byrne said. 'I tried to comfort her and tell her that everything would be all right. Then I looked at the soldier. I did not know whether to finish him off or not.'

'Well, he is only a soldier,' Byrne thought to himself. 'So I told him not to stir for fifteen minutes.'

'As we came out of the house, fire was opened on us from a house on the other side of the street. We retreated down Mount Street, at the same time keeping the house, from where the firing came, under fire.'

Meanwhile Saurin was still in the house. 'In my anxiety to make a thorough search I was unaware that the squad had left and, hearing some shooting in the street, I walked to the door of Bennett's room,' he explained. 'I heard a noise and, looking down the hall, I saw a British soldier outside the room where the two bodies were. I wheeled to shoot but the soldier jumped into the room.

'Come on,' Tom Ennis cried. He was on the doorstep. The batman across the street was shooting at the retreating squad with what appeared to be a .22 automatic. Ennis and Saurin fired at the batman who jumped back into the doorway of his house. It was only afterwards that they learned that the officer across the street was Major Carew, a much-wanted intelligence officer. He was the man who had led the group against Seán Treacy. It was later mistakenly suggested that he was one of the targets on Bloody Sunday, 'but he put up a good show and escaped,' according to Mark Sturgis. 'A party went to his house,' Sturgis added. 'He did not let them in and fired from the window hitting two – this lot made off and he escaped unharmed.'

Byrne and his men crossed Mount Street, turned right into Verschoyle Place, and continued down until they came to Lower Mount Street. 'As we came near the corner, the firing was very heavy,' he recalled. 'I saw Tom Keogh dashing across Mount Street and, as he was running across the road, he dropped one of his guns. He quietly turned back and picked it up again.' At this time the firing had eased somewhat. Keogh went down Grattan Street, while Byrne and his men went down the lane behind Holles Street hospital.

'Here I came upon my first-aid man again,' Byrne noted. He was very excited.

'Oh, Vinny, what will I do with this?' he asked, taking out the .38 pistol.

'Give it to me and you make yourself scarce and away from us,' Byrne replied, feeling sorry for the man who was getting on in years. 'The remainder of us carried on until we came to the quays on the South Wall, where we expected a boat to carry us across the river, but, when we arrived there there was no boat, it being on the other side. However, it crossed back for us, and we all safely boarded it.'

Meanwhile Ennis and Saurin had retreated down to Sir John Rogerson's Quay, where they took the ferry across the Liffey to the north side. 'I had to walk to the east side of Clontarf, armed, and with my pockets full of enemy documents,' Saurin explained. 'Amongst the papers I had Ames' notebook which showed their system of intelligence work was similar to ours insofar as they had agents or touts working on identity numbers for patrol purposes.'

CHAPTER 15

'THE MOST DISGRACEFUL SHOW'

Having left Mount Street on the morning of Bloody Sunday, Crozier went to Dublin Castle, and had just got there when word came though about what had been happening around Dublin. Crozier felt the intelligence officers there were a snobbish bunch. They were 'mostly "hoy, hoy lah-di-dahs" in mufti', he wrote, and, on reflection at any rate, he seemed to take a certain vicarious satisfaction at seeing them taken down a peg

'What!' exclaimed an officer holding a telephone as he went distinctly pale.

'About fifty officers are shot in all parts of the city – Collins has done in most of the secret service people.'

Cabs, sidecars and all modes of conveyance began arriving at Dublin Castle as undercover agents sought information and refuge. 'Panic reigned,' David Neligan noted. 'The gates were choked with incoming traffic – all the military, their wives and agents.' They were seeking protection within the castle walls. 'A bed was not to be found for love or money,' he added. 'Terror gripped the invincible spy system of England. An agent in the castle whose pals had been victims, shot himself. He was buried with the others in England. The attack was so well organised, so unexpected, and so ruthlessly executed that the effect was paralysing.' Neligan concluded that 'the enemy never recovered from the blow. While some of the worst killers escaped, they were thoroughly frightened.'

On the afternoon of Bloody Sunday a mixed force of RIC, auxiliaries and military, raided a Gaelic football match between Dublin and Tipperary. They approached the grounds from different directions. The auxiliaries stated that people just outside the grounds fired on them as they approached from the Royal Canal end. 'The firing was returned and a number of casualties was sustained by people who were watching the match,' read the official statement issued that evening from Dublin Castle.

There were undoubtedly IRA men at the game as there was a great deal of overlapping in membership between the IRA and the Gaelic Athletic Association. Indeed, in many areas the IRA companies were established on the basis of GAA clubs. It was, therefore, quite conceivable that some shots were fired at the approaching crown forces.

People at the game though said that it was the auxiliaries who fired first. The castle authorities stated that the intention was for a British officer to go out on the field about fifteen minutes before the end of the game and announce with a megaphone that all males were going to be searched leaving the stadium and that any men who tried to get out by other means than the exits would be shot. However, even before he reached the ground the shooting had started about fifteen minutes into the game.

All the witnesses stated that the shooting started at the canal end at the southwest corner of the stadium near where Jones' Road crossed the Royal Canal. This shooting led to panic. One of the armoured cars at the St James' Avenue exit opened up with a machine gun burst of fifty shots in the air to stop people rushing out of that exist. In the panic people took off their overcoats to allow them to run faster. Men, women and children were knocked down and trampled upon as they tried to run up the steep embankment

When it was all over fifteen people lay dead or fatally wounded including a ten-year-old boy, Jeremiah O'Leary, who was shot in the head, John Scott aged fourteen, and Jane Boyle, who had gone to the game with her fiancée. They were due to marry five days later. The other people killed were Michael Hogan, the fullback on the Tipperary team, as well as Thomas Hogan, Thomas

Ryan, James Burke, James Matthews, Thomas Boyle, Patrick O'Dowd, William Robinson, Joseph Traynor, Michael Feery, James Teehan and Daniel Carroll. There were over sixty people requiring hospital treatment and eleven of those were detained in hospital.

There was no proper inquest, just a military inquiry held in camera and the result of which was not published for over eighty years. The auxiliaries testified that they were fired on.

'I was in the first car of the convoy detailed to go to Croke Park,' one of them testified. 'Immediately we came to the canal bridge on the rise overlooking the park I observed several men rushing back from the top of the bridge towards the entrance gate of the park. I observed three of them turning backward as they ran and discharging revolvers in our direction. Almost immediately the firing appeared to be taken up by members of the crowd inside the enclosure. At this time the members of our party were jumping out of the cars. Most of them rushed down the incline towards the entrance gate.'

'I was in the second lorry of the convoy to Croke Park,' another auxiliary testified. 'The lorry halted just over the canal bridge. I saw no civilians on the bridge. There were some civilians in the passage leading to the turnstiles. I got out and went to the turnstiles as quickly as I could. As I got to the turnstiles I heard shots. I am certain they were revolver shots, a few shots fired quickly. They were fired inside the field. I tried to get through the turnstiles and found that they were locked. When getting over them a bullet hit the wall convenient to my head. This was the wall on the right hand side inside the archway and splinters of brick and mortar hit me in the face. It could not have been fired from outside the field. As I got inside I landed on my hands and feet. I saw young men aged between 20 and 25 running stooping among the crowd, away from me between the fence and the wall. I pursued and discharged my revolver in their direction.

'Having been fired at, I used my own discretion in returning fire,' the second auxiliary continued. 'I aimed at individual young men who were running away trying to conceal themselves in the crowd. I used a .45 revolver and service ammunition. I chased them across the ground nearly to the wall on the east side. I then saw that a number of people were going back towards the main gate by which I came in. I rushed to that gate and took up my position outside to try and carry out my duties of identification. I stayed there until the ground was cleared.'

Two DMP officers, who testified that they were in the vicinity of the canal bridge on Jones' Road, said nothing about the auxiliaries being fired on, or any civilians acting in a threatened manner. One officer testified that the men in the first lorry to arrive ran down towards the entrance of the stadium. He did not know what started the shooting. A military officer raced up to him.

'What is all the firing about?' he asked. 'Stop that firing.'

Another DMP testified that he was on duty at the main gate in Jones' Road. 'At about 3.25 p.m., I saw six or seven large lorries accompanied by two armoured cars, one in front and one behind, pass along the Clonliffe Road from Drumcondra towards Ballybough,' he testified. 'Immediately after a small armoured car came across Jones' Road from Fitzroy Avenue and pulled up at the entrance of the main gate. Immediately after that, three small Crossley lorries pulled up in Jones' Road. There were about ten or twelve men dressed in RIC uniforms in each. When they got out of the cars they started firing in the air which I thought was blank ammunition, and almost immediately firing started all round the ground.'

The auxiliaries fired a total of 228 rounds of small arms fire, in addition to the fifty rounds fired from the armoured car. The court of inquiry found that the shooting was unauthorised and excessive, even if some members of the crowd fired on the auxiliaries first. Following the inquiry Major-General G. F. Boyd, commanding officer of the British soldiers in Dublin, concluded that the firing on the crowd, which began without orders, was both indiscriminate and unjustifiable.

Brigadier General Frank Crozier, who would shortly resign in protest against what he believed was the condoning of the misconduct of his men, publicly stated that one of his officers told him that the auxiliaries started the shooting. 'It was the most disgraceful show I have ever seen,' one of his officers told him. 'Black and Tans fired into the crowd without any provocation whatever.'

It has generally been stated that all of the Squad stayed away from Croke Park because they expected trouble, but some of them were definitely there, although they had dumped their guns beforehand. 'Tom Keogh asked Joe Dolan and myself to go to the football,' Dan McDonnell recalled. 'We went there. His theory was that if there was any sudden raid we would be much safer there. We parked ourselves on the famous Hill 16, and the match had just started when, as far as we could see, there was a rumble and bustle going on around the entrance gate at the Hogan Stand side. (I personally had no interest in the match.) We suddenly realised that the whole ground was under rifle and machine-gun fire. We scattered and separated from one another on the hill. My hat fell off and while I was picking it up the man in front of me was shot. I was very fit in those days and I ran across the slob lands at the back of Hill 16 over to the Ballybough gate. I ran so fast that I was nearly the first to reach it.'

'Next morning we knew the actual number of British agents who had been disposed of. We were disappointed with the result,' Dan McDonnell recalled.

'The fact is that the majority of raids by the IRA were abortive,' Todd Andrews noted. 'The men being sought were not in their digs, or in several cases the men looking for them bungled the jobs. It is not clear how many people were actually on the overall list. At one point there were apparently more than fifty, but some names were dropped at the insistence of Cathal Brugha. About thirty-five still remained, which meant that the IRA actually got less than a third of those targeted. Nevertheless the British agents were terrified and many went to ground.

'My one intention was the destruction of the undesirables who continued to make miserable the lives of ordinary decent citizens,' Collins wrote. 'I have proof enough to assure myself of the atrocities which this gang of spies and informers have committed. Perjury and torture are words too easily known to them. If I had a second motive it was no more than a feeling such as I would have for a dangerous reptile. By their destruction the very air is made sweeter. That should be the future's judgment on this particular event. For myself my conscience is clear. There is no crime in detecting in wartime the spy and the informer. They have destroyed without trial. I have paid them back in their own coin.'

In London Lloyd George and members of the cabinet were very jittery, according to Sir Maurice Hankey. Greenwood provided weapons for all his domestic staff, though – unlike the prime minister – he was able to joke about his own predicament. 'All my household are armed,' the chief secretary told the cabinet, 'my valet, my butler, and my cook. So if you have any complaints about the soup you may know what to expect.'

When the House of Commons next met, there were some ugly scenes. Joe Devlin, the nationalist MP from Belfast, provoked uproar from the benches when he asked why members were asking about the deaths of the officers in the morning and ignoring what had happened in Croke Park in the afternoon.

'Sit down!' members shouted. 'Sit down!'

'I won't sit down,' Devlin replied. 'I want to know from the prime minister why the House has not been made acquainted in this recital with the entrance of the military into a football field of 15,000 people, the indiscriminate shooting, and the ten men killed. Why have we not heard of this?'

'I was never asked that question,' Hamar Greenwood replied, on walking to the despatch box. 'But I am prepared to answer it now.' The chief secretary rummaged among his papers as members on the government benches beneath Devlin were on their feet shouting at him to sit down. Devlin turned to Major John Molson on the Conservative bench below him and said something. The major grabbed Devlin around the neck with his right arm and tried to drag him into the row below. A violent scuffle ensued as Devlin broke loose and traded punches with government MPs.

'Kill him, kill him,' members from all sides of the house shouted. Other members rushed to break up the scuffling. Devlin's coat had been pulled from him in the struggle. T. P. O'Connor and James M. Hogge, the Liberal MP, restrained Devlin from behind.

'This is a fine specimen of your English courage and chivalry – to attack one man among six hundred,' Devlin taunted his attackers.

'If there is a fight I am in it,' Jack Jones of the Labour Party said as he imposed himself in front of Devlin.

'I declare the sitting suspended,' the speaker said.

The public gallery was cleared, but some members remained rooted to their benches. Lloyd George, Bonar Law, Winston Churchill and Austen Chamberlain sat together on the treasury bench, while Greenwood, Sir Eric Geddes and Sir Lionel Worthington-Evans stood staring at where Devlin sat, pale and angry, flanked by O'Connor and Hogge. A number of members went to Devlin and shook hands with him, while some Conservatives engaged in animated discussion with him. Those included Viscount Curzon and Sir Harry Brittain. The session resumed after about a twenty minute recess.

The three men arrested in the hours before the 9 a.m. strike, McKee, Clancy and Clune, were being held in the old detective office in the Exchange Court. The room was being used as a kind of guardroom in which beds, other furniture and some stores were kept, including a box of handgrenades. Even though there were three windows in the room overlooking an alley, it was dark because of the high building on the other side. The prisoners supposedly got hold of the handgrenades and threw them, and one of them was also said to have got hold of a rifle. But all three – McKee, Clancy and Clune – were shot dead before they could do any damage.

'I stood erect, and saw one of the prisoners with a rifle, which he levelled and fired at the guard commander, who had just entered the room,' one of the guards later testified. 'The prisoner then swung round and fired a shot at me. I fired at the prisoner with my revolver, and he dropped. The guard commander also fired at the prisoner with his revolver.'

'I heard a scuffling noise and rushed into the guardroom,' the commander of the guard testified. 'The prisoner McKee fired at me with a rifle; the shot passed my head and buried itself in the wall. McKee also fired a shot at the sentry, who appeared above the table. I fired at McKee with my revolver and he dropped. I saw Clancy with a shovel strike at one of our men twice and miss him. A guard fired at him, and I saw Clancy fall.'

A sentry on duty at the window testified that he and a colleague heard noise behind them and, looking round, noticed that two of the prisoners had thrown handgrenades at them and dived behind some mattresses. When the grenades did not detonate, Clancy seized a shovel and aimed to hit the sentry. 'I fired at the prisoner, Clancy, killing him,' the sentry explained. A fourth witness told much the same story, and he, too, said that he had seen Clancy holding a shovel and being shot and killed.

When the bodies were released to the families there were extensive signs of discolouring that seemed to indicate extensive bruising, but the army doctor said that large staining could occur after death, depending on the position in which a body was lying after death. Clancy had been hit by up to five bullets, which made eight wounds, McKee had three wounds caused by two bullets, while Clune had nine wounds cause by seven bullets at most. He said there were no bayonet wounds, but there was a bullet lodged underneath McKee's skin in the right side of the chest. David Neligan was quite adamant that they were not bayoneted.

The bodies were handed over for burial. While Clune's body was sent to Quin, County Clare, Collins requested that some volunteers who were not prominent should collect the bodies of

McKee and Clancy. Pat McCrae of the Squad was detailed to find such volunteers but could only get Tom Gay and one other man, so he went himself as well. They were brought to a small chapel at the pro-cathedral. Collins had doctors examine the bodies 'so that the minds of their comrades could be satisfied that they had not been tortured, as their imaginations had led them to think,' according to Ernie O'Malley. But Piaras Beaslaí told a very different story. He contended that the examination showed that McKee had been savagely mistreated, a bayonet thrust had punctured his liver and he had suffered broken ribs. The bodies were then dressed in the uniforms of the Irish Volunteers.

Collins was distraught at the deaths. They were 'two men who fully understood the inside of Collins' work and his mind, and who were ever ready and able to link up their resources of the Dublin brigade to any work that Collins had in hand, and to do so promptly, effectively and sympathetically,' Richard Mulcahy noted. Next morning Collins, Cullen, Thornton and Gearóid O'Sullivan, the adjutant-general, helped to carry the bodies out to the waiting hearses. A photograph of Collins and Cullen at the head of one of the coffins actually appeared in the *Evening Herald*. He attended the requiem mass and went on to the graveside, where he was actually filmed as he stepped out of the crowd to lay a wreath on the grave. Attached was a note signed by himself: 'In memory of two good friends – Dick and Peadar – and two of Ireland's best soldiers.'

'Look, there's Michael Collins,' a woman said as he stepped forward.

'You bloody bitch!' he snarled.

The auxiliaries of F Company based at Dublin were responsible for the deaths of McKee, Clancy and Clune, but Collins had little inside information on them, 'Occasionally I visited the Auxies' canteen with McNamara,' Neligan said. Their quarters were situated just inside the castle lower gate in a building known as the Exchange Court.

Dick Foley suggested that a Major Reynolds in F Company would possibly be willing to provide information to the IRA in return for money. Collins had Frank Thornton sound him out. 'I met Reynolds regularly in different public houses and gave him certain jobs to do, which he did successfully,' Thornton said. 'At the beginning, however, we were not too satisfied about his trustworthiness, and on every occasion that I met Reynolds either Dolan or Joe Guilfoyle was conveniently nearby and were armed. However, as the time went on, Reynolds became more useful and secured quite a lot of very valuable information in the form of photographs of the murder gang – F Company, Q Company and other companies of the auxiliaries.'

Of course, the British also set about reorganising their intelligence operation.

'A number of British intelligence officers were drafted into Dublin Castle,' according to Lily Mernin. 'A new department was opened up in the Upper Castle Yard. My work did not bring me in contact with this department.' She was asked to provide descriptions of the men involved.

'These intelligence officers used come into our office,' she explained. 'The three girls of the staff were curious to know who they were. Some of the girls would ask "Who was so-and-so that came in?" In this way we got to know the names of the various intelligence officers. Some of the girls in the office were very friendly with them and used go around with them. General conversation would give a lot of information concerning their whereabouts, things that were said, etc. Any information obtained was immediately passed by me to IRA intelligence.'

Following Bloody Sunday the British engaged in raids throughout the country to round up as many of the rebels as possible. Dan McDonnell did not go home for a couple of days after Bloody Sunday. When he did go home, he never forgot the scene. 'I found my home in chaos,' he said. 'My mother, extraordinary though it may seem, was as cool as a cucumber, and quietly informed me that the military and Tans had been in the house looking for a Daniel McDonnell. "Your Dad was here when they called," she said.'

'I am Daniel McDonnell,' his father had replied. He was taken away and the woman whom his son and Dolan had slapped around in the bed in Renelagh was brought to look him over. Of course, they had the wrong Dan McDonnell, but he was interned anyway in Ballykinlar.

Arthur Griffith was arrested and jailed on 26 November 1920, much to the annoyance of Lloyd George, who felt that the British government should have been consulted before such a high profile individual was arrested. Now the British felt that somebody much more militant would inevitably take over as president, because Griffith was the most moderate of the Sinn Féin leaders.

When the dáil met to elect his replacement, the secretary produced a letter from Griffith's solicitor nominating Cathal Brugha to take office or Austin Stack, in the event of Brugha being unable or unwilling to fill the post, and Michael Collins, should Stack not wish to serve. J. J. O'Kelly presided at the meeting. 'Cathal would not act; his army work engaged all his thoughts and all his energy,' O'Kelly wrote. Brugha explained that he had already served as president before de Valera's election. Stack said that he could not act, as he was too busy setting up republican courts and organising a republican police force.

'Come, Micheál,' O'Kelly said to Collins, 'sit in this chair, and we'll all do our best to help you.'

'As no one else will,' he said, 'I suppose I must.'

Collins was acting president for four hectic weeks, amid a welter of peace rumours. The strain was tremendous. 'Those of us who were in constant touch with him always possessed the fear that he would collapse under it,' Seán Ó Muirthile wrote. Now those fears became all the more real when Collins – still deeply upset over the brutal killings of McKee and Clancy – assumed the extra strain of the presidency.

He was not even in his new post two full days when the British-based IRA fire-bombed more than a dozen warehouses in the Liverpool docks area, causing millions of pounds worth of damage. That same day in Kilmichael, County Cork, Tom Barry led an IRA ambush on a convoy of auxiliaries and killed seventeen of them.

Lloyd George had been making peace overtures behind the scenes for some weeks and he opened up a new peace channel on 1 December 1920. He asked the Irish-born Roman Catholic archbishop of Perth, Australia, Patrick J. Clune, to meet the Irish leader in Dublin and sound him out about negotiations and a possible ceasefire. Clune was a former chaplain-general to the Australian forces who also happened to be an uncle of the late Conor Clune, the young man killed with Clancy and McKee.

Griffith, who met the archbishop in Mountjoy Jail, advised Collins against a meeting because of the danger that British agents were watching Clune, but Collins met him without difficulty on 4 December at a school run by Louise Gavan Duffy on St Stephen's Green. Even if the secret service were keeping an eye on the archbishop, they would have considered his visit to her school quite natural, as she was a daughter of Sir Charles Gavan Duffy, a former Young Ireland leader who had risen to the top in Australian politics having migrated there in the mid-nineteenth century. 'I wonder how it is that the archbishop sees Collins apparently without difficulty in Dublin and our intelligence fails to find him after weeks of search,' Mark Sturgis wrote in obvious exasperation.

Although Collins was highly sceptical of the British government's intentions, he gave Clune a written outline of ceasefire terms agreeable to the dáil cabinet. When the archbishop returned to London, Lloyd George told him it would be necessary to hold off on actual talks for a while longer. If the Irish would keep things quiet for about a month, he predicted the atmosphere would be more conducive for negotiations. He also added it would help matters if Collins and Mulcahy left the country for a while. He told the House of Commons that the 'extremists must first be broken up' before there could be a negotiated settlement, and he announced the introduction of martial law throughout the southern counties of Ireland.

Next evening the Black and Tans and auxiliaries ran amuck in Cork, burning much of the business centre of the city in a frightening rampage of arson and looting. Collins was clearly disillusioned. 'It seems to me that no additional good result can come from further continuing these discussions,' he wrote to Griffith. 'We have clearly demonstrated our willingness to have peace on honourable terms. Lloyd George insists upon capitulation. Between these there is no mean, and it is only a waste of time continuing.' Collins feared the British might think the IRA was desperate for peace because it was on the verge of collapse. 'Let Lloyd George make no mistake,' Collins continued, 'the IRA is not broken.'

Nevertheless the archbishop brought back proposals suggesting the British would stop arrests, raids and reprisals for a month in return for a ceasefire on the Irish side. 'A truce on the terms specified cannot possibly do us any harm,' Collins wrote to Griffith. Clune returned to Griffith on 17 December, however, with news that the British had appeared to harden their attitude again. Dublin Castle was now insisting that the IRA should first surrender its arms. Griffith told him without hesitation that it would not even be considered.

That evening the Squad killed a prominent RIC officer, District Inspector Philip J. O'Sullivan, a native of Bantry, County Cork, where his father was a solicitor. Philip, who had served in the Royal Navy during the Great War, was just twenty-two years old. A qualified solicitor, he had only been in the RIC for five months and he was based in the office of the RIC's deputy inspector general at Dublin Castle. Ned Kelliher was given the task of identifying him and suggesting the best time to shoot him. 'When I identified him I trailed him for about a week,' he explained. It was decided to shoot him early on an evening in December 1920.

'I was instructed, with others, to proceed to Henry Street to assist in the shooting of D.I. O'Sullivan. About four of us comprised the party,' recalled Joe Byrne, one of the newer members of the Squad. 'A couple of us were detailed not to take part in the actual shooting but to cover off the men who were to do the job.'

'I pointed him out to members of the Squad,' Kelliher said.

O'Sullivan met his fiancée in Henry Street as usual around 6.15 p.m. She had been waiting for him and had noticed two men in a doorway across the street. As soon as O'Sullivan came along, they walked towards Sackville Street. The two men crossed the street, took out revolvers and shot him from close range. She grappled with one of the men while the other stood over O'Sullivan on the ground and fired another shot at him. The two assailants promptly disappeared into the rush hour crowd.

'I saw the D.I. being shot by a member of the Squad and when the shooting was over we returned to Morelands,' Byrne noted. Curiously none of the older members of the Squad left any details of this shooting.

A passing military lorry took the wounded police officer to Jervis Street hospital, where he died within minutes.

His fiancée said afterwards that she had recently received a warning herself. 'You are walking out with a Black and Tan – Beware.' She had told O'Sullivan, but he did not attach much significance to it.

Next day Collins met Archbishop Clune for a second time. 'Our interview was not a lengthy one,' Collins wrote. 'We had both, practically speaking, come to the conclusion that no talk was necessary, seeing that the new proposal from the British government was a proposal that we should surrender.' It would seem that the killing of O'Sullivan was the Big Fellow's real answer to the British.

CHAPTER 16

'TOO GOOD TO BE TRUE'

Eamon de Valera had received cabinet approval for his plans to stay longer in the United States, but he changed his mind on hearing the news from Dublin that Griffith had been arrested and that Collins had taken over as acting president. He arrived home on Christmas eve and lost no time in complaining about the way the IRA campaign was being waged.

'Ye are going too fast,' he told Mulcahy. 'This odd shooting of a policeman here and there is having a very bad effect, from the propaganda point of view, on us in America. What we want is one good battle about once a month with about 500 men on each side.' It was certainly insensitive to criticise the way the campaign had been run without, at least, waiting to consult a few people at home.

Collins had his narrowest escape yet from arrest that evening. The *Police Gazette: Hue and Cry* had come out that day with a good photograph of him taken only the previous year on its front page. He had arranged a stag party with some friends at the Gresham hotel, but the auxiliaries raided the party and all were questioned and searched.

'They were very suspicious of me,' Collins told friends next day. 'I was questioned over and over again. One officer actually drew an old photograph of me out of his pocket, and compared it with my face, drawing my hair down as it was in the picture. It was touch and go. They were not quite satisfied, and hesitated long before they left us.' Throughout it all Collins remained cheerful, and the raiding party eventually departed, leaving him to get very drunk.

Relations between Collins and both Brugha and Stack had become distinctly strained, and they would become even worse now that de Valera had returned. De Valera got cabinet approval for the idea of sending Collins to the United States, but the Big Fellow refused to go, as he believed the whole thing was a plot to get rid of him.

'That long whore won't get rid of me as easy as that,' Collins remarked.

A new threat began to grow in the form of the so-called Igoe Gang. The Igoe Gang was a group of undercover RIC men whose job it was to identify active republicans from Dublin and from the provinces who had set up in Dublin, such as Dan Breen, Seán Treacy and their gang. Their leader was Head Constable Igoe from Galway. They gradually began playing a very active role.

Even though they wore civilian clothes, they were heavily armed. They began moving about on the footpaths, covering each other on both sides of the road, walking some yards apart so that they would be inconspicuous as they looked for wanted men from Dublin or the country. IRA intelligence never fully identified the personnel of Igoe's party, beyond establishing that they comprised members from different 'hot spots' in the country. They were nearly all Irishmen with considerable experience and service in the RIC, and they were effective in picking up volunteers. Igoe's gang became a difficult and dangerous force in the eyes of the Squad and IRA intelligence.

'We received orders to concentrate of locating Igoe's gang,' Frank Thornton explained. 'On several occasions our intelligence officers would pick them up and, leaving one to keep on trailing them, the other reported back to our Headquarters, when we got in touch with our Squad which then tried to intercept the gang. Their tactics, however, defeated our efforts on numerous occasions as they redoubled on their tracks and we lost contact.'

'One particular day we had actually contacted them up in Thomas Street, our Squad coming down with intelligence officers on one side of the road going towards James' Street while they were coming down on the other side, when all of a sudden a military patrol of about twenty-five men came up a side street and started to come down in our direction in extended order across the road.' Thornton continued. 'We had no option but to disperse as quickly as possible as we would have found ourselves between two fires and would have been completely out-numbered.'

The first thing they had to do was recognise Igoe. None of the intelligence people knew what he looked like, so Thomas 'Sweeney' Newell was brought from Galway to help identify him. For three weeks he walked the streets of Dublin looking for Igoe. He did see him a couple of times but on each of those occasions Igoe disappeared before the Squad could act. Newell saw him a third time on 7 January 1921 as he was going to meet his companion for the day. Igoe was with sixteen or eighteen men near O'Connell's Bridge and Newell followed them into Dame Street. 'They crossed Dame Street into Trinity Street and into Wicklow Street,' Newell recalled. 'In Wicklow Street I met Charlie Dalton and told him that Igoe and his gang had gone into Grafton Street. We both went back to Headquarters, Crow Street, where he reported the matter.'

Dalton assumed that Igoe was heading for Harcourt Street railway station, and he told those at headquarters that he would go with Newell to Stephen's Green and wait there for the Squad. 'After a few minutes Dalton came back and told me that he and I would walk on one footpath, and Jim Hughes and Dan McDonnell would walk on the opposite side.' None of them was armed. They were just trying to locate Igoe for the Squad, which was to join them. It just so happened that Tom Keogh, Jimmy Slattery and Vinny Byrne arrived at intelligence headquarters moments later. 'We met Liam Tobin, who asked us had we our guns with us,' according to Byrne.

'No,' they replied.

'For God's sake, get them quick. Igoe is on his way to Harcourt Street railway station.'

'Go and get the guns and we will meet you in Stephen's Green,' Keogh said to Byrne.

'I made a dash down the stairs and away over to the dump at Moreland's,' Byrne explained. 'I collected the guns – Jimmy's long Webley, Tom's Peter and short Webley, and my own Peter. Tom Keogh always carried a Webley, in case his Peter would jam. I buckled on my belt beneath my light dustcoat, and slung the guns, which were all in holsters. Leaving the dump, I proceeded to Liffey Street and crossed the Metal Bridge.' He was heading for St Stephen's Green to meet the rest of the Squad and Newell, but Dalton and Newell had already run into trouble.

'Newell and I proceeded to Grafton Street by the shortest route, and when we had almost reached Weir's jewellery stores in Grafton Street, I noticed that we had been passed by some men who I instinctively recognised as Igoe's party, although Newell had not had time to confirm this. When they had passed us out, they wheeled on us.'

'I felt a hand gripping the collar of my coat,' Newell recalled. 'I turned to see who was holding me. It was Igoe.'

'Come on Newell,' he said. 'I want you.'

'My name is not Newell.'

'I know you anyway,' Igoe said and told his colleagues to arrest Dalton.

'Pedestrians passed by, unaware that anything unusual was happening,' Dalton explained. They were then told to walk in the direction of Suffolk Street, down Trinity until they came to No. 38 Dame Street, which was an insurance office. They were told to stand against the wall. Newell and Dalton were kept some distance apart and surrounded by Igoe's men. Igoe questioned both of them but they could not hear each other's answers.

Dalton saw Vincent Byrne cutting across Dame Street on his way to St Stephen's Green to the rendezvous. 'As I was crossing Dame Street I noticed a group of men standing along the wall and, speaking to two of them, was Charlie Dalton,' Bryne recalled. 'I did not know any of the other men, and I thought to myself that the group was probably the southside ASU. I carried on up Dame Street and, as I was passing Charlie, I gave just a slight nod of my head towards him. He did not recognise me. I thought it was strange.'

'When I arrived at Stephen's Green, I met the remainder of the Squad and intelligence,' Byrne continued. 'I told Tom Keogh that I had seen Charlie in Dame Street with a gang of fellows, but that I did not know any of them. As far as I can remember, we proceeded to Harcourt Street station, but there was no sign of Igoe or his gang, or anybody looking like his party.'

Meanwhile Dalton and Newell were still being interrogated. 'In reply to the questions put to me, I gave my correct name and address,' Dalton said. 'I stated that I was a believer in home rule and that my father was a J.P. (Justice of the Peace) and did not agree with the Sinn Féin policy.'

'Newell endeavoured to bluff also, and we were asked how we came to know one another. I stated that he was a stranger I had met on the street who had got into conversation with me and that I was directing him somewhere or other. I failed to realise at the time that Igoe was aware of Newell's position in the Galway Volunteers and knew him quite well. Under the interrogation Newell lost his temper and abandoned pretence.

'I know you, Igoe, and you know me.' This outburst ended any further questioning and Dalton was let go.

'I was told to walk on and not look back,' he recalled. 'I walked on in the direction of Trinity Street, knowing from the footsteps behind me that I was under cover by some of Igoe's men. I moved fairly slowly at first, not being physically able to go any faster. I moved through Trinity Street, Suffolk Street and into Wicklow Street, gaining a few yards on each bend and when I turned the corner of Wicklow Street I made a dash of about thirty or forty yards and entered a building where my father had his commercial offices. I went up to the two flights of stairs into his office and was practically in a state of collapse on reaching it. My father's typist was in the office, but I did not speak to her as I expected to hear the sound of steps on the stairs any second. After about five minutes, as nothing happened, I asked her to put on her hat and coat and accompany me, which she did. We walked out from the office and cut up Clarendon Street as far as St Stephen's Green, where I parted with my pilot and located the squad.

'Having told Tom Keogh what happened, I got hold of a gun and we all returned to Dame Street in the hope of overtaking some of Igoe's party. We searched several streets in the area without coming across them. We assumed that they must have entered the castle, as they were nowhere to be seen.'

Newell had been marched off with two of Igoe's men in front of him, one on either side and two behind him. He was taken to what he later learned was Greek Street, where they stopped. 'Igoe again questioned me as to how I came to be in Dublin.' But Newell refused to answer. 'Four of Igoe's gang were beside me and two on the opposite corner.'

'Run into the street,' Igoe told Newell, pointing to Greek Street.

'If you want to shoot me,' Newell replied, 'shoot me where I am standing.'

'He gave me a hell of a punch which sent me several yards into the street and immediately opened fire on me,' Newell added. 'I fell and I was not able to get up as I had received four bullet wounds, one in the calf of the right leg, two in the right hip and one flesh wound in the stomach. I then saw Igoe blow a whistle. Within a minute a police van arrived. I was put roughly into it, and taken to the Bridewell. I was questioned as to where I lived in Dublin. I refused to tell them. I was beaten on the head with the butt end of a revolver; four of my teeth were knocked out and three or four others broken. I was left lying on the floor for some hours and was then taken in an ambulance to King George V hospital.'

While the Dublin brigade was targeting the auxiliaries and

British troops in general, Collins and the Squad were still targeting individuals, such as Willie Doran, the night porter at the Wicklow hotel. Collins had information from Paddy O'Shea within the hotel that Doran was giving information about guests of the hotel to the British. People like Collins, Tobin, Cullen, Gearóid O'Sullivan and Diarmuid O'Hegarty often used the hotel. Despite a number of warnings Doran persisted, and the Squad was sent to kill him.

'Tobin turned to me one day and asked me would I carry out the execution,' Joe Dolan recalled. 'I said I would if I got Dan McDonnell to go along with me, so the two of us were detailed to carry out the job.' McDonnell already knew Doran. The two of them walked to the door of the hotel on 29 January 1921. Just as they entered the lobby Doran came out of one of the rooms.

'That's Doran,' said McDonnell.

'I produced my revolver and shot him through the head and the heart,' Dolan added. 'McDonnell shot him through the stomach. We had a covering party and we had no difficulty in getting away.'

Doran, aged forty-five, was married with three young children. His wife knew that Doran had helped Collins in the past and she assumed that her husband had been murdered by the crown forces, so she appealed to Sinn Féin for money for her children. Collins ordered that she should be given the money and not be told what had actually happened.

'The poor little devils need the money,' he said.

There was a curious incident on 1 February when Vincent Fouvargue from Ranelagh was being moved from Kilmainham Jail to Dublin Castle for questioning. 'While passing along the South Circular Road fire was opened on the lorry', read an official statement issued from Dublin Castle. 'The lorry was stopped and all the escort alighted and pursued the attacking person or persons. In the excitement the prisoner escaped, and has not since been recaptured.'

McNamara and Neligan thought the story was 'too good to be true' when the British military command notified the DMP about the escape. 'We thought it highly suspicious that this man should have escaped in broad daylight from an escort consisting of British intelligence officers who fired no shots,' said Neligan. 'We conveyed our suspicions to Collins.'

'Collins afterwards told us that he [Fouvargue] had recently joined the Volunteers and on being arrested betrayed his comrades and volunteered to work for the English. He was shot in England afterwards by the IRA over there.' Joe Shanahan, who acted as the driver, told Neligan that Reggie Dunne killed Fouvargue at a lonely part of Ashford Golf Course in Middlesex, outside London. Fouvargue's body was found on 3 April 1921 with a note: 'Let spies and traitors beware. IRA.'

Also early in the year Collins learned that Corporal John Ryan of the British military police was responsible for the arrest of Dick McKee and Peadar Clancy in the early hours of Bloody Sunday. The Squad was told to kill him.

Paddy Kennedy was the intelligence officer selected to identify him. 'Before the two men were detailed to carry out the execution, I asked to be allowed to take part in it as I felt very keenly about the murder of Dick McKee,' Bill Stapleton explained. 'I fought in 1916 and served subsequently with him in the second battalion. My request was granted and the second man instructed to accompany me was Eddie Byrne.'

Kennedy located Ryan at about 10.30 a.m. on 5 February in Hynes' public house at the corner of Old Glouchester Place and Corporation Street. He went into the bar along with Stapleton and Byrne, while Jimmy Conroy remained on guard. 'I saw Ryan standing facing the counter reading a newspaper and he was identified by the Intelligence Officer [Kennedy],' related Stapleton. 'Before doing the job we held him up and searched him but he had no guns or papers on him.'

'You are Ryan?' they asked.

'Yes, and what about it?'

'With that we shot him. I have an idea that the chap behind the counter was one of our intelligence officers' contacts as he made himself very scarce as we entered. We left the place then and proceeded towards the Gloucester Diamond and as usual the remainder of the Squad were following up to cover our retreat. We went back to the Squad dump, which was in a stable off North Great Charles St near Mountjoy Square and that concluded the operation as far as we were concerned.'

While watching for the Igoe gang Ned Kelliher noted that four RIC men were in the habit of travelling to Dublin Castle in an open Ford touring car, and they would then walk down to a restaurant in Ormond Quay for dinner. He reported this and was told to continue to observe the men.

'I was instructed to proceed to the Ormond hotel to find out if it would be a good place to shoot whatever policemen would be found there,' Jim Slattery recalled. 'Examining the hotel I thought it would not be a good place for the operations, as some innocent people might be hurt, and besides that there might be many enemy agents in civilian attire in the hotel itself. Viewing the position between the Ormond hotel and the castle, I thought the best spot would be Parliament Street, at the junction of Essex Street and Parliament Street.'

Paddy Kelly, one of the headquarter's drivers, brought Ben Byrne, Jimmy Conroy and Mick O'Reilly to Essex Street around dinnertime on 23 February 1921. They took up positions near the Dolphin hotel, from where they could see the intelligence officer, Ned Kelliher, who had taken up a position on the opposite side of Parliament Street, near to Honan's tobacconist shop, from where he was to signal the approach of the three RIC men – Constables Martin J. Greer of Cootehall, County Roscommon; Edward McDonagh from Tuam, County Galway; and Mick Hoey of Portarlington, who was a brother of Daniel Hoey, the DMP detective killed in September 1919.

'I took up a position facing the Squad members,' Kelliher explained. 'The signal I had arranged to give was to raise my bowler hat when the RIC men were passing the Squad members. As they were passing, I gave the sign.'

The Squad had already been given descriptions of the three men, so they were ready when the three approached together heading in the direction of Ormond Quay when Kelliher raised his bowler. 'Without any further ado,' Byrne said, 'Conroy, myself and O'Reilly descended on the three victims and, in less time than it takes to relate, two of them were lying on the ground dead.'

Hoey and Greer were killed almost instantly. Although McDonagh also went down, he got up and started running towards the river amid a hail of bullets. He then turned back and ran into Honan's shop as bullets shattered the glass in the door. He tried to vault the counter. The shop owner helped him into a back room and tried to comfort him. McDonagh was shot in the chest and leg. He was taken to King George V hospital, where he died that night.

Despite assertions to the contrary, the Squad never did get Igoe or any of his gang. The three men killed in Parliament Street were not connected with him. 'It was later learned that their names were Constables Greer, McDonagh and Hoey,' Kelliher noted. 'Nobody had even bothered to find out their names before targeting them in error.'

'Those poor wretches were mere dispatch riders and were mistaken for members of the Igoe Gang,' Neligan also admitted. After the shooting, however, the police were more circumspect about leaving Dublin Castle for lunch.

Many prominent IRA people were caught up and held in the round ups, but the British failed to appreciate the significance of those they were holding, because they had not identified them. Paddy O'Daly was taken under an assumed name and and spent time in Arbour Hill and Kilmainham jails, before being transferred to Ballykinlar internment camp near Newcastle, County Down, without the British ever knowing who they were actually holding. Rory O'Connor was taken and brought to Dublin Castle, where Neligan told the auxiliaries that he was only a crank.

They did not realise he was one of the more dangerous men. O'Connor was a middle-aged man with a distinctly unhealthy appearance – short, very thin, with a haggard pale face. Despite his hangdog look, he was a cheerful individual, a great talker, and fearlessly brave. He managed to escape without being recognised. Ernie O'Malley was taken in Kilkenny in somewhat similar circumstances. Even though they had not identified him, he was transferred to Kilmainham Jail in Dublin, where he was held with a number of men arrested for involvement, or supposed involvement, in the Bloody Sunday killings.

During January and February 1921 the British charged ten men with murder in relations to the Bloody Sunday killings. Only one of them, Frank Teeling, was involved in the killing with which he was charged, but four of them were convicted of murder, another as an accessory, while the other five were acquitted of all charges.

The first to be tried were Thomas Whelan of 14 Barrow Street, Michael J. Tobin of 19 Upper Sherrard Street, James McNamara of 81 Lower George's Street in Kingstown and James Boyce of 10 Aungier Street. They were accused of murdering Captain G. T. Baggallay at 119 Lower Baggot Street. The case against Tobin was dropped at the opening of the trial, and McNamara and Boyce were found not guilty, largely on the basis of the evidence of witnesses who testified that the accused were at nine o'clock mass when Baggallay was killed. One woman swore that she sat in the same pew as Whelan at mass at the same time in Ringsend, while a man testified to meeting him leaving the church after mass at 9.40, and a bar worker who had gone out to purchase a newspaper said that he saw the accused at the same time coming out of the church with the crowd after mass. But the officer who was shaving in the bathroom at the time Baggallay was killed identified

Whelan as one of the men in the hallway. This was a military court and Whelan was convicted and sentenced to death.

Frank Teeling, who had been wounded and captured during the shoot-out at 22 Mount Street, was tried along with three others for the murder of Lieutenant H. Angliss (alias Paddy McMahon). Others charged were William Conway of 32 Upper Mount Street and Edward Potter of 41 Rathmines Road. Daniel Healy of 86 Phibsborough Road was also charged with this murder but he was granted a separate trial and was subsequently acquitted.

The officer who had been sharing the bed with Angliss identified Teeling and Potter as having been among the gunmen that broke into their room at 22 Lower Mount Street, while Conway was identified by a maid in the house. 'I declared before Almighty God that I am not connected with any political organisation,' Potter testified on his own behalf. 'I am not guilty of the charge. I have never used a revolver in my life.' Conway was equally forceful in proclaiming his innocence. 'I am innocent of the charge brought against me,' he told the court. 'I know nothing of the transaction whatever, and I have never been in 22 Mount Street in my life. I fired no shot, and I have never used a revolver.'

Teeling spoke up on their behalf. 'These people who have been arrested for this affair, I honestly swear, were not there at all, and had nothing to do with it,' he told the court. 'I, therefore, do not like to see them suffer when wholly innocent.'

Before sentence could be pronounced on Teeling, he escaped from Kilmainham Jail on 15 February, along with Simon Donnolly and Ernie O'Malley, who was being held under the false name of Bernard Stewart. They wanted Paddy Moran to come with them. He had led the assassination team in the Gresham hotel on Bloody Sunday morning, but he was being tried for the murder of Captain Peter Ames in Upper Mount Street, along with Joseph Rochford of 11 Elm Park Avenue. Rochford stated that he was at home in bed until 11 a.m. on the Sunday morning, while Moran said that he had attended eight o'clock mass and had a witness that saw him there and others who saw him in Blackrock, where he lived, after nine o'clock. Only then had he gone into the city centre on the tram.

'I'm not going,' Moran said when O'Malley tried to persuade him to escape with them. 'I won't let down the witnesses who gave evidence for me.'

'Someone has to die for this,' O'Malley warned. 'Maybe Teeling or myself, but they'll hang you for certain if we get through.'

Following the escape from Kilmainham, Collins cycled out to meet O'Malley in his hiding place. The Big Fellow shook his hand for a long time. 'You're born to be shot,' Collins said. 'You can't be hanged! Why didn't Paddy Moran come with you?'

'I don't know,' O'Malley replied. 'He thought there was no case against him.'

'They'll hang him as a reprisal now,' Collins said.

Joseph Rochford was acquitted of the murder of Ames, but Moran was wrongly convicted of that killing. He and Whelan were hanged on 13 March for crimes they did not commit. Of course, in Moran's case he was responsible for the two killings in the Gresham hotel, but Whelan hadn't had an involvement in any of the killings. Conway and Potter were both sentenced to life in prison, even though they had no involvement in the killings either. James Green, the hall porter at 38 Upper Mount Street, who was acquitted of the murder of Lieutenant-Colonel Hugh F. Montgomery, was convicted of assisting the man that Major Woodcock's wife had seen in the back garden. She saw Green unlock a side door to let that man out after the killings. For this he was sentenced to two years in jail.

CHAPTER 17

'SOMEONE HAS TO DIE FOR THIS'

On New Year's Eve the flat of Eileen McGrane at 21 Dawson Street was raided and a huge cache of Collins' papers were discovered. The documents found included the carbon copies of reports supplied by Ned Broy, and the daybook that Collins had taken in April 1919 during the night he spent in the G Division archives.

'That damned old daybook of yours was twice nearly getting me shot,' Joe O'Reilly told Broy.

Collins warned Broy that the documents had been found and that it would only be a matter of time before he would come under suspicion. Broy received a further warning from Superintendent John J. Purcell, who had replaced Owen Brien.

'Every vestige of political duty was immediately removed from the Brunswick St office to the castle,' Broy wrote. British intelligence ceased to give any further confidential information to the DMP.

'I continued to meet Collins almost every night during this time and, of course, had to take extra precautions in doing so.' He found Collins 'very perturbed' about cabinet pressure both to ease off on the war that he had been engaging in against individuals and to get him to go to the United States. Even though Collins had built up a formative intelligence network, his most valuable police spies had lost their effectiveness. Joe Kavanagh died in September 1920 from a blood clot after an operation for appendicitis in Jervis Street hospital. Sergeant Jerry Maher came under suspicion at the county inspector's office in Kildare, and quit the RIC. He was replaced by then Sergeant Patrick Casey, who was already supplying Collins with information. He was able to continue until March, when he too came under suspicion and was transferred to Downpatrick. Broy and McNamara's effectiveness as spies was ended when they came under suspicion as a result of the captured documents.

'I was in charge of the office from which the documents were taken and, consequently, was not likely to have given out the documents myself, as I would have been obviously the first to be blamed,' Broy argued in his own defence. When he was brought before the commissioner of the DMP he was handed a sensitive report drawn up by a detective who had watched over Broy as he typed it up. Broy had not been able to make an extra carbon of that report, but he had given the file copy to one of Collins' people with the instruction that they should type up a copy and return the original to him without delay. Thus it was the re-typed copy that was found and Broy was quick to notice that this was typed on an elite typewriter with ten characters to the inch, as opposed to the typewriters at G Division headquarters, which were all pica models with just eight characters to the inch. This was enough to raise some doubts about Broy's guilt. He argued that if he had been supplying Collins with the information, he would have fled once it became clear that he was under suspicion, yet he stayed around for more than a month before his arrest.

The man that Broy had to fear within the DMP was Detective Chief Inspector Joe Supple who was expected to prepare the case against him. He was a slight man with a goat face, according to Neligan. Supple began every day by attending mass in Mount Argus near his home, and McNamara suggested that Collins warn Supple that if he took the case he should pick out his spot in Mount Jerome cemetery beside Mount Argus.

'By God,' Collins said, 'I'll go up there tonight!'

Collins arranged for a man to deliver the warning without delay. 'I have a grave warning to give you!' the man told Supple. 'It concerns someone called Broy, of whom I know nothing. I am to tell you that if you go on with the case against him, you will be shot!'

Collins enlisted the help of former Detective Sergeant Pat McCarthy, who had tried to play on both sides of the fence in the DMP for a time. His brother was active in Sinn Féin and had told Collins that Pat was not involved in political work. However, the Big Fellow was able to produce a report in which the detective sergeant had detailed the names, addresses and usual haunts of prominent Sinn Féiners. In the circumstances Pat McCarthy resigned from the DMP and emigrated to London. Now Collins contacted him and, in order to deflect suspicion from Broy, asked him to flee to America as soon as secret transportation could be arranged. 'McCarthy agreed, and sent me word that under no circumstances would he make a statement to the British or come to Dublin,' Broy explained. 'When the Civil War was over, I had the pleasure of reinstating McCarthy in the Dublin Police and promoting him to inspector and later superintendent.'

Among the papers found at Eileen McGrane's there was apparently evidence that prompted the intelligence people to look at the whole affair about the American seamen bringing arms into Dublin again and McNamara came under suspicion for having leaked the document to the IRA. Upon his return to Dublin from Glasgow, McNamara was summoned to the office of the DMP inspector general and summarily dismissed from the force.

'Listen, Mac!' Neligan warned him, 'don't go to your father's house tonight or any other night.'

'You are lucky,' Collins told McNamara. Obviously the British did not have much on him, or they would not have let him go. But henceforth he went on the run, with the IRA.

Meanwhile Collins was still living a charmed life. Following Bloody Sunday, the British had arrested thousands of suspects, but it took some time to reorganise their intelligence network. They regularly cordoned off city blocks and searched the buildings within the area. One night Frank Thornton was in Jim Kirwan's pub in Parnell's Street with Sergeant Maurice McCarthy of the RIC from Belfast, the man who had helped to supply him with the photograph of Forbes Redmond a year earlier. Collins rushed into the pub.

'Get out quick and see what the auxiliaries are doing,' Collins said to Thornton. 'There is a crowd of them coming up the road in extended order.'

'I went out the back way and down the lane into Parnell Street, and as I got to the end of the lane I was held up by the auxiliaries, demanding where I was going and so forth, and after searching me for a gun I was let go,' Thornton recalled. 'I turned to the right and walked into Kirwan's by the front entrance and walked down towards the rear of the shop to find that Collins had left the snug and was standing at the counter in one of the partitions and I stood in the next. We both called for drinks, but didn't recognise one another.'

The auxiliaries searched the snug where McCarthy was still sitting. He produced his identification card and his revolver. One of the auxiliaries bought a drink for McCarthy and warned him that carrying a gun in Dublin was dangerous because if he were not careful the republicans would take his gun and might shoot him as a spy. This was one of the many occasions in which Collins was allowed to slip through the enemy's net.

In addition to the uncovering of most of his main police spies in Dublin, some of Collins' hideouts were being uncovered. On 31 January the British raided Cullenswood House because they had become suspicious about a number of seemingly unnecessary structural alterations that they had noticed on a recent raid. They decided to inspect the alterations, only to discover that the changes included false walls and false doors, and a false wardrobe with a secret spring which opened into a chamber that appeared to be a secret office. In one of the rooms secret doors and secret cupboards were found. There were nine existing doors giving access to adjacent fields. During the investigation a revolver and some ammunition were found in one of the dummy walls. There was nobody on the premises but in one room supper had been laid, apparently for people on the previous night.

The spy ring within the DMP had practically disintegrated but it was no longer that important because the DMP had ceased to be any real threat to the IRA. There was no longer that much information to be picked up within the force, because British intelligence did not now share any information with the DMP as it had proved so unreliable. Collins therefore had to recruit new spies in other branches of the security forces. He suffered a further set back when Major Reynolds, his informer within F Company of the auxiliaries, was transferred to Clare, where he continued to work for the IRA. Liam Tobin managed to recruit another auxiliary named McCarthy, but Tobin and the others were always deeply suspicious of paid informers like Reynolds and McCarthy.

Willie Beaumont had a scare one day when Major Stokes, one of the senior British intelligence officers, produced some of the notes that Seán Beaumont had submitted about what Willie had told him. 'I'll show you what these Sinn Féiners are able to do,' he said as he produced the notes. Willie Beaumont thought he was in trouble, but Stokes never linked the notes to him.

Willie actually became disillusioned about the lack of activity in targeting undercover people that he had identified. 'He told me that he had come to the conclusion that Collins did not want to prosecute the war vigorously against the Auxiliaries,' his brother Seán noted. 'I don't know whether he actually had an interview with Collins or with one of the Squad but he accused them anyway of not acting vigorously enough and more or less washed his hands of any further activity.'

David Neligan concluded that he was wasting his time in the DMP. 'Now I was alone in the castle,' he said. 'I carried on for some time.' He decided to try to get into British intelligence. 'I told Collins the facts,' Neligan said. 'It was useless staying there any longer. The British secret service had taken over and we were completely in the dark. I told him I intended trying to join the British secret service, which I did in a few days.'

Neligan, who was interviewed by Major Stokes, was told that

he been highly recommended. He was therefore promptly sworn into the service the same day. The oath he took was:

> I ___ do solemnly swear by Almighty God that I will faithfully perform the duties assigned to me as a member of His Majesty's Secret Service; that I will implicitly obey those placed over me; that I will keep forever secret such membership and everything connected therewith, that I will never, in any circumstances betray such service or those connected with it even when I have left the Service. If I fail to keep this Oath in every particular I realise that vengeance will pursue me to the end of the earth, so help me God.

'I was assigned to the district of Dalkey, Kingstown and Blackrock,' Neligan explained. 'I got a curfew pass signed by General Boyd, O/C., Dublin District.'

'Join the IRA by all means, if you can,' Major Stokes told him. 'We will be glad if you get in.'

Stokes then called in a Captain Woolridge, a British army intelligence officer. They arranged to meet him in Kingstown a couple of days later.

'When I told Collins the next day he was pleased his Squad already knew Woolridge, but they didn't know the Major,' Neligan said. Cullen and Tobin had followed Woolridge from the North Dublin Union before but had lost him. Neligan was not supposed to go into Dublin proper, so Collins agreed to come out to meet him in Keegan's Bar in Blackrock.

'I met plenty of the British secret service after this,' Neligan added. 'They were scattered in various private houses about the city. These houses were all owned by loyalists and they were carefully screened by the British before the agents were allowed to go into them, a very wise precaution! These loyalists, whose houses lodged the secret service men, were, for the most part, Freemasons and were of course largely staffed by Protestant servants.

'The other secret service men I knew were practically all Englishmen,' Neligan explained. 'Those fellows were good types. They could not understand why I, a Catholic and an Irishman, was hostile to my own countrymen and they clearly told me that I should be ashamed of myself and that if they were Irishmen they would be Sinn Féiners.'

'I was expected to make an intelligence report once a week,' Neligan continued. 'Collins often helped me to write these reports; in fact, he wrote them himself. Many a good laugh we had over them! He used to say in these reports that the IRA was in no way short of arms or ammunition; recruits were simply falling over each other; they had plenty of money; new columns were being formed to fight the British.'

Captain Woolridge complimented Neligan on his reports and said that he knew the IRA had plenty of ammunition, because they were deliberately feeding the republicans with booby-trapped ammunition so that the IRA would use it. 'We are dropping stuff here and there,' Woolridge explained. 'If they use them, they will get a shock.'

The doctored bullets were marked 'ZZ'. Neligan passed this on to Collins, who had a warning circulated.

Collins was under intense pressure and had a number of narrow escapes, but the British still had no idea what he looked like, or where to look for him. There were a number of unfounded reports of his arrest. On 10 January 1921 John Foley, a former secretary of the lord mayor of Dublin, was arrested while having lunch in Jammet's restaurant with a former high sheriff of Dublin, T. J. McAvin. 'Come on, Michael Collins, you have dodged us long enough,' one of the arresting officers said. The two men were taken to Dublin Castle before they could establish that Foley was not Collins. In fact, he did not even look remotely like him.

Soon after a man whose real name was Michael Collins was arrested in the Prince of Wales hotel where he was a barman working under the name of Corry. The *Daily Sketch* reported that

Collins had been shot off a white horse while trying to escape from Burgatia House on the outskirts of Rosscarbery, County Cork, on 2 February, even though he was not within a hundred miles of the place. IRA intelligence intercepted a telegram from Dublin Castle asking for confirmation. 'Is there any truth that Michael Collins was killed at Burgatia?' the telegram read.

'There is no information of the report re Michael Collins, but some believe he was wounded,' came the reply from Cork.

'We are hoping to hear further confirmation about poor Michael Collins,' the Big Fellow remarked on being shown the telegrams. On 8 February a news agency circulated a report that Collins had been killed in Drimoleague, County Cork; obviously untrue.

The amazing stories of his escape were according him enormous notoriety. 'He combined the characteristics of Robin Hood with those of an elusive Pimpernel,' Ormonde Winter wrote. 'His many narrow escapes, when he managed to elude almost certain arrest, shrouded him in a cloak of historical romance.'

The ASU (Active Service Unit) was established from among the Dublin brigade with over one hundred men on full time service under the direction of Oscar Traynor. It engaged in two or three ambushes daily against the auxiliary lorries as they moved about Dublin. The lorries were caged to prevent the IRA throwing grenades into them. However, the IRA came up with methods to bomb the trucks, so the British resorted to carrying hostages. A wooden post was erected in the truck and an imprisoned member of the dáil was handcuffed to it as the truck travelled about the city. IRA headquarters decided to retaliate by taking members of the British parliament hostage. The headquarters intelligence section was given the task of planning the retaliation.

'We were instructed to be ready on a suitable date within any one week to arrest twelve members of the then British government,' Frank Thornton recalled. 'This number was to include cabinet ministers if possible.'

Thornton, Seán Flood and George Fitzgerald went to London to check out the habits of government members of the British House of Commons. They were in regular contact with Sam Maguire and Reggie Dunne of the London IRA. 'One day when Seán Flood and I were going out to Acton on a routine check-up on the Underground Metropolitan Railway, we ran into Westminster Station to find the lift gates just closing,' recalled Thornton.

'I'll race you to the bottom down the runway,' Flood said.

'It was a long winding passage with about three bends on it,' Thornton explained. 'Seán raced off in front and disappeared around the second last bend about a few feet in front of me. I heard a terrific crash and on coming around the corner I fell over two men on the ground, one of whom was Seán Flood. We picked ourselves up and both assisted in helping to his feet the man who Seán Flood had knocked down. To our amazement two other men who were with him ordered us to put up our hands. We more or less ignored them and started to brush down the man and apologise to him when to our amazement we discovered that the man we had knocked down was Lloyd George, the prime minister.'

Lloyd George told the two guards to put their guns away. They pointed out the two men were obviously Irish from their accents.

'Well, Irishmen or no Irishmen, if they were out to shoot me I was shot long ago,' the prime minister replied.

After about a month, during which they got some interesting insights into the extracurricular activities of members of the British parliament, they had a list of twenty-five members of parliament who had regular patterns for certain nights of the week. They provided the details to the London IRA whose members helped them draw up a list of addresses from where those people could be kidnapped. But the London operation was abandoned when the British quit the practice of using dáil deputies as hostages.

Local leaders like Dan Breen in Tipperary, Tom Barry and Liam Lynch in Cork, Tom Maguire in Mayo and Seán MacEoin in the Longford area, had generally acted independently of IRA headquarters, but Collins was always quick to endorse their actions.

This generated the impression that their actions were being orchestrated centrally. As a result the British often accused Collins of involvement in skirmishes with which he had no connection.

Brugha wanted to resurrect his old scheme to kill members of the British cabinet. This was abandoned after Tobin concluded it would be suicidal. Collins realised this would be the same mistake that the British had made in Ireland. The IRA was not beating the British despite such successful ambushes as Kilmichael and Clonbannin, which undermined Lloyd George's contention that he had 'murder by the throat'. But more and more British people began to question the democracy of a kind of paramilitary chaos in which the rule of law was being ignored. The reprisal policy was not intimidating the Irish but it was embarrassing the British and forcing more and more people to question both the morality and the efficacy of a policy of reprisals in which the crown forces were engaging in counter murder, arson and looting without regard to any law.

Brigadier General Frank Crozier resigned in disgust as leader of the auxiliaries after General Tudor, the head of all police operations, had undermined his efforts to discipline some of his men for outrageous conduct. Crozier had ordered the arrest of the auxiliaries responsible both for arson and looting in Trim and for the killing of the two young men in Drumcondra. Eighteen-year-old Patrick Kennedy and twenty-seven-year-old James Murphy had been arrested on the night of 9 February and taken to Dublin Castle, where they were questioned and slapped around. Neither was a member of the IRA. They were supposedly released but were in fact taken out to Drumcondra and shot. The auxiliaries said that the two were 'trying to escape', but the *Irish Times* noted that 'the postures suggested that the two men had been placed side by side and with their backs to the wall before being shot.' Kennedy was found dead and Murphy mortally wounded. He died a couple of days later in hospital, but not before making a deathbed statement about what happened to them.

Three auxiliaries – Captain William L. King, Temporary Cadets Herbert Hinchcliffe and F. J. Welsh – were subsequently charged with murder. King was particularly notorious in the eyes of republicans because he was believed to have been involved in the mistreatment and killing of McKee, Clancy and Clune. Murphy's deathbed statement was not admitted in evidence and the three were acquitted.

The growing hostility of British opinion was causing political problems for the Lloyd George government, but Collins realised that killing cabinet members would drive the British people to support the militants. Sinn Féin had been able to project the British campaign as an affront to democracy in Ireland, but killing the British cabinet would have been seen as a challenge to democratic government in Britain, and the British people could easily be roused to defend their own democracy against an Irish assault, especially in the light of the sacrifices in defending that democracy against the might of the German empire in the recent Great War. Hence Collins opposed Brugha's plan to kill British cabinet members.

'You'll get none of my men for that,' he declared.

'That's all right, Mr Collins, I want none of *your* men. I'll get my own.'

Brugha called Seán MacEoin to Dublin and outlined the scheme to him. MacEoin reluctantly agreed to lead the attack.

'This is madness,' Collins thundered when MacEoin told him. 'Do you think that England has the makings of only one cabinet?'

Collins suggested that MacEoin should discuss the matter with the chief-of-staff, Richard Mulcahy.

'I was appalled at the idea,' Mulcahy wrote. He reprimanded MacEoin for coming to Dublin and ordered him to have nothing further to do with the idea. On 3 March MacEoin was spotted on the train and when he got off at Mullingar the crown forces were waiting for him. He was shot trying to escape and was brought to King George V hospital in Dublin. 'It is simply disastrous,' Collins said. 'Cork will be fighting alone now.' He actually wrote that he 'would almost prefer that the worst would have happened' than MacEoin would have fallen into the hands of the enemy. He began trying to arrange MacEoin's escape.

The heaviest fighting in the country was in County Cork with the result that some of the most blatant reprisals occurred there. Unlike elsewhere in the country, the British army took a particularly active role in Cork, under Major A. E. Percival of the Essex regiment. He became a target of the IRA. Collins introduced Frank Thornton to Bill Aherne, Pa Murray and Tadhg Sullivan in Kirwan's pub in Parnell Street, one Sunday. The three Cork men had been selected to kill Percival in England when he was on holidays in March, and Thornton was to help them.

On arriving in London they tracked Percival with the help of Sam Maguire and Reggie Dunne, but their plan to shoot the major in Dovercourt proved impractical, because Percival was staying in a military barracks there. 'However, our contact man succeeded in getting the information that Percival was returning to Ireland on 16 March and would arrive at Liverpool Street Station, London, at about 3 o'clock in the afternoon,' Thornton noted. 'We made our plans and our party, augmented with a few more from London, took up our positions in Liverpool Street Station.'

About fifteen minutes before Percival was due to arrive at the station, Sam Maguire arrived to call the whole thing off, as he had learned from one of his contacts in Scotland Yard that the police had made plans to surround the place. 'We got out as quickly as possible,' Thornton added. 'We learned afterwards that at about five minutes to three a cordon of military and police was thrown round the station and every passenger had to pass through this cordon, some of them being held for hours. The unfortunate part about it was that Percival was able to get back to Cork safely.'

Captain Cecil Lees was brought back from the east in 1921 as the British felt that he would be an excellent man for intelligence work in Ireland. He came with a very high reputation as an ace intelligence officer, and he became part of Colonel Hill-Dillon's staff.

Collins was anxious that he should be dealt with as soon as possible, and intelligence made concerted efforts to locate him. Ned Bolster, who believed that Lees had a reputation for using torture to extract information from suspects, learned from his contacts that the 6'3" tall Lees was staying in St Andrew's temperance hotel in Wicklow Street. Tom Keogh and Ben Byrne kept an eye on the place but saw no sign of Lees. He seemed to vanish for about three weeks and they suspected that he must have returned to Britain, before they picked up his trail again.

'Tom Keogh and I were in the dress circle of the Scala picture-house, and just prior to the commencement of the programme a lady and gentleman proceeded to their seats,' Ben Byrne recalled, 'Keogh nudged me and said, "I think that is Lees". We decided to keep a watch on this gentleman and, whether he was Lees or not, find out where he was living. After the show was over we followed him and found that he was staying in St Andrew's.'

Next morning, 29 March, Keogh succeeded in rounding up Ned Bolster and Mick O'Reilly to join Byrne and himself to wait for Lees, because they knew that if it was him, he would be heading for Dublin Castle about 9.30. 'Bolster and myself were detailed to do the actual shooting,' related Byrne. 'Lees appeared without any undue delay, and, as he was already known to me, there was no need for any further identification. He was accompanied by a lady, but we had no interest in her. We opened fire on Lees, and he fell mortally wounded.'

CHAPTER 18

'SHE WANTS TO SEE GENERAL MacEOIN'

Temporary Cadet McCarthy had been passing on information about F Company of the auxiliaries based at Dublin Castle since he was recruited following the transfer of Temporary Cadet Reynolds to Clare. McCarthy gave documents to Tobin and Dan McDonnell in return for money. 'On a few occasions he brought out files which we were able to copy and hand back to him,' remembered McDonnell. 'All went well for some time until about May 1921, when an incident occurred which shook our confidence in McCarthy and, as a matter of fact, rather convinced us that he had started to double-cross us.'

Tobin, Cullen and McDonnell had been having lunch regularly in La Scala restaurant, which was attached to the La Scala cinema (which later became the Capital theatre). 'We went there for lunch every day and we went to the one waitress,' McDonnell explained. One Friday Tobin was wearing a new brown suit. 'Sitting across the room from us was McCarthy, the auxiliary, with two other fellows whom we didn't know. McCarthy made no attempt to recognise us, which didn't create any suspicion in our minds at the time.' Next day the three of them were discussing operations in their Crow Street headquarters, along with Frank Saurin and Charlie Dalton, when Tobin was called away for a meeting with Collins. Cullen then went somewhere else and McDonnell headed off for lunch at La Scala with Saurin.

Crossing the Halfpenny Bridge he noticed a convoy of army and auxiliaries crossing O'Connell Bridge, heading north, but he did not take much notice as it was by then a regular occurrence. 'I went on towards the La Scala, crossed over towards the old *In-*

dependent office and went up on the left-hand side of Middle Abbey Street going towards O'Connell Street,' McDonnell said. 'When I reached the narrow laneway running between Middle Abbey Street and Princes' Street two auxiliaries stepped out and held me up, demanding to know where I was going. I was searched, and on informing them that I was on my way home, was propelled by their boots.' He found O'Connell Street occupied by soldiers and auxiliaries. Later he learned that they had raided the La Scala restaurant and detained the patrons there for up to two hours.

'When the raiding party entered the Restaurant they immediately went to the table that we had been at for the previous week and demanded of the waitress the names of the three men, giving a very accurate description of the three of us, and particularly describing the tall thin man wearing a new brown suit,' McDonnell noted. 'They insisted that we must have come into the building and that we must be hiding somewhere. However, they ransacked the place from cellar to garret, but needless to remark they didn't get us because we weren't there.' Paddy Morrissey, the volunteer who had first introduced the auxiliary McCarthy told McDonnell that he had an uneasy feeling about McCarthy. 'These, however, were the chances which had to be taken when dealing with men of the McCarthy type, who after all were only working for the pay they received,' McDonnell concluded. 'One possibly couldn't expect anything else to happen, and we can only congratulate ourselves that we escaped so luckily on occasions like this.' They were not sure that McCarthy had betrayed them, so they did not retaliate against him, but they never used him again.

Ever since the capture of Seán MacEoin, Collins was particularly taken up with plans to arrange his escape. The first attempt was to be made immediately after his capture. He was known to have been wounded and assuming that he would be transferred to King George V military hospital the Squad was sent to intercept the convoy bringing MacEoin from Mullingar to Dublin.

'We left Morelands and got the tram as far as Lucan,' Vinny

Byrne recalled. 'We proceeded along the road towards the Spa hotel. A few yards beyond the hotel the road takes a sharp turn, with a high bank on the left-hand side.' They decided to lie in ambush there behind a hedge, as the position commanded a good view of the road.

They lay there for four or five hours, but no cars or trucks of a military nature passed, and they decided to call off the attack.

'We observed a small car coming along the road, going towards the city and we held it up,' Byrne said. 'We ordered the driver to take us to town. He refused point-blank, stating he was an ex-British army officer. I must admit he was a brave man.'

'If any of you can drive, you can have the car and I will travel along with you,' the driver said. 'I promise on my word of honour I will not draw attention to anyone, or give any trouble whatsoever.'

They put him in the back seat with one man on either side of him but none of them could drive. Ben Byrne said that he knew a little about driving.

'I am not going to risk my neck,' Tom Keogh said. 'I am going to walk home.' He handed over his gun to those in the car and took off across the fields and walked home along by the canal. The others drove to Islandbridge, where they ordered the British officer out and told him that he could collect the car in Park Gate Street, at the entrance to Phoenix Park.

A number of efforts were planned to rescue MacEoin from King George V hospital. While he was in Dublin (before his capture) MacEoin had met Brigid Lyons and asked her to visit him if he was ever captured. So hearing that MacEoin had been shot, she assumed that he would have been taken to King George V hospital, and she went to visit him. 'I met the officers in charge there and I told them I wanted to see General MacEoin,' she recalled. 'There were a few little titters.'

'She wants to see *General* MacEoin,' they remarked to one another in amusement.

'I told them that I wanted to write to his mother to tell her how he was, so they had a little pow-wow and they said it would be all right and they would bring back an answer,' she continued. He responded to her message with a note assuring her that he was all right but add facetiously that he could do with sugar as the place tended to be rather sour. She called at the hospital a couple of other times, and then someone told her that MacEoin had been moved to Mountjoy Jail.

MacEoin wrote to her suggesting that she get permission from Dublin Castle to visit him in prison. She pleaded with the authorities there for permission. 'Why do you want to see MacEoin?' they asked. She was pretending to be a girlfriend. As she was a medical student she said she wished to assess his condition for herself, so that she could inform his mother. This worked and she was given permission to visit him in the hospital area of the prison, which was on the ground floor.

Shortly afterwards Joe O'Reilly asked Brigid to meet Collins at 46 Parnell Square, the Keating's branch of the Gaelic League, at 11 o'clock the following morning. Collins often used the building for intelligence meetings.

'I took to the air,' she said at the thought of meeting Collins. 'I was never so thrilled or excited in my whole life.' She cut class to race over to Parnell Square for the meeting.

When she arrived at the house in Parnell Square there was a little girl taking dancing lessons in one of the rooms. Collins charged in to meet her and greeted her with a firm handshake. 'Have you seen Seán?' he asked.

She said that she had.

'I want you to get detailed information on where he's confined in Mountjoy,' he said. 'Pay particular attention to exactly where you see him – the room, where it's situated, how you get in, where you go inside, the number of locked doors, the number of sentries, who is present at the interviews, and all the details concerned with your visits.'

The interview with the Big Fellow lasted about three minutes.

Each time she went to the prison wardresses searched her. 'They were courteous enough, but they made certain you couldn't carry anything in,' she noted. He had asked for sugar 'to prevent him going sour,' but she had to leave that at the gate. 'I usually held a written note between my fingers and I managed to slip that to him, and collect his note when I first went in or as I was about to leave. Once while he was in the prison hospital, I failed to get the note to him.'

'Brighid, have you nothing to say to me,' Seán asked in desperation with an auxiliary guard looking on.

'I have,' she replied, 'but I can't say it with that fella looking on.'

'Get on with it, Missie, and be quick,' the auxiliary said, turning his back.

She quickly slipped the note under his pillow.

'Tell me more and get every detail,' Collins would say to her when they met, 'because I must get him out.'

In mid April Dublin Castle refused permission for further visits. Collins surmised this was because of the impending execution of Tom Traynor. The IRA took RIC District Inspector Gilbert N. Potter hostage and offered to exchange him for Traynor, but this was rejected. After Traynor's execution, Potter's captors apparently did not wish to kill him but they received orders from headquarters in Dublin to carry out the reprisal.

When Brigid Lyons was next allowed to visit MacEoin he had been transferred from the prison hospital to the top floor of the prison, and she saw him in the office of the deputy governor. As she was parting the deputy governor and the auxiliary present discreetly turned their backs and she palmed him a note from Collins, who was well advanced on the escape plans.

Ted Herlihy, one of the friendly warders, gave Seán Kavanagh one of the prisoners, a .38 Webley. 'This was brought around for Seán MacEoin,' Herlihy explained. Kavanagh was to hide it in his cell until it was needed. He did this by burying it in a box of sand that surrounded the pipes by the cell wall to deaden the sound as the men tried to send messages to each other in Morse code on the pipes.

Collins was working on an elaborate plan to send an armoured car into the prison to pick up MacEoin, supposedly from Dublin Castle. The first part of the plan involved highjacking an armoured car. Michael Lynch, a volunteer and superintendent of the corporation's abattoir on North Circular Road, suggested that they could seize the armoured car that called at the abattoir. Each morning at around 6 a.m., it escorted a lorry bringing meat to Portobello barracks. Lynch was 'on the run' himself, but his wife and family were living in a house attached to the abattoir. Tobin instructed Charlie Dalton to report this to a meeting at the Plaza hotel in Gardiner's Row one night in late April.

'When I walked into the room I saw several staff officers assembled. Among them was the director of intelligence, Michael Collins,' Dalton recalled. 'I knew Michael by sight, but this was the first occasion on which I met him face to face. He was sitting at a table, and he gave me a friendly nod when I reported to him. I felt very important to be in such company, but at the same time the presence of Michael completely overawed me. I was very vexed with myself not to be able to be at my ease, as I was most anxious to make a good impression.'

'I want you to go to the Superintendent's house,' Collins told Dalton, 'and observe the movements of the crew and see if there is any possibility of capturing the car.'

'The next night, shortly before curfew, I went to the house,' Dalton said. While talking to Lynch's wife he was looking out the window for a possible escape route in the event the house was raided during the night. The area was bathed in moonlight and to his horror he saw shoals of rats moving about. 'I withdrew hastily from the window, making up my mind that, if that were my only way out, I would cheerfully allow myself to be murdered in my bed,' he said.

Mrs Lynch called him in the morning in time to witness the arrival of the armoured car, which parked in front of the drawing-room window. 'Kneeling down, I could see through the lace fringe at the bottom of the blind all that was going on,' Dalton explained. 'I saw the arrival of the armoured car. It accompanied two lorries and pulled up exactly on the spot opposite the window, only a dozen paces away.' The lorries went further up the yard to be loaded with the meat.

'I saw the door of the car opened,' Dalton continued. 'Four soldiers got out. They were dressed in dungarees and each had a revolver on the holster of his belt. Lighting cigarettes, they stood chatting. It was a double-turreted car, and I knew the crew consisted of six men. On getting out, one of the soldiers had locked in the other two by fastening a small padlock on the door.'

Each morning Dalton took up his position at 6 a.m. and watched the process. 'Every morning I made observations and every day I reported them to Liam [Tobin],' he said. 'After a week I was summoned to another meeting at brigade headquarters. On this occasion we met at Barry's hotel, a few doors from the Plaza, where to my surprise, and gratification, I again saw Michael Collins.'

'I described the arrival of the car, the several journeys it made, and the conduct of the crew. I produced a sketch of my own, showing the position usually occupied by the car when in the abattoir. They heard me out without interruption.'

'I take it from your report you consider it possible to capture the car?' Collins said.

'I do, sir,' Dalton replied, 'but our success depends upon the exact arrival of our men at the opportune moment, which may only occur very occasionally'.

'Only on one occasion did the whole crew leave it,' Dalton said. 'Until such another occasion arose we could not capture it. When it did arise, it would be necessary for our men to be at hand to seize it instantly. This seemed to satisfy Michael.'

Collins then asked Pat McCrae, one of the Squad drivers, if he would be able to drive the armoured car. He had never driven that make – a Peerless – but he was confident he could do so. 'I could see that his assurance was quite enough for Michael, who immediately proceeded with the rest of the business.' He explained his plan in detail. The armoured car had to be stolen without the alarm being raised at the nearby Marlboro barracks. Three gunmen would accompany McCrae. Having seized the car they would pick up two more men dressed in the uniforms of British officers, and go to Mountjoy, where the officers would present bogus documents at the prison governor's office demanding the release of MacEoin for transfer to Dublin Castle. MacEoin was to try to be in the governor's office at the time, filing some complaint.

Charlie Dalton's brother, Emmet, was an obvious choice for one of the officers. Emmet had served as an officer in the British army during the First World War and he still had some of his old uniforms. Just who would accompany him was a bit of a problem.

After his arrest in the round up following Bloody Sunday, Paddy O'Daly had taken the unusual step of signing himself out of Ballykinlar internment camp by solemnly proclaiming to an interviewing board that he would have nothing to do with the republicans following his release. This was an option that was open to everyone, but very few of the prisoners availed of it. O'Daly's hardest job had been convincing the prisoners' committee in the camp that he was doing the right thing. 'I told the committee that the Volunteers outside were beginning to think that there were too many getting themselves locked up for safety, and that the war would have to be won outside,' O'Daly noted. 'I told the committee I had Michael Collins' approval of my plan, that I would like to have their blessing but I would sign the form and tell the British I[ntelligence] O[fficer]s all the lies necessary.' While the committee was still considering the matter, O'Daly applied for release.

He was brought before an interviewing board consisting of a judge and two military officers. He explained that he was a widower with four young children, the eldest of whom was just eight years old. This was the truth. The judge appeared very sympathetic, but one of the officers was clearly sceptical. He asked if O'Daly knew Michael Collins.

'I said I did not,' O'Daly explained. He then asked me did I ever hear of him. I told him I did, but that I thought he was like the banshee, something we were asked to believe in but never saw.'

'Why do you say that?' the judge asked.

'I think Collins is a bogey-man,' O'Daly replied. 'I never met the man who could tell me he met him.'

'Do you think you are talking to fools?' the second officer asked.

'Oh, no, sir, but I know from every book and history I have read that the British intelligence is the best in the world, and I cannot believe that there is any man in the whole of Ireland wanted by the police or military who could not be picked up at least within a month. Certainly he would not go on for years, as this Collins is supposed to do.'

'A likely story,' the second officer grunted. 'A pack of lies.'

'If you saw anyone shooting a soldier or a policeman would you give information to the authorities?' the first officer asked.

'I would not,' O'Daly replied. 'Let those who go about with guns look after that. I want to live to rear my family.'

'So you would be afraid,' the officer said. 'You must be a poor type of citizen.'

'Would you blame any citizen for being afraid?' O'Daly asked the judge. 'Sure we can't walk the street of Dublin between the lot of them.'

'That will do,' the judge said. 'Your case will be considered by the proper authorities.' A couple of weeks later O'Daly was released and returned to Dublin.

The Squad had lost most of its clout while O'Daly was in prison. According to George White of the ASU, there was too much indiscipline within the Squad, because some members, especially its leader, Tom Keogh, had been drinking too much. Collins ran into problems when he tried to have O'Daly take over the Squad again. Keogh refused to hand over the reins and the majority of the Squad backed him. At a joint meeting of the ASU and the Squad, presided over by Oscar Traynor, members of the Squad were 'definitely disobedient and they cut up rather rough,' reported White. The meeting had been called to arrange an ambush that never took place, because the British failed to take the bait.

In the planning of the attempt to rescue MacEoin, there were questions over whether O'Daly or Joe Leonard should accompany Emmet Dalton.

When Collins outlined the plan earlier in a private room of Kirwan's pub, O'Daly was anxious to go but two of the friendly warders from Mountjoy – Daly and Breslin – objected.

'You won't deceive the Governor with Paddy,' they said. 'The Governor knows him well. Sure he has been in twice in the last twelve months.' Leonard was therefore suggested.

'I told Michael Collins that Joe was in the same category as myself,' O'Daly noted.

'The warders said that Joe would have some chance, as it was nine months since he was in Mountjoy and he was not as well known as myself,' Breslin said. 'Sure Paddy was in the Governor's office every day when his wife was dying. The Governor could not but recognise him.'

Leonard was therefore chosen. Arrangements were made with Seán MacEoin to find some excuse to have an interview with the governor every morning at ten o'clock and to delay over the interview and be in the passage as much as possible. They hoped that MacEoin would actually be in the office when the car arrived. The operation involved the whole Squad, members of the ASU and some of the intelligence staff from headquarters.

On the first morning that they waited at the abattoir, only four of the soldiers got out of the armoured car, so the whole thing was called off. The same thing happened next morning, 14 May, but this time Charlie Dalton felt that there was something carefree about the attitude of the soliders, and he felt that that there might be a better chance when the car returned on another run later, so everybody stood at the ready. Four soldiers got out of the armoured car again, but this time they did not lock the door. As the four wandered off into the abattoir to watch the animals being killed, the other two soldiers emerged from the car.

'On stepping out, they lit cigarettes, and one of them shut the door, locking the padlock and putting the key in his pocket,' Dalton noted. 'I rushed into the room from which my signal was to be given and I raised the blind.'

He then saw Tom Keogh and another volunteer pass the window. Rushing back to the drawing room window he saw the two soldiers with their hands up, while their revolvers were being taken from them. The other Volunteers went in search of the remainder of the crew.

Pat McCrae and the others were putting on dungarees similar to those worn by the British soldiers. McCrae took the cap off one of them but it was too small for him. He forced it on his head anyhow. He then searched the soldiers for the key of the padlock and unlocked the door of the car.

'The remainder of us,' Vinny Byrne said, 'walked quietly into the slaughter-house and, as we came near the Tommies, shouted: "Hands up!" At the same time a few shots rang out and one of the Tommies fell dead.' He did not know 'what caused some of our men to open fire, for we had already received instructions that, if at all possible, the operation was to be carried out without any shooting.' The remainder of this part of the operation went off without a hitch.

Charlie Dalton locked Mrs Lynch and the children in a bedroom to give the appearance that they had been held captive. He then hurried off on his bicycle around the corner on to North Circular Road to the house where his brother, Emmet, and Leonard, were waiting, dressed and armed like British officers. 'Emmet was wearing his own British uniform and, having worn it for a long time before, had all the appearance and manner of a British Officer,' said Joe Leonard. 'He knew how to adopt the right tone in serving a Prisoner's Removal on the Jail authorities. I had served six months in Mountjoy and knew the prison well. Besides, Emmet's second uniform fitted me to perfection.'

'Come on,' Charlie said to them somewhat breathlessly, 'the car will be along any minute.'

They went out to the street as the car appeared with McCrae driving. They joined Tom Keogh, Bill Stapleton, and Jack Caffrey in the car. Charlie Dalton then cycled to Middle Abbey Street where he saw Collins, who was waiting for news. Dalton did not have to say anything as the Big Fellow could read his expression. 'There was no need to ask,' Dalton explained.

'I hope the second part will be as successful,' Collins remarked.

Some of the Squad were left guarding the British soldiers at the abattoir for about fifteen minutes. The armoured car had no problem getting into Mountjoy. 'Emmet Dalton who was sitting outside as the officer usually was, waved an official looking paper at the look-out warder,' said Leonard. 'The gates opened wide and shut-to with a clang after us. Two more iron gates were opened for us. McCrae turned the armoured car in such a way that the second gates could not be closed.

'Dalton and myself jumped smartly out of the car,' Leonard continued. 'We posted Tom Keogh, dressed in British dungarees and a Tommy's uniform cap, outside the main entrance door to cover our rear or give the alarm if necessary. Dalton and I entered the main door at 10.30 a.m., as the warders were coming from their quarters on duty. One of them, Warder Kelly, had known me as a prisoner and was so surprised at seeing me in British uniform that he said, "Oh, cripes, look at Leonard", and then, clapping his hand over his mouth, dashed back upstairs.'

Dalton and Leonard went to the office of Governor Charles Munroe, where there were a number of warders. The plan was for MacEoin to be there, but there was a change in the auxiliary guards at the prison that day and they were being shown the prisoners at the time. MacEoin was not allowed to visit the prison governor's office. On being presented with a forged order to hand over the prisoner, Munroe decided to telephone Dublin Castle to get the message verified. His suspicions were apparently roused by the presence of Leonard. 'I sprang for the telephone and smashed it while Dalton, drawing his gun, held the staff at bay, and then began tying the staff up with hope of securing the master keys,' Leonard explained.

Meanwhile Seán Doyle was in charge of a group outside the jail that included Frank Bolder of the Squad and Jack Walsh of the intelligence staff. Paddy O'Daly, who had cycled over from the abattoir, arrived in time to see the drama unfold. Annie Malone handed a parcel in at the wicket gate, while Doyle and others rushed the gate and forced their way in by holding up the warders at the gate. They then proceeded to open the main gate.

A sentry, seeing what was happening, fired a shot, which ricocheted and wounded Jack Walsh in the hand. Tom Keogh fired at the sentry and possibly hit him because the man's rifle fell to the ground. Once the shooting started Dalton and Leonard headed back to the armoured car. As they emerged from the jail, Leonard noticed the sentry's rifle on the ground and he barked out orders to the auxiliaries on the roof and soldiers on the ground to withdraw. 'Acting the part of a British Officer I ordered them to retire,' Leonard continued, 'and on their refusal to obey I took up the rifle, knelt down and threatened to fire. The soldiers, seeing an officer kneeling in the firing position, retired to their quarters.' Leonard then casually vaulted into the car, and one of them told McCrae 'to let it rip'.

He drove to where Joe Hyland, the other Squad driver, was waiting in his hackney car to collect Leonard and Dalton. Hyland had waited there for the past three of four mornings until Joe O'Reilly had come to tell him 'that there was nothing doing for that day'. But this day there was no sign of O'Reilly, so he waited.

'After a considerable delay I saw an armoured car approaching me,' Hyland said. 'By the way it was travelling with steam issuing from the engine I sensed that it was our men.' The vehicle was clearly in trouble.

When the armoured car reached where Hyland was parked, Leonard and Dalton alighted. 'They jumped into my car and told me to get away as fast as I could,' Hyland said. 'They were both dressed as British Officers. I went straight down the North Circular Road to Portadown Row, to the North Strand and turned towards Clontarf.'

The armoured car went off in the direction of Ballybough. It overheated in the Marino area, and the others abandoned it, but not before dismantling the Hotchkiss gun and setting fire to what they could. They made across the fields to Paddy Belton's house in Donnycarney, where they dumped the gun and the military overalls and came back to the city.

McCrae had already headed back to work for his brother Bob, who was the proprietor of Peter Murphy's provisions shop in Great George's Street. The business had a contract with Portobello barracks, where Pat casually made a delivery that afternoon. All of the troops seemed at the ready.

'What's on today?' he asked one of the sergeants. 'You seem to be all on the move.'

'Tell no one, but the blinking Sinn Féiners are after stealing an armoured car,' the sergeant whispered.

Pat laughed and said he did not believe it.

'It is a fact,' the sergeant insisted. 'They may be around the city shooting all before them. All armoured cars are being called back to barracks.' An aeroplane then scoured the area looking for the missing car.

McCrae realised that he had left his collar in the armoured car, and there was a danger that if it had not been burned he could be identified by the laundry number. Paddy O'Daly got some men to raid the Phoenix Laundry on Jones' Road. 'The Scotsman who was manager was surprised when we cleared out all the files and lists of customers and were taking them with us,' O'Daly said. 'We warned him that if he gave the name and address of any customer to the police he would be shot.'

'You'd better take this too,' the manager said going to the press and taking out a big ledger. 'Now you have all the customers' names and address so don't blame me for anything, but if you could let me have the books back in a few days you will save me a lot of trouble.'

'I told him that depended on his own conduct,' O'Daly said. 'We were able to let him have the books back when the intelligence staff had gone through them.'

'The men worked glorious and gallantly, but they just failed to achieve complete triumph,' Collins wrote to the adjutant of the Longford brigade the next day. 'It was nobody's fault. There were no mistakes made. Things went on splendidly up to the last moment, and then there was a mishap. Our men fought their way out of the prison, and sustained only one slight casualty.'

CHAPTER 19

'MISS, YOU'LL BE LUCKY IF YOU GET OUT WITH YOUR LIFE'

A certain amount of friction developed between Éamon de Valera and Michael Collins over the former's plan for major military confrontations. Collins did not believe that the IRA could maintain such a campaign. Oscar Traynor, the officer commanding the Dublin brigade, recalled one top level meeting at 40 Herbert Park, the home of the family of The O'Rahilly, who had been killed in the Easter Rebellion. Those in attendance included Cathal Brugha, Austin Stack, Michael Collins, Seán Russell, Traynor and others.

'Something in the nature of a big action in Dublin was necessary in order to bring public opinion abroad to bear on the question of Ireland's case,' de Valera argued according to Traynor. 'He felt that such an action in the capital city, which was as well known abroad as London or Paris, would be certain to succeed. He suggested that the seizing of the headquarters of the Black and Tans, which was situated in Beggar's Bush barracks, would capture the imagination of those he had in mind, apart from the serious blow it would constitute to the enemy. As an alternative to this he suggested the destruction of the Custom House, which was the administrative heart of the British civil service machine in this country. It was the headquarters of the Inland Revenue and various tax offices, the assay office, local government and the Companies Registration office. As officer commanding the Dublin brigade, Traynor was given the task of considering the two operations and reporting to the army council.

'I immediately set to work and was given the help of GHQ intelligence. Two weeks were spent on the investigation and examination of the possibilities of capturing Beggar's Bush. The experience of the men engaged on this work was such that they reported against such an operation. My activities were then turned to the alternative suggestion – the Custom House.'

Traynor examined the building himself and then took Tom Ennis, the officer commanding the second battalion, into his confidence and asked him to examine the building. He got plans of the Custom House from Liam O'Doherty of the fifth battalion. There was no military guard in the building – they had been withdrawn a short time before.

As it was in the second battalion's area, Ennis was given the task of burning the Custom House. The first battalion was to protect the outside of the building in the event of a surprise attack by the enemy, as well as deal with any fire station in their area. The third and fourth battalions were likewise to ensure that the fire brigades in their areas were blocked. The fifth was to cut communications between the Custom House and Dublin Castle.

The Custom House operation on 25 May 1921 was the largest single action in Dublin since the Easter Rebellion. Tom Ennis was anxious to have all the former members of the second battalion who had joined the Squad. Collins apparently did not want any of his men to be involved, but Ennis insisted and got his way. Paddy O'Daly was then concerned at what amounted to the break up of the Squad for the operation.

'I appealed to Michael Collins to have us all included as I was afraid it would cause dissension amongst the men if any of them would be left out,' O'Daly noted. After consultations with Traynor, O'Daly said that it was decided that the Squad would be the only unit other than the second battalion engaged in the Custom House itself.

'The Squad was to take charge of all the entrance doors of the Custom House,' said O'Daly. 'I posted my twenty men at the various doors. Their instructions were to allow nobody to leave the building once they went into position, but any civilian entering the building on business was to be admitted and then held prisoner so that the outside public would not be given the information that the building was held by the Volunteers.'

The operations were supposed to begin around 12.45 p.m. and the Squad were to take control of all the doors at the same time 'to prevent anybody finding one door closed getting out by another door,' according to O'Daly. 'This was the only job allotted to the Squad.' It was significant that none of the people from intelligence headquarters were involved. Collins gave strict orders 'that on no account were we to go near the Custom House, the reason being that he did not want to have everybody involved in it,' related Dan McDonnell.

Ennis planned the whole thing with each officer having a number of men under him. There were people to round up the civil servants in the building and people to set the fires. The other Dublin battalions and the ASU were assigned the task of frustrating any effort by the crown forces to intervene and volunteers were also assigned to prevent sections of the fire brigade going to put out the fire at the Custom House. Despite O'Daly's assertions that Ennis had planned the whole thing meticulously, there was obviously a breakdown, because the Black and Tans arrived early, with little difficulty, and surrounded the building.

Vinny Byrne went into the Custom House with Tom Keogh and Jimmy Slattery. 'As we entered the hall, we met Tom Ennis who said he was short of a couple of men,' Vinny recalled. Ennis asked if he could take Vinny to burn some of the offices on the second floor. Keogh agreed and Byrne complied.

'I was assigned the task of holding the Beresford Place door,' Jim Slattery recalled. 'My instructions were to collect the policeman outside the door, take him inside, and allow nobody out once they entered the Custom House.

'I went to the policeman at about five minutes to one on that day, and asked him to come inside with me, which he did reluctantly only after I showed him my gun,' Slattery continued. The main body of the IRA arrived and carried in tins of fuel and bales of cotton, which had arrived in a lorry driven by Tom Kilcoyne. The fuel and cotton were then brought upstairs.

Vinny Byrne got a tin of petrol and went to the second floor. 'I opened the office door, and sitting inside were a lady and gentleman, civil servants, having tea,' he said. 'I requested them to leave, stating that I was going to set fire to the office.'

'Oh, you can't do that!' the man replied.

'I showed him my gun and told him I was serious,' Byrne continued. 'He got very worried about the whole thing.'

'You had better get out at once, unless you want to be burned alive,' Byrne said.

The lady asked if she could get her coat.

'Miss, you'll be lucky if you get out with your life,' Vinny told her.

All the civil servants were ordered to the ground floor, where they were held with their hands on the heads for around half-an-hour.

'I started on a tour of inspection, entering by the main door facing the Liffey,' Paddy O'Daly recalled. 'I could not make my way through the inside owing to the herding of the staff and the various groups of Volunteers running to their positions, so I came out, went round the outside and found that all the men under my charge were in the positions allotted to them. As I came out the main door facing Liberty Hall I saw Oscar Traynor, who beckoned me over. I told him what I knew, that everything was going on perfectly as far as I could see. He took out his watch. He was very anxious at seeing no sign of smoke and said that the building should be on fire by now.

'As we were speaking a Tan lorry swung around from the quays and pulled up right beside us,' O'Daly continued. 'At that moment a young lad, identified as Dan Head, a mere boy, threw a hand-grenade right into the lorry. Before the lorry came I had seen this lad standing near us, but I did not take him to be a Volunteer, he looked about fifteen years of age.'

'Run,' O'Daly said to Traynor. 'I darted towards Abbey Street. 'With the explosion of the bomb the whole place seemed to rock, and one Tan fell out of the lorry right in front of me as I was running past making for Abbey Street. Shots were fired and struck the wall of Bairds, the big ironmongers. Whether the shots were from the Tan lorry or from our own men firing on the Tan from the Custom House I do not know, as I was right in the line of fire from both parties.'

'I mingled with the crowd in Abbey Street and saw an armoured car and more lorries,' O'Daly continued. 'The Tans were dismounting and spreading out, so I made my way around Marlboro street. Outside the Abbey Theatre I met Oscar Traynor, and I was glad to see him alive. We went round by Talbot Street into Store Street, but could not get near enough even to see the Custom House.'

Things were clearly going awry. The Tans had managed to arrive at the building unopposed. 'The Tans lay down on the square facing the building, and I went outside and fired a couple of shots from a Peter the Painter,' Slattery recalled. 'There is going to be sport here today,' he told Tom Flood on darting back into the cover of the building. He was making light of the whole thing to boost morale. Shortly afterwards an armoured car arrived and there was general firing.

The signal to set the fires was to be given with a whistle. Somebody blew a whistle but nothing happened. Tom Ennis came down the stairs,' Slattery noted. 'I asked him if the fires had been stated and he said no. He wanted to know did I hear the whistle and I told him I did. He started cursing and went back again.'

Vinny Byrne was busy preparing to torch the office he had taken over. 'I opened the safe and removed all the ledgers, which I placed on the table which was in the centre of the office,' he explained. 'I collected all other papers and files I could find and placed them on the table. I then proceeded to pour the petrol all over the office and on the papers. On hearing the signal – the whistle – I stepped outside. I lit a ball of paper, and slightly opening the door, I flung it into the office. In a flick the whole office was ablaze.'

Some of the men got out of the building with the staff when they were allowed to leave. 'We mixed with the staff and eventually found ourselves outside the Custom House dock,' James Harpur of the ASU recalled. 'In passing out there was a gentleman there with some auxiliary officers who was identifying the staff but who did not identify myself, Tom Flood, Tom Keogh, Ned Breslin or Mick Dunne as members of the staff, and we were separated from them and brought down to another party on the Quays ... We were searched and during the search a hole was discovered in the lining of Ned Breslin's pocket and on feeling around at the back of his coat a round of ammunition was discovered and the auxiliaries who were searching him took him out and gave him an unmerciful hiding.'

'All the men who were upstairs taking part in the burning of the Custom House crowded down the main hall,' remembered Slattery. 'Nobody was keen on going out, but I was very anxious to go out because I did not think I would stand a chance if I was arrested. I tried to get the lads to burst out with me. A few of them did, but the Tans opened fire when we got outside the door. Seán Doyle, whose brother had been executed, broke through. He did not want to be arrested because he knew he stood no chance.

'When we were almost halfway across the square there was a burst of machine-gun fire and I was hit on the hand. I called Doyle, who was slightly in front of me, and I saw blood trickle down his chin,' Slattery said. He had been shot through a lung.

'As I was coming down the stairs, I heard a burst of revolver and rifle fire from inside and outside the building,' Vinny Byrne recalled. 'When I came to the hall, everyone was dashing from place to place. I ran along the corridor towards the docks and, as I came to the end, I could see the Auxies on the quay, firing. I retreated back to the hall. There was not a soul to be seen.'

There was a glass partition on top of a timber base in the hall, inside the main entrance. There were sandbags behind the timber frame. As Byrne approached the entrance an armoured car drove up and fired a burst of machine gun fire into the hall. 'I flung myself down to the floor,' Byrne said. 'It was a blessing the sandbags were there.' They saved him and he waited until the car withdrew. 'I could see the Auxies standing out on the roadway,' Byrne continued. 'At this time, the whole building was a raging inferno. It meant either being burned or shot. I decided to have another go to get out. The first time I had fired from my Peter I did not realise that I had emptied it. I had a look to see how many rounds I had left, and I re-loaded the gun. Just then two Auxies appeared a few yards from the doorway. I opened fire on them and missed them. After firing the second time, my gun went silent – no more ammunition. I said to myself: "This is where you finish". I walked out. As I came to the door, I heard a shout, "hands up". I threw up my hands and found myself covered by an Auxie with a rifle.'

'Come over here,' the auxiliary shouted. He lowered his rifle and struck Byrne in the face. He then ordered him to walk in front of him across a green patch to Brooks Thomas' premises. 'Every minute I was expecting a bullet in the back, which never came,' Byrne explained. 'He marched me over to Brooks Thomas' wall and, when another auxiliary joined him, he remarked: "this bastard came out of the building." I got a few more blows on the face and body. He asked me what I was doing in the building.

'I was on a message for my boss, sir,' Byrne replied. 'He struck me again, saying, "don't sir me" and when I did not "sir" him, he struck me for not "sirring" him.'

'You don't stir from here,' the auxiliary warned Byrne, turning to other auxiliary saying a specific colleague 'got it this time'.

'The two auxiliaries left me and turned their attention to the body of a dead man a few feet away from me. He was a civilian. Catching him by the hair of the head, they lifted up his body and felt his pockets, letting him fall back again on to the ground.

'Across the road I could see all the Squad men and members of the second battalion, standing under the middle arch. Needless to say, I did not recognise them. At the same time, I noticed a big crowd of civilians standing outside the entrance to Brooks Thomas. A major or some high-ranking officer arrived and held a conversation with a few men in civilian clothes. Then I noticed that the crowd started to file past them and go into Brooks Thomas. On observing this, I started to move up, inch by inch, towards the entrance until I came in front of the officer. As I was moving along, I thought I got a strong smell of petrol from my hands. I took a few cigarettes out of my pocket, wet them and rolled them very well into my hands, giving a smell of tobacco.'

Now it was Byrne's turn to go before the officer.

'Could I go home now?' he asked.

'What are you doing here?' the officer asked.

'Sir, I was on my way to Brooks Thomas to buy some timber.'

The officers frisked Byrne and pulled out a carpenter's rule and a few pieces of paper on which he had jotted different sizes of pieces of timber to bolster his cover as a carpenter. 'Get the hell out of this,' he said, returning the ruler and pieces of paper.

'Thank you, sir.'

Before the operation, many of the Squad had met in the geographical society's offices in Gardiner Street, and Byrne knew that Tom Keogh had left his bicycle there. 'Accordingly, that was the first place I made for, in order to get Tom's bike. I then cycled to O'Connell Bridge and saw all the boys being carried away in military lorries. It was a standing joke ever after – Where are you going, Vincie? Is it for your timber?'

'The military and police officers, amazed that the fire brigades had not answered the fire calls, despatched a party to investigate,' reported the *Irish Times*. 'When they reached Tara Street fire station, they learned that the firemen had been warned by the IRA that they would move at their own peril. Once assured of an auxiliary escort, they promptly manned the engines and rushed to the

Custom House, but by then the fire had taken hold and the building was eventually gutted.

That evening Michael Collins wished to see the state of the Custom House for himself. Johnny Dunne and Joe Byrne of the Squad went with him. 'We walked down from the Engineer's Hall in Gardiner's Row and mingled with the people,' said Byrne. 'Collins did not say anything but smiled when he saw the place was still burning, and then moved off. We went up Abbey Street, turned into O'Connell Street and to Parnell Street. Immediately on entering Parnell Street, auxiliaries were holding up people and Collins was held up. I heard him abuse the auxiliary.'

'How dare you!' Collins said. 'Do you know who I am? Give me your name and number. I'll deal with you later.'

'The auxiliary apologised and Collins went on his way,' Byrne continued. 'Apparently the auxiliary was so excited about the incident that he left us by also. We proceeded to Kirwan's public-house, Parnell Street, and Collins stood us two glasses of malt.' Dan McDonnell observed that Collins 'was not too happy about the results.' There were over a hundred men involved in the operation, and over eighty of them were captured. Paddy O'Daly, Joe Leonard and Vinny Byrne had managed to escape but most of the members of the Squad were arrested.

Seán Doyle and Jim Slattery were seriously wounded. They actually got to talk to one another in the Mater hospital. 'On the night of the burning of the Custom House,' Slattery noted, 'a party of British military and medical men came to the Mater hospital and examined our charts. The nun warned me beforehand to pretend I was asleep if they came. I pretended to be asleep and they looked at the chart.' Doyle died the following day, while Slattery remained in the hospital for nearly a fortnight.

In reality the attack on the Custom House was a military disaster, but de Valera was interested in its propaganda value. It turned out to be a propaganda success and a political victory, because the British government came under intense international pressure to try to negotiate a settlement.

Collins had a very narrow escape a couple of days later. He should have been in his finance office at 22 Mary Street when it was raided, but he had been delayed and was warned off once the raid was in progress. They raced through the offices first merely counting those present as they went in search of Collins himself. Alice Lyons, his secretary, had put on her hat and coat and promptly walked out of the building as the security forces were combing the building. Later all of the people in the building were interviewed and the officer in charge noted that one person was missing.

'I distinctly remember meeting a lady in the inner office when we first entered,' he said. 'Where is she now?'

'That must be Mick Collins who escaped disguised as a lady,' someone suggested in an undertone. Of course, this added to the myths surround the elusiveness of Collins. While his mystique continued to grow, his influence within the IRA was on the wane.

The remaining members of the Squad were amalgamated with the ASU, which became known as the Dublin Guard, under the leadership of O'Daly, but not without some controversy. He spoke to a joint meeting of the remaining members of the Squad, the ASU and the intelligence officers at the Plaza hotel in Upper Gardiner Street.

'O'Daly addressed all present and stated that he had now been appointed to command the ASU,' stated Joe McGuinness of the ASU. 'He said that owing to the very much reduced strength of the ASU on account of arrests and other casualties, it was now proposed to reorganise it and that, from that day on, the Squad, the ASU and intelligence would merge and form one unit under his control.'

The combined strength of the two amalgamated units was 120 men. This was divided into two half companies, with Joe Leonard of the Squad in charge of the half-company covering North Dublin.

Even though the opposition to O'Daly from within the Squad

had evaporated following the arrest of Keogh and the other dissidents during the Custom House operation, the transition was still far from smooth. Paddy Flanagan, the head of the Dublin ASU, resigned, as did his adjutant, Mick White, following O'Daly's appointment. 'When I took over I told the men that we were having no staff officers,' he explained. 'Every officer and non commissioned officer would be a leader in attack. The lieutenants would not alone take orders from me, but they would look for jobs and keep the men employed. Every Tan and military lorry was fair game, but no individual shootings of civilians must take place; no man had the right to say who was a spy. Headquarters were the only people who would give an order for an execution.'

'An all out effort was being made by those still at liberty to increase the number of attacks, so that the enemy would not be aware of the depletion the Custom House arrests had made in the ranks of the active volunteers in Dublin,' noted Charlie Dalton. Instead of targeting only specific individuals, members of the former Squad were targeting any enemy personnel. But some individuals remained targets, such as Ormonde Winter, the head of British intelligence operations. On the afternoon of 2 June a small group of IRA men ambushed the RIC car in which Winter was travelling along Thomas Street approaching the junction with James' Street. A grenade was thrown at the car and several revolver shots were fired, but Winter escaped with just one minor bullet wound.

Plans were also made to attack the British hangman, John Ellis, and his assistant, William Willis, the following week, as they arrived from England to hang Edward Foley and Patrick Maher in Dublin on 7 June. Ellis was the chief British hangman. He had already carried out the executions of Roger Casement and Kevin Barry, along with all seven others already hanged in Dublin during 1921. Even though members of the IRA staked out Kingstown to kill the two hangmen as they arrived, both had already slipped in without being noticed. It was only much later that the IRA learned that Ellis and Willis always arrived some days in advance.

Collins was still director of intelligence, but he had effectively lost control of the Squad, and all of his moles within the police in Dublin had been uncovered. David Neligan did remain undetected. 'After a while I suggested to the British that it would be better for all the British secret service men to meet some place where we could have a discussion,' Neligan noted. 'The meeting took place in the North Dublin Union. About forty or fifty of those fellows turned up there. I got to know several of them and where they were living too.

'There was to be another Bloody Sunday, but the Truce came along and it saved those fellows,' he added. Indeed, there was also a plan to kill as many auxiliaries as possible on the streets of Dublin but it too was called off.

Lloyd George had been anxious to negotiate ever since the previous autumn, but his wing of the Liberal Party was only a small minority within the coalition government. The Conservatives actually enjoyed a clear overall majority in both houses of parliament. They could therefore bring down the government at will. While Hamar Greenwood was contending that the security forces were winning, Lloyd George had to wait, if only to strengthen his own negotiating position. The attack on the Custom House seemed to undermine the contention that the security forces were getting the better of the IRA, because in May 1921 the British suffered their heaviest casualties since the Easter Rebellion.

The number of attacks on the security forces in the first six months of 1921 was supposedly down, but the number of casualties was dramatically up. The total casualties for the second half of 1920 were 174 killed and 310 wounded, whereas 317 were killed and 638 wounded in the first half of 1921. In the circumstances it seemed unlikely that the IRA was about to collapse.

There was a noticeable relaxation on the part of British officials. De Valera had been arrested and quickly freed and told to await a communication from the British prime minister. This turned out to be an invitation to London to discuss terms for a peace conference. De Valera demanded a truce first and the terms of a truce were agreed on Saturday to come into effect on the following Tuesday. Brigid Lyons was passing Mountjoy Jail on Sunday when, on impulse, she went up to the door to request permission to see MacEoin. 'There's a one outside wanting to see MacEoin,' he said to someone inside the gate.

'What do you want to see him for? he asked. 'Do you have a permit?'

When she replied that she did not, he slammed the wicket. Then she heard the bolt on the door being withdrawn and a well dressed man came out. She did not know him, but later learned he was Sir Alfred Cope, the assistant secretary at Dublin Castle.

'I am trying to get into to see Commandant MacEoin,' Brigid said to him, 'and they won't let me see him.'

'That's too bad,' he said. 'Are you a friend?'

When she said she was, he turned to the warder and said, 'Take the visitor to see Commandant MacEoin.' She was as surprised at the use of MacEoin's title as she was at being taken to see him.

EPILOGUE

The Truce came into effect on 11 July 1921. Collins sent a message to Brigid Lyons that night that he would like to accompany her to see MacEoin on Wednesday afternoon at 2.15. She made arrangements for herself and 'James Gill' to visit. The Big Fellow entered the jail as Gill.

'It was a joy to see Seán MacEoin's surprise when he saw Mick Collins walk into Mountjoy that day,' remembered Brigid. 'Seán just greeted him as a visitor but there was no hiding his inner delight.'

The following day MacEoin wrote to Brigid. 'I don't know how to explain to you how grateful I am to you for your visit yesterday. My old heart beat high with joy and all I could do was stare and murmur to myself "Thank God". I am sure you understand how I felt,' he wrote.

'I will be forever grateful to you for that visit,' he continued. 'Never were you so welcome and that welcome will always remain so long as I remain.'

There was no doubting the intensity of MacEoin's appreciation at Collins' gesture. Later the Big Fellow caused a certain amount of disquiet within Sinn Féin circles by announcing that the dáil would not consider peace terms offered by the British unless MacEoin was first released. The British had already announced that all the other members of the dáil would be released, but they were holding on to MacEoin because he had been sentenced to death. Collins had no authority for his pronouncement, but it worked and the British promptly released MacEoin.

Part of the loyalty that Collins attracted was prompted by the sense of caring that he generated. Men believed that he really cared about them as individuals and that he would go to extraordinary lengths to try to rescue them. After the Anglo-Irish Treaty was accepted by the dáil in January 1922, Collins became chairman of the Provisional Government. Some of his subsequent behaviour though raised questions about whether he would ever have been able to adapt from the part of gang leader to a more restrained role in civilian government.

On 21 January 1922 Collins thought he had an understanding with Sir James Craig, the prime minister of Northern Ireland, in accordance with which prisoners would be released. These included ten 'Monaghan footballers' who were arrested crossing the border on 14 January. They were supposedly going to play a football game, but were actually planning to spring three prisoners from Derry Jail who were under sentence of death for killing a warder.

When it became apparent that he had overestimated the significance of his understanding with Craig, Collins came up with a plan to kidnap about a hundred Orangemen and hold them as hostages for the three men under sentence of death. General Eoin O'Duffy, who took over as chief-of-staff from Richard Mulcahy when the latter became minister for defence, arranged the overall operation, which was supposedly undertaken by anti-Treaty forces. On 7 February forty-two unionists were kidnapped and held hostage. The whole thing was a reckless act, especially when it was learned that the three men had already had their sentences commuted earlier that day. If the sentences had not been commuted, would Collins have had some of the hostages executed?

He even tried to have the hangman and his assistant killed. Having failed to intercept John Ellis and William Willis on their way to Dublin on previous occasions, Collins sent two men over to England to kill them in their homes.

'Charlie Byrne and I got instructions to report to Collins at the Gresham hotel where he had his office at the time,' Dolan said. 'Collins explained to me what he wanted done. We were told to get in touch with a man named Paddy Daly, who was one of the Liverpool Irish Volunteers, that he would show us where to go to find the men who we were to shoot, and that he would give us the assistance of whatever number of Liverpool Irish Volunteers as we might consider necessary.'

They met Daly as arranged and then went by train to Manchester. 'I undertook the shooting of Ellis, and six or seven of the Liverpool men came along with me,' Dolan continued. Byrne went after the hangman's assistant, William Willis, with some of the Manchester Volunteers. Willis lived in Accrington and they went by car.

'We went by train to Rochdale where Ellis lived, and some of the Liverpool Volunteers conducted me to the house and pointed it out to me. I walked up to the door alone and knocked at the door, which was opened by Mrs Ellis. At this stage I noticed that the other fellows had all disappeared, but I decided to go ahead with the job on my own. Mrs Ellis informed me that her husband was not in, that he had gone to Ireland, but as I did not believe her at the time, I forced my way into the house and looked around. There was no one there and I had to accept her assurance that he had left already for Ireland. Our boats had probably crossed.'

Charlie Byrne's mission had also proved abortive. Their car broke down. Byrne wanted to commandeer a car, but the others would not hear of it. So he too came up empty handed. Willis had probably already left for Ireland anyway.

In the early 1950s Dolan caused a sensation by disclosing that in June 1922 Collins had been behind the killing of Field Marshal Sir Henry Wilson in London. This was the incident that had essentially ignited the Civil War in Ireland. The British thought that republican forces occupying the Four Courts were responsible and they warned that if Collins did not clear out the Four Courts without delay, they would do so. In fact, General Sir Nevil Macready was ordered to clear out the Four Courts, but he delayed in the hope that Collins would eventually do so, which he did the following day.

Dolan was not involved in the shooting of Wilson, who was

killed outside his London home by Reggie Dunne, the officer commanding the London IRA, and one of his men, Joe O'Sullivan, who had lost a leg in the war. There was also believed to have been a third man driving a getaway car, but he apparently fled when the two were chased and captured by people at the scene.

'I was then a Staff Captain in the National Army attached to the military intelligence branch at Oriel House,' Dolan recalled. 'Naturally, we all discussed the shooting, or the report of it that had appeared in the newspapers, but I don't think I spoke to anyone who knew any more about it than I did at the time.' Before Dunne and O'Sullivan went on trial Collins summoned Dolan to his office in Portobello barracks.

'Collins was a man who wasted no words; he always spoke snappily and to the point,' Dolan said. 'Having mentioned the shooting of Sir Henry Wilson, he immediately came to the point by saying that he wanted to effect a rescue of Dunne and O'Sullivan if at all possible. He said he wanted me to change into civilian attire immediately, report to Sam Maguire in London and there to see what could be done towards effecting a rescue at all costs. The idea was not that I should attempt to rescue immediately but that I should explore the possibilities and report back to Collins without delay.'

'I left for London by the mail boat that evening and reported to Sam Maguire as arranged,' Dolan continued. 'The rendezvous with Maguire was at Peel's public house in Fetter Lane, which is off Fleet St. That was the usual place where Maguire could be contacted. When I met Maguire, I discussed my mission with him, and I gathered from him that he already knew of the rescue project. He called over another man who was there at the time – Seán Golden, whom I already knew – and told me that Golden would show me around. Golden, who was one of the London Volunteers also, had been standing nearby in the same pub but had not been in Maguire's company when I came along, and he was instructed by Maguire to show me the way around and assist me to explore the likely places where a rescue might be attempted.'

Dolan concluded there might be an opportunity of rescuing Dunne and O'Sullivan as they travelled between the prison and the court. Some three days later he reported to Collins, but then became involved in the Civil War, which had already begun. Afterwards Sam Maguire told Dolan that Collins had sent Tom Cullen to check on Dolan's suggestions, and apparently ruled out any rescue.

'There is nothing more I can say from my personal knowledge on this incident except to express my firm belief that Collins did instruct Dunne to carry out the execution of Wilson,' Dolan added. 'The Belfast pogrom was still going on and we all knew that Wilson was one of the chief forces at the back of it. Before the Truce it would have been perfectly legitimate to have Wilson executed, but perhaps it was only after the Truce that his responsibility in this matter was identified and his activities had not ceased with the Truce.'

These were not the actions of someone committed to a democratic constitutional process. Whether Collins would ever have adapted to a role in civilian government must be open to question in view of his efforts in trying to kill the British hangman and his assistant, as well as the subsequent murder of Sir Henry Wilson. There is little doubt that some of his men were not able to make the transition after Collins was killed at Béalnabláth on 22 August 1922.

Major General Paddy O'Daly was in charge of the Free State's soldiers in Kerry who committed the worst atrocities of the Civil War, and he presided over the subsequent army inquiry, which was a proverbial whitewash. Liam Tobin, Charlie Dalton and Frank Thornton were leading figures in the Army Mutiny of 1924. Eoin O'Duffy became commissioner of the garda siochána during the 1920s, but he tried to organise a coup d'état to prevent Fianna Fáil coming to power in 1932, while David Neligan, the head of the special branch, stood idly by. O'Duffy and Neligan were ousted the following year. Ned Broy became garda commissioner and loyally served the de Valera government.

Most of those closest to Collins were unable to make the adjustment to civilian authority. They were virtually leaderless without him. They tried to live up to his ideals, but as the Big Fellow was such a secretive individual, nobody was ever quite sure where he really stood.

BIBLIOGRAPHY

Manuscript Sources
Robert Barton Papers, TCD
Michael Collins Papers,
 Marquette University,
 Milwaukee, Wisconsin
Michael Collins Papers, Liam
 Collins, Clonakilty
Richard Mulcahy Papers, UCD
Ernie O'Malley Papers, UCD
Austin Stack Papers, Nanette
 Barrett, Tralee

Bureau of Military History Statements, National Archives
Ahern, Maurice, WS 483
Archer, Liam, WS 819
Barton, Robert, WS 979
Beaumont, Seán, WS 709
Berry, Patrick J., WS 942
Bolger, John C., WS 1,745
Broy, Eamon, WS 1,280,
 WS 1,284, WS 1,285
Byrne, Bernard C., WS 631
Byrne, Joseph, WS 461
Byrne, Vincent, WS 423
Coghlan, Francis X., WS 1,760
Culhane, Seán, WS 746
Dalton, Charles, WS 434
Dalton, Emmet, WS 641
Dolan, Joe, WS 663, WS 900
Doyle, Gerald, WS 1,511
Duffy, Thomas, WS 1,409
Fitzgerald, George, WS 684
Fox, Thomas, WS 365
Gay, Thomas B. WS 780
Harpur, James, WS 536
Hyland, Joe WS 644
Kelliher, Edward J., WS 477
Kelly, Paddy, WS 726
Kennedy, Patrick, WS 499
Kennedy, Tadgh, WS 135, 1413
Kenny, James, WS 174
Knightly, Mike, WS 833
Lawless, Sr Eitne (Eibhlín),
 WS 410
Lawson, Patrick, WS 667
Leonard, Joseph, WS 547
MacNeill, Hugo, WS 1,377
Mannix, Patrick, WS 502
McCorley, Roger, WS 389
McCrae, Patrick, WS 413
McDonnell, Daniel, WS 486
McDonnell, Michael, WS 225
McElligott, T. J., WS 472
McGarry, Seán, WS 368
McGuinness, Joseph, WS 607
McMahon, Liam, WS 274
Mernin, Lily, WS 441
Mullen, Patrick J., WS 621
Neligan, David WS 380
Newell, Thomas 'Sweeney'
 WS 572, WS 698
Nunan, Seán, WS 1,744
O'Connor, Mrs Batt, WS 330

O'Connor, Patrick J., WS 608
O'Daly, Patrick, WS 220, WS 368
O'Donoghue, Florence, WS 554
O'Donoghue, Patrick, WS 847
O'Donovan, Daniel, WS 1,480
O'Hegarty, Seán, WS 54
O'Keeffe, Patrick, WS 1,725
O'Reilly, Michael W., WS 886
Peppard, Thomas J., WS 1,399
Saurin, Frank, WS 715
Slattery, Jim, WS 445
Stafford, Jack, WS 818
Stapleton, W. James, WS 822
Thornton, Frank, WS 510, WS 615
Tobin, Liam, WS 1,753
Traynor, Oscar, WS 340
Tully, James, WS 626
White, George, WS 956

Published Works

Abbott, Richard, *Police Casualties in Ireland, 1919–1922*, Cork: 2000.
Andrew, Christopher, *Secret Service: The Making of the British Intelligence Community*, London: 1985.
Andrew, C. M. and Dilks, David N., eds, *The Missing Dimension: Government and Intelligence Communities in the Twentieth Century*, London: 1984.
Andrews, C. S., *Dublin Made Me: Autobiography*, Dublin and Cork: 1979.
Beaslaí, Piaras, 'How it was Done – IRA Intelligence' in *The Kerryman*, ed., *Dublin's Fighting Story, 1916–21*, Tralee: n.d.
– *Michael Collins and the Making of the New Ireland*, 2 vols, Dublin: 1926.
– 'Twenty Got Away' in *The Kerryman*, ed., *Sworn to be Free: The Complete Book of IRA Jailbreaks, 1918–21*, Tralee: 1971.
Bennett, Richard, *The Black and Tans*, New York: 1959.
Breen, Dan, *My Fight for Irish Freedom*, Dublin: 1950.

Callwell, C. E., *Field Marshal Sir Henry Wilson: His Life and Diaries*, 2 vols, London: 1927.

Coleman, Marie, *County Longford and the Irish Revolution*, Dublin: 2003.

Coogan, Tim Pat, *Michael Collins*, London: 1990.

Cowell, John, *A Noontide Blazing: Lyons Thornton, Rebel, Soldier, Doctor*, Dublin: 2005.

Crozier, Frank, *Ireland for Ever*, London: 1932.

Deasy, Liam, *Towards Ireland Free: The West Cork Brigade in the War of Independence, 1917–21*, Dublin and Cork: 1973.

Dwyer, T. Ryle, *Big Fellow, Long Fellow: A Joint Biography of Collins and de Valera*, Dublin: 1998.

– *Michael Collins: The Man Who Won the War*, Cork: 1990.

– *Tans, Terror and Troubles*, Cork: 2001.

Figgis, Darrell, *Recollections of the Irish War*, London: 1927.

Forester, Margery, *Michael Collins: The Lost Leader*, London: 1971.

Gaughan, J. Anthony, *The Memoirs of Jeremiah Mee, R.I.C.*, Dublin: 1975.

Gleeson, James, *Bloody Sunday*, London: 1962.

Griffith, Kenneth and O'Grady, Timothy E., *Curious Journey: An Oral History of Ireland's Unfinished Revolution*, London: 1982.

Hart, Peter, ed., *British Intelligence in Ireland, 1920–21*, Cork: 2002.

Herlihy, Jim, *The Royal Irish Constabulary: A Complete Alphabetical List of Officers and Men, 1816–1922*, Dublin: 1999.

– *The Dublin Metropolitan Police: A Complete Alphabetical List of Officers and Men, 1836–1925*, Dublin: 2001.

Hopkinson, Michael, *The Irish War of Independence*, Dublin: 2002.

Jones, Thomas, *Whitehall Diary, Volume 3: Ireland 1918–25*, edited by Keith Middlemass, London: 1971.

Macardle, Dorothy, *The Irish Republic*, London: 1968.

McBride, Lawrence W., *The Greening of Dublin Castle: The Transformation of Bureaucratic and Judicial Personnel in Ireland, 1892–1922*, Washington DC: 1991.

McColgan, John, *British Policy and Irish Administration*, London: 1982.

MacEoin, Uinseann, ed., *Survivors*, Dublin: 1980.

Macready, General Sir Nevil, *Annals of an Active Life*, London: 1924.
Neligan, David, *Spy in the Castle*, Dublin: 1968.
O'Broin, Leon, *Michael Collins*, Dublin: 1980.
O'Connor, Batt, *With Michael Collins in the Fight for Irish Freedom*, London: 1929.
O'Connor, Frank, *The Big Fellow: Michael Collins and the Irish Revolution*, Dublin: 1965.
O'Donovan, Donal, *Kevin Barry and His Time*, Dublin: 1989.
O'Donoghue, Florence, *Tomás MacCurtain: Soldier and Patriot*, Tralee: 1971.
O'Halpin, Eunan, 'British Intelligence in Ireland, 1914–21' in Christopher Andrew and David Dilks, *The Missing Dimension*, Illinois, USA: 1984.
O'Malley, Ernie, *On Another Man's Wound*, Dublin: 1936.
Roskill, Stephen, *Hankey: Man of Secrets*, vol. 2, London: 1974.
Stapleton, William J., 'Michael Collins' Squad' in *The Capuchin Annual*, 1969, pp. 368–77.
Street, C. J. C., *Administration of Ireland*, London, 1921.
– *Ireland in 1921*, London: 1922.
Sturgis, Mark, *The Last Days of Dublin Castle: The Mark Sturgis Diaries*, Dublin: 1999.
Taylor, Rex, *Michael Collins*, London: 1958.
The Kerryman, ed., *Dublin's Fighting Story, 1916–1921*, Tralee: n.d.
– *Sworn to be Free: The Complete Book of IRA Jailbreaks, 1918–1921*, Tralee: 1971.
Townsend, Charles, *The British Campaign in Ireland, 1919–21: The Development of Political and Military Policies*, London: 1975.
– 'The Irish Republican Army and the Development of General Warfare, 1916–1921', *English Historical Review*, 94, pp. 318–45.
Winter, Ormonde, *Winter's Tale*, London: 1955.

INDEX OF NAMES

Aherne, Bill 224
Allen, Eileen 152
Ames, Captain Peter 163, 168-169, 182-183, 185, 211, 212
Anderson, Sir John 108, 118-119, 141
Andrews, Todd 174-176, 190
Angliss, Lieutenant H. R. 143, 166-168, 178-180, 211
Archer, Liam 86-88, 132
Ashe, Thomas 16, 82

Baggallay, Captain 168, 177, 210-211
Barrett, Ben 52-53, 67-68, 71, 89, 92
Barrett, Denis 82, 108, 146, 148
Barry, Kevin 139, 154-156, 251
Barry, Tom 197, 222
Barton, Detective Sergeant Johnny 62, 66-70, 82
Barton, Robert 27-29, 43, 83-85
Beaslaí, Piaras 29, 32, 42, 45, 55-56, 59-60, 96, 167, 194
Beaumont, Seán 127-128, 217
Beaumont, Willie 127-128, 163, 217
Beecham, Sir Thomas 24
Bell, Allen 70, 88, 98-101, 124
Bennett, Lieutenant George 163, 168-169, 181-183
Berry, Patrick Joseph 16, 28, 32
Blythe, Ernest 51

Bobrikov, Nicholai 65
Boland, Harry 12, 19, 24-25, 29, 34, 40, 44-45
Bolder, Frank 238
Bolster, Ned 225
Boyce, James 210
Boyd, Major-General G. F. 189, 218
Breen, Dan 22-23, 65, 71-72, 146, 149-151, 153, 201, 222
Brennan, General Michael 85
Brennan, Jim 146
Brennan, Joseph 74, 108
Brennan, Robert 76
Breslin, Ned 246
Breslin, Warder 16, 235
Brien, Detective Superintendent Owen 11-12, 17, 40-41, 78, 86, 146, 148-149, 213
Brooke, Frank 123-124
Broy, Ned 10-12, 18-20, 35, 37-38, 40-42, 50-51, 63, 76, 80, 96, 130, 148-149, 213-215, 258
Brugha, Cathal 26, 30, 37, 39, 45, 54, 64, 120, 168, 190, 196, 200, 222-223, 241
Bruton, Detective Inspector John 77, 146-148
Burke, Peter 139-140
Burke, William P. 140
Byrne, Ben 208-209, 225
Byrne, Bernard 66

Byrne, Charlie 14, 255-256
Byrne, Joe 199, 249
Byrne, John Charles 79-80, 88-90, 99, 110
Byrne, Constable Matt 129
Byrne, Sir Joseph 74-75
Byrne, Vinny 66-67, 71, 81, 83, 87, 90-92, 97-101, 103-105, 123, 147, 153, 169, 181-184, 202-204, 228, 236, 243-249

Caffrey, Jack 237
Caldow, John 178
Callaghan, Hugh 176
Carew, Major 183-184
Carroll, Patrick 150
Carson, Edward 48, 75
Casey, Sergeant Patrick 213
Chamberlain, Austen 192
Childers, Erskine 116
Churchill, Winston 106-107, 110-111, 135, 144-145, 155, 192
Clancy, Peadar 32-33, 55, 83-84, 111, 150, 168, 170, 192-194, 197, 207, 223
Clayton, Inspector 95
Clune, Archbishop Patrick J. 197, 199
Clune, Conor 170, 192-194, 197, 223
Cody, Jack 120
Coffey, Detective Sergeant Denis 153-154

Coghlan, Francis X. 174-176
Collins, Michael 7-10, 12-13, 16-20, 22-32, 34-45, 48-60, 63-66, 69-70, 74-82, 86-87, 89, 92, 94-97, 99, 101, 108-109, 112-114, 116-118, 120, 123-124, 126-130, 133-134, 136-139, 141, 143, 146, 148-149, 151, 155, 163-165, 168, 170, 176, 186, 191, 194-201, 206-207, 212-220, 222-227, 229-235, 237, 240-243, 249-250, 252, 254-259
Connolly, Con 56
Connolly, W. J. 74, 108
Connor, District Inspector Henry 78
Conroy, Herbie 181-182
Conroy, Jimmy 92, 207-209
Conway, John 160
Conway, William 211
Cope, Alfred 108, 141, 253
Corringham, Joseph 150
Cotton, A. T. 123
Crozier, Brigadier General Frank 180-181, 187, 190, 222
Culhane, Seán 120-121, 123
Cullen, Tom 13, 28, 32, 80, 88-91, 98, 101, 112, 127, 131, 134, 146-147, 150, 163-164, 167-168, 194, 206, 218, 226, 258

Dalton, Charlie 14, 17, 90, 132, 146-147, 165-168, 172-

173, 202-204, 226, 231-232, 236-237, 251, 258
Dalton, Detective Constable Laurence 102-103, 124, 153
Dalton, Emmet 233, 235, 237-239
de Valera, Éamon 9-12, 23, 25-27, 29-31, 34, 37, 39-40, 42, 44-45, 48, 108, 154, 196, 200-201, 241, 249, 253, 259
Dempsey, Jim 180
Devlin, Joe 191-192
Dolan, Joe 14, 89-91, 99-100, 103, 111, 132, 151-152, 174-175, 190, 195-196, 206, 255-258
Donnolly, Simon 211
Doran, Seán 56
Doran, Willie 206
Dowling, Major C. M. G. 173
Doyle, Seán 52-53, 81, 92, 174, 182-183, 238, 246, 249
Duffy, George Gavan 27
Duffy, Sir Charles Gavan 197
Duffy, Tom 182
Duggan, Eamonn 13
Dunne, Jackie 181
Dunne, Johnny 249
Dunne, Leo 172
Dunne, Lil 166
Dunne, Mick 246
Dunne, Reggie 207, 221, 224, 256-258

Earle, Hubert 174
Edgeworth-Johnson, Colonel Walter 17, 35, 74-75, 148, 152

Ennis, Tom 46, 51, 169, 181-182, 184-185, 242-243, 245

Feely, Peter 130
Figgis, Darrell 29-31
Fisher, Sir Warren 49, 107
Fitzgerald, Captain John 177
Fitzgerald, George 53, 56, 109, 221
Fitzgerald, Michael 115, 154
Fitzmaurice, Constable 151-153
Flanagan, Constable Thomas 72
Flanagan, Paddy 172-173, 251
Fleming, Paddy 32-33
Flood, Seán 221
Flood, Tom 245-246
Foley, Dick 195
Foley, Edward 251
Foley, John 219
Foley, Michael 18
Fouvargue, Vincent 206-207
Fox, Tom 121-122
French, Sir John 64-65, 70-74, 95, 99, 123, 133, 137-138, 159
Furlong, Matt 151

G., Lieutenant 165, 168
Garniss, Frank 179
Gay, Thomas 11, 35, 41-42, 194
Gibbons, John 140
Golden, David 111
Golden, Seán 257
Gooding, J. L. 137-139
Gough, Sir Hubert 145
Green, James 172, 212
Greenwood, Sir Hamar 64, 107,

109-111, 116, 118, 150, 160, 162, 176, 191-192, 252
Greer, Constable Martin J. 208-209
Griffin, Paddy 92
Griffith, Arthur 12, 26, 29, 31, 37, 39, 137-139, 145, 154, 196-198, 200
Guilfoyle, Joe 14, 99-100, 128, 195

Hales, Donal 94
Halley, Detective Sergeant Nicholas 40, 72
Hankey, Sir Maurice 107, 145, 191
Hardy, F. Digby, see Gooding, J. L.
Harpur, James 246
Hayes, Michael 164
Hayes, Seán 60
Headlam, Maurice 74, 108
Healy, Daniel 211
Healy, Mary 26
Healy, Tim 19, 43
Henderson, Frank 150
Henderson, Leo 150
Herlihy, Ted 230-231
Hill-Dillon, Colonel 15, 96, 225
Hoey, Detective Constable Daniel 51-52, 60, 82, 208
Hoey, Mick 208-209
Hogan, Michael 187
Houlihan, John 157, 160
Hughes, Jim 202
Hughes, Thomas 115
Hurley, James 61-62, 66
Hyland, Joe 238-239

Igoe, Head Constable, 201-205, 209

Jameson, John, see Byrne, John Charles

Kavanagh, Detective Sergeant Joseph 11, 35, 41, 63, 213
Kavanagh, Seán 170, 230-231
Kelliher, Ned 14, 174, 198-199, 208-209
Kells, Detective Constable Henry 101-102, 124
Kelly, Paddy 208
Kelly, Tom 29
Kennedy, Mick 46
Kennedy, Patrick 14, 90, 176, 207, 222-223
Kennedy, Tadgh 63, 156
Kennedy, Tim 125-127
Keenlyside, Captain B. C. H. 172-173
Kenny, James 174-176
Keogh, Tom 46-47, 52, 64, 66-67, 71, 81, 90-92, 97-99, 102, 104, 111-112, 123, 147-148, 151-152, 167, 169, 178, 184, 190, 202-205, 225, 228, 235-238, 243, 246, 248, 251
Kerr, Inspector 51
Kerr, Neal 27
Kilcoyne, Tom 46, 51, 89, 244
Kileen, Pat 130
Knightly, Mike 68-69, 99

Law, Bonar 48, 75, 107, 118, 143-

144, 192
Lawless, Eibhlín 49-51
Lawless, Frank 60
Lawless, James 140
Lawless, Matthew 55
Lawless, Michael 183
Lees, Captain Cecil 225
Leonard, Joe 33, 46, 52-53, 60-61, 66-68, 71, 81, 92, 102, 146-147, 167, 177, 235, 237-239, 249-250
Leonard, Seán 121-122
Lloyd George, David 74-75, 95, 106, 110, 118, 136, 143-144, 163, 191-192, 196-198, 221-223, 252
Lodge, George 56-57
Logue, Michael Cardinal 141
Love, Detective Inspector George 49
Lynch, Fionán 77
Lynch, John 143, 146, 166, 168
Lynch, Liam 143, 222
Lynch, Michael 60, 231
Lyons, Alice 250
Lyons, Brigid 228-230, 253-254

MacCurtain, Tomás 93-95, 97, 120-121, 123-124
MacEoin, Seán 222-224, 227-231, 233, 235, 238, 253-254
MacLean, Captain Donald L. 177-178
MacLean, Kate 178
MacMahon, James 73, 107-108, 141
MacNeill, Eoin 37, 102
MacNeill, Hugo 102, 146
Macpherson, Ian 48, 73, 95, 107-108
Macready, General Sir Nevil 106, 108-109, 111, 136, 256
MacSwiney, Terence 137, 146, 148, 154, 157-158
Maguire, Sam 57, 221, 224, 257-258
Maguire, Tom 222
Maher, Jerry 63, 213
Maher, Patrick 251
Malone, Thomas 32, 34, 238
Mannix, Sergeant Patrick 130-131, 178
Markievicz, Constance 37, 97, 116-117
McCabe, Inspector 148-149
McCan, Pierce 29
McCarthy, Detective Sergeant Pat 215
McCarthy, Paddy 56
McCarthy, Sergeant Maurice 64, 75, 216
McCorley, Roger E. 120-122
McCormack, Captain Patrick 176
McCrae, Pat 90, 112, 194, 233, 236-239
McDonagh, Edward 208-209
McDonnell, Constable James 22
McDonnell, Dan 14, 127, 134, 174-175, 190, 196, 202, 206, 226-227, 243, 249

McDonnell, Mick 45-47, 51-54, 64, 66-72, 83, 92, 97, 99-100, 102, 104, 146
McElligott, Sergeant Thomas J. 78-79
McEvoy, Paddy 130
McGarry, Seán 23, 26
McGrane, Eileen 213, 215
McGuinness, Joseph 9, 250
McKee, Dick 45, 52-53, 60, 150, 165, 168-170, 192-194, 197, 207, 223
McLean, Billy 179
McMahon, Liam 26-27
McNamara, James 210
McNamara, Jim 41, 63, 76, 79-80, 89, 127, 147, 149, 195, 207, 214-215
Mee, Constable Jeremiah 115-117
Mernin, Lily 15, 96-97, 165-167, 195
Milroy, Seán 23, 25-26
Molloy, Fergus Bryan 96-98
Montgomery, Lt-Colonel Hugh F. 172-173, 212
Moran, Paddy 169, 176, 211-212
Morris, Cecil A. 179
Moynihan, Pat 132
Mulcahy, Dick 23, 28, 32, 45, 52, 54, 65, 79-80, 120, 164, 168, 170, 194, 198, 200, 224, 255
Mulhern, William 77-78, 124
Murphy, Dick 120-121, 123
Murphy, Fintan 24-25, 60
Murphy, Greg 18

Murphy, James 222-223
Murphy, Joseph 154
Murphy, Peter 239
Murray, Lieutenant R. G. 173
Murray, Pa 224

Neary, Constable John 130
Neligan, David 41, 59, 66, 102-103, 125-127, 131, 134-135, 143, 149, 151-154, 186, 194-195, 207, 209-210, 214-215, 217-219, 252, 258
Newbury, Captain W. F. 177
Newell, Thomas 'Sweeney' 202-205
Nunan, Seán 37-38

O'Brien, Art 79-80, 136
O'Brien, Detective Constable Denis 40, 78
O'Brien, Nancy 64
O'Connell, Daniel 31
O'Connell, J. J. (Ginger) 49, 130
O'Connell, Patrick 22
O'Connor, Batt 20, 29, 58-59, 79-80, 96
O'Connor, Rory 28, 55, 79, 210
O'Connor, Simon 160
O'Connor, T. P. 115-116, 160-161, 192
O'Daly, Paddy 16, 32-33, 51-53, 60-62, 67-73, 81, 84, 92, 99, 102-104, 112-114, 146-147, 153, 169, 209, 233-235, 238, 240, 242-245, 249-251, 258

O'Dea, Mick 130
O'Donnell, Constable Alexander 112
O'Donoghue, Florence 165
O'Donoghue, Paddy 24-26, 55-56
O'Donovan, Dan 60, 128
O'Donovan, John 115
O'Donovan, Julia 130
O'Duffy, General Eoin 255, 258
O'Hanlon, Gertrude 61
O'Hanrahan, Harry 10-11
O'Hegarty, Diarmuid 60, 206
O'Keeffe, Paudeen 50-51
O'Kelly, J. J. 196
O'Kelly, Paddy 208
O'Kelly, Seán T. 27
O'Kelly, Ted 43
O'Kelly, Tom 30
O'Leary, Jeremiah 187
O'Malley, Ernie 194, 210-212
Ó Muirthile, Seán 76, 86, 196
O'Reilly, Constable Terence 130
O'Reilly, Joseph 13, 28, 34, 43, 59, 213, 229, 239
O'Reilly, Mick 92, 208-209, 225
O'Rourke, Sergeant Thomas 63, 125
O'Sullivan, Constable P. 130
O'Sullivan, Denis M. 157
O'Sullivan, Dermot 132
O'Sullivan, Fr Charles 115
O'Sullivan, Gearóid 130, 194, 206
O'Sullivan, Joe 257-258
O'Sullivan, Philip J. 198-199

Peel, Mr 143, 166-168, 178, 180
Percival, Major A. E. 224-225
Plunkett, Count 37, 97
Potter, Edward 211-212
Price, Captain Leonard 173
Purcell, Superintendent John J. 149, 213

Quinlisk, Henry Timothy 76, 86-87
Quinn, Fergus 82, 108

Redmond, Inspector W. C. Forbes 75-82, 108, 124, 216
Redmond, William 10
Reid, Daniel 152
Revell, Sergeant Richard J. 103-105, 124
Reynolds, Major 195, 217, 226
Robinson, Seamus 71, 146
Roche, Sergeant Daniel 151-153
Rochford, Joseph 211-212
Russell, Seán 83, 168-169, 241
Ryan, Corporal John 207

Saurin, Frank 13, 15, 91, 97, 163, 167, 182, 184-185, 226
Savage, Martin 71-73
Scott, John 187
Shanahan, Joe 207
Shaw, General Frederick 74, 106
Sheehan, Paddy 50, 60, 126
Sheeran, Constable Patrick 115
Slattery, Jim 45-47, 51-52, 64, 66-67, 71, 81-83, 85, 90-92, 97-100, 102, 111, 123, 151-152,

178-180, 202, 208, 243, 245-246, 249
Smith, T. J. 70, 74-75, 95
Smith, Thomas Herbert 177
Smyth, Detective Sergeant Patrick 45-48, 60, 82, 108
Smyth, Gerald Brice Ferguson 114-118, 149-150
Stack, Austin 27, 31, 42-43, 55-56, 68, 126, 196, 200, 241
Stapleton, Bill 64, 93, 177, 207, 237
Stove, Captain F. Harper 91
Sturgis, Mark 108-109, 136-137, 141, 146, 155, 184, 197
Sullivan, Tadhg 224
Supple, Joe 214
Supple, Kerry Leyne 63
Swanzy, District Inspector 95, 120-121, 123-124

Taylor, Sir John J. 70, 74, 108
Teeling, Frank 180-181, 210-211
Thomson, Sir Basil 70, 80-81, 138
Thornton, Frank 13-15, 32, 75, 80, 88-89, 91, 127, 131, 137, 150-151, 163-164, 168, 194-195, 201-202, 216, 221, 224, 258
Tobin, Liam 13-14, 16, 32, 53, 56, 79, 88-92, 97-100, 102, 104, 134, 150-151, 163-165, 168, 202, 206, 217-218, 222, 226, 231, 258
Tobin, Michael J. 210
Tracy, Patrick 10

Treacy, Seán 22, 71, 146, 149-151, 153, 184, 201
Traynor, Oscar 132-133, 220, 235, 241-242, 244-245
Traynor, Tom 230
Tudor, Major-General Henry 108, 115-116, 136, 141, 150, 222

Wall, Tommy 159-160
Walsh, Constable John M. 88
Walsh, D. P. 56
Walsh, Detective Sergeant Thomas 26
Walsh, J. J. 32, 34, 102, 129, 238
Walsh, James 94
Wharton, Detective Sergeant Thomas 60-62, 66
Whelan, Thomas 210-212
White, Captain A. P. 150
White, George 234-235
White, Mick 251
Wilde, L. E. 176
Wilson, District Inspector Percival Lea 111-113
Wilson, President Woodrow 27, 42
Wilson, Sir Henry 106, 109, 111, 136, 143-145, 256-258
Winter, Sir Ormonde 108, 135, 149, 164, 220, 251
Winters, Superintendent John 113-114
Woodcock, Major W. 172-173
Wylie, William E. 108, 119, 141

Other T. Ryle Dwyer Titles

HAUGHEY'S FORTY YEARS OF CONTROVERSY

A lively and succint reassessment of one of the most controversial and
significant political leaders of twentieth-century Ireland.
Dwyer delivers his conclusions on the Haughey Years.

MICHAEL COLLINS,
THE MAN WHO WON THE WAR

The story of a charismatic rebel who Arthur Griffith referred to as
'the man who won the war'. Who was this Michael Collins and
what was his real role in the War of Independence?

TANS, TERRORS AND TROUBLES
Kerry's Real Fighting Story 1913–23

Told in a fast-paced and readable style, this book gives
the full story of the events in Kerry in the dark days from
November 1913 to the end of the Civil War in April 1923.